P9-APE-755

radical
possibilities

The *Critical Social Thought* Series
edited by Michael W. Apple, University of Wisconsin–Madison

radical
possibilities

public policy,

urban education,

and a new

social movement

j e a n a n y o n

ROUTLEDGE
NEW YORK AND LONDON

Published in 2005 by
Routledge
Taylor & Francis Group
270 Madison Avenue
New York, NY 10016

Published in Great Britain by
Routledge
Taylor & Francis Group
2 Park Square
Milton Park, Abingdon
Oxon OX14 4RN

© 2005 by Taylor & Francis Group, LLC
Routledge is an imprint of Taylor &Francis Group

Printed in the United States of America on acid-free paper
10 9 8 7 6 5 4 3

International Standard Book Number-10: 0-415-95098-8 (hardcover) 0-415-95099-6 (softcover)
International Standard Book Number-13: 978-0-415-95098-5 (hardcover) 978-00-415-95099-2 (softcover)

No part of this book may be reprinted, reproduced, transmitted, or utilized in any form by any electronic, mechanical, or other means, now known or hereafter invented, including photocopying, microfilming, and recording, or in any information storage or retrieval system,without written permission from the publishers.

Trademark Notice: Product or corporate names may be trademarks or registered trademarks,and are used only for identification and explanation without intent to infringe.

Library of Congress Cataloging-in-Publication Data

Anyon, Jean.
  Radical possibilities : public policy, urban education, and a new
social movement / Jean Anyon.
    p. cm. — (The critical social thought series)
  Includes bibliographical references and index.
  ISBN 0-415-95098-8 (hardback : alk. paper) — ISBN 0-415-95099-6
(pbk. : alk. paper)
  1. Education, Urban—Social aspects--United States. 2. Educational change—
United States. 3. Social change—United States. I. Title. II. Series:
Critical social thought.
  LC5131.A56 2005
  379.173'2--dc22

                                                                2004023037

Taylor &Francis Group
is the Academic Division of T&F Informa plc.

Visit the Taylor &Francis Web site at
http://www.taylorandfrancis.com

and the Routledge Web site at
http://www.routledge-ny.com

I dedicate this book to my parents,
who lived the struggle,
and to Jessie and C, with love

Contents

Part III
Social Movements, New Public Policy,
and Urban Educational Reform

Series Editor's Introduction

Public Policy, Urban Education, and a New Social Movement

Reading Jean Anyon is like coming home. She and I have similar political and personal histories. Both of us come from politically active families. Both of us taught in inner-city schools that seemed all too often to almost be purposely organized in ways that made the lives of students and teachers extremely difficult. The two of us share a sense of profound anger at the ways in which not only schools, but nearly all of this society's major institutions are organized to maintain massive inequalities. And like so many others who share this anger, we want to participate in struggles to alter these conditions.

Many people who are concerned about education have been deeply affected by such books as Jonathan Kozol's *Savage Inequalities* (Kozol, 1991). These books are absolutely essential in illuminating the ways in which such things as our systems of educational funding participate in reproducing inequalities and what the class and race effects of such inequalities are. The stories that are so powerfully told by authors such as Kozol lead to one of the most crucial questions we can ask. What is to be done?

In 1932, George S. Counts published a short book with the title of *Dare the Schools Build a New Social Order?* (Counts, 1932). It was a call to activism, a call to use the schools to create a society in which equality and social justice would be the fundamental aims of all economic, political, and cultural policies and practices. In hindsight, we might admit that Counts was a bit naïve. However, the question raised in the title still has resonance today. Can schools play a role in making a more just society possible? If not, why not? If so, what can they do?

There has been a long history of work on these questions. But few people have been as honest about the complex, but still doable, politics involved in answering them as Jean Anyon is in this book.

Radical Possibilities stands directly within the lineage of the tradition of Counts and other critically democratic educators. It not only swims within the vast river of democracy but it wants to keep that river flowing in the direction of increased social justice for all people in this nation. As in her previous and justly well-respected book (Anyon, 1997), Jean Anyon directs most of her attention to urban schools and the economic and educational crises that have been so very damaging to economically and culturally dispossessed people in our cities and neighborhoods. However, what she has to say is crucial to everyone who is concerned with what is happening in education in this society.

She is not romantic in believing that education can alone radically alter the roots of the crises we are experiencing. However, she is optimistic that it can play a large role—along with other institutions and movements—in providing the conditions and resources that contribute to the struggle for a more just society. The book's basic claims can best be seen in Anyon's own words:

> [E]ven though economic justice may be a prerequisite for educational justice, more equitable macroeconomic policies will not by themselves create high quality urban schools. Macroeconomic policy will need to be augmented by educational reform. Providing economic opportunity and realistic hope in urban neighborhoods will be necessary to create the conditions that allow for and support successful urban schools, but these nurturing conditions will have to be supplemented by reforms that prevent racial tracking, low-level curriculum, and poor teaching (for example).

As she goes on to say:

> [T]he disastrous state of the educational systems in urban areas today could provide impetus to organizing a new social movement. Education already has a strong tradition of critical pedagogy and social justice activism to call upon.

A key phrase in the above statement is "a new social movement." Anyon recognizes something I too have argued at greater length elsewhere—that it is social movements that are the driving forces behind social and educational transformation (Apple, 2000). In my own case, I have directed much of my critical attention to the forces and movements behind current neo-liberal and neo-conservative policies, what I have called conservative modernization, for two reasons. First, whether we like it or not, these movements have been increasingly powerful in transforming our core ideas about democracy and citizenship. The social, economic, and educational effects of the policies that have come from the Right often have been strikingly negative, especially for those who have the least in our own and other societies (Apple, 2001; Apple et al., 2003). Second, I think that we have much to learn from the forces of the Right. They have shown that it is possible to build an alliance of disparate groups and in the process to engage in a vast social and pedagogic project of changing a society's fundamental way of looking at rights and (in)justice. Radical policies that only a few years ago would have seemed outlandish and downright foolish are now accepted as commonsense. While we should not want to emulate their often cynical and manipulative politics, we still can learn a good deal from the Right about how movements for social change can be built across ideological differences.

Whereas I have focused on critically understanding why the Right is winning and what we can learn from them, Jean Anyon shifts the focus powerfully. She directs our attention to the historical and current progressive mobilizations that have made a difference in society. She sets about examining the specifics of such social movements, documenting why and how they pushed this society, sometimes against great odds, toward a greater commitment to social justice.

While many of the movements examined in *Radical Possibilities* are concerned with economic justice and racial oppressions outside of education, Anyon also includes a number of others within cultural and educational institutions. In this, she understands what Nancy Fraser has taught us. Fraser (1997) reminds us that we can (analytically) distinguish two kinds of political movements, a politics of redistribution and a politics of recognition. Neither is a substitute for the other. Both are crucial at this historic moment. Our task is to work on both simultaneously so that gains along one set of dynamics (class and the economy, for example) do not contradict and are not contradicted by the other set of dynamics (struggling for curricula and teaching that respond to oppressed groups' cultures, identities, and histories, for example). Of course, in the real world it is almost impossible to differentiate totally between redistributive movements and those involving recognition. For instance, African Americans and Latinos/as suffer economic discrimination and levels of exploitation at a tragic rate. But this can more easily occur because of the history of racism and of being constructed as a category of "despised others." Thus, racism and a retrogressive politics of whiteness cohere with exploitative economic relations. As this book demonstrates, schools can play crucial roles in raising critical questions about and building movements to challenge both the ways in which the economy now functions unequally and the ways in which the politics of race operates in every one of our institutions.

In the process of telling the stories of different kinds of movements, Anyon also shows how, by participating in political actions, new activist identities are formed by dispossessed groups at the same time as very real progress is made culturally, educationally, politically, and economically. But activist movements don't just help to transform economic, political, cultural, and educational institutions and policies. They also have profound effects on other sympathetic organizations. Movements making what seem at the time to be utopian and radical demands historically have pushed more mainstream organizations along, creating a situation where they too must support fundamental changes in policies that are deeply discriminatory and harmful (Sewell, 2004).

Anyon is very honest about what is actually required to change schools. This is more than a little refreshing, since all too often we seem to be content with critical slogans, rather than examine what actually is possible and how we might bring these possibilities into existence in the real world of schools and communities. It is from this basis of honestly confronting the realities we face that *Radical Possibilities* is able to offer ways of engaging in and with schools and communities that have a much greater chance of making a difference in the long run.

I want to say more about this rare combination of honesty and hope. Anyon is not content to simply critically analyze the current situation—although she is very good at doing that. Unlike many others, she goes beyond bearing witness to the negativities of current social and educational conditions and policies. One of the most useful things that she does is to provide something of a handbook of what is to be done. This cannot but help all of us in our continuing struggles to build an education that is worthy of its name and that serves all of us. *Radical Possibilities*, thus, lives up to its name. It is a book that confronts reality squarely in the face and points to where we can go to make a difference.

Michael W. Apple
John Bascom Professor of Curriculum and Instruction
and Educational Policy Studies
University of Wisconsin, Madison

REFERENCES

Anyon, J. (1997). *Ghetto Schooling: A Political Economy of Urban Educational Reform.* New York: Teachers College Press.
Apple, M.W. (2000). *Official Knowledge: Democratic Education in a Conservative Age.* New York: Routledge.
Apple, M.W. (2001). *Educating the "Right" Way: Markets, Standards, God, and Inequality.* New York: RoutledgeFalmer.
Apple, M.W. et al. (2003). *The State and the Politics of Knowledge.* New York: RoutledgeFalmer.
Counts, G.S. (1932). *Dare the School Build a New Social Order?* New York: The John Day Company.
Fraser, N. (1997). *Justice Interruptus.* New York: Routledge.
Kozol, J. (1991). *Savage Inequalities.* New York: Crown.
Sewell, S.K. (2004). The "Not-Buying" Power of the Black Community, *Journal of African-American History, 89,* 135–151.

Acknowledgments

My family, friends, colleagues, and students worked with me to make this a better book. I would like to thank them all. In our weekly seminar, students were brilliant and unafraid: Janice Bloom, Lori Chajet, Michael Dumas, Kathleen Nolan, and Emily Schnee. Students Takiema Bunche-Smith, Mark Dunetz, Greg Tewksbury, Eve Tuck, and Jen Weiss also gave me smart, helpful advice. Friends and family who read and critiqued former drafts include Annette Lareau, Roz Mickelson, Alan Sadovnik, and my brother Bob Anyon. Editors Mike Apple and Catherine Bernard provided crucial, careful comments. Others who assisted in so many ways include Yolanda Anyon, Olivia Araiza, Stanley Aronowitz, John Beam, Lori Bezalher, Tony Bryk, Marta Civil, Tony DeJesus, Leigh Dingerson, Liz Ellsworth, Terrie Epstein, Norm Fruchter, Marilyn Gittell, Norm Glickman, Sun Kim, Joyce E. King, Pauline Lipman, Kavitha Mediratta, Carmen Mercado, Janet Miller, John Mollenkopf, Jeannie Oakes, John Rogers, Aaron Schutz, Dennis Shirley, Stephen Smith, and Julia Wrigley.

Introduction

Born in the 1940s to parents who had been active in the radical
social movements of the 1930s, I was a "red-diaper baby." Both
parents had been labor organizers, and continued their activism
during my youth. In the mid-1950s, Senator Joseph McCarthy
called my father to Washington, D.C., on charges that he had
been a member of the Communist Party almost twenty years
before. The president of the elite university where my father was
by then a tenured faculty member stepped in, and McCarthy
desisted, but had my father's passport revoked.

Early on, I imbibed the family passion for social justice. I
believed I should, and could, fight against the racial and class
oppression I observed. During my high school and college years,
the civil rights movement deeply engaged me, and I became active
in a Northern branch of CORE (Congress of Racial Equality)—
picketing, marching, and sometimes organizing. I raised money
for the movement in Mississippi during "Freedom Summer" of
1964. Three years later, political activist Abbie Hoffman and I
opened a store in New York City where we sold leather and
cotton goods made by an African American women's collective
in South Carolina; we sent the proceeds South to support the collective and civil rights activity.

During the late 1960s and early '70s I taught elementary grades
in inner-city schools in Washington, D.C., and Bedford Stuyvesant, Brooklyn—ever hopeful for Black civil rights, as victories
followed major protests in the South. During those years, I joined

protests against the Vietnam War, and rejoiced when the 10-year-old movement met with success and U.S. troops were withdrawn from Vietnam in 1973.

After seven years, I left city classrooms for doctoral studies, and then a position in the Teacher Education Department of Rutgers University in Newark, NJ—wanting very much to make a difference in the struggle against what I perceived to be racial and class oppression in urban schools. I wrote *Ghetto Schooling: A Political Economy of Urban Educational Reform*, in part to demonstrate that the failure of city school systems such as Newark was a function of 100 years of urban political and economic history, rather than a result of an influx of Black Southern families in the 1950s and '60s—as many whites assumed.

This book is another attempt to intervene against injustice. In it, I examine ways in which the current political economy maintains the damage that U.S. history inflicted on cities. While historical decisions and policies severely delimited the capacity of cities to support their schools, current public policy maintains this disadvantage.

Specifically, I will argue that macroeconomic policies like those regulating the minimum wage, job availability, tax rates, federal transportation, and affordable housing create conditions in cities that no existing educational policy or urban school reform can transcend.

Thus, in my view, low-achieving urban schools are not primarily a consequence of failed education policy, or urban family dynamics, as mainstream analysts and public policies typically imply. Failing public schools in cities are, rather, a logical consequence of the U.S. macroeconomy—and the federal and regional policies and practices that support it. Teachers, principals, and urban students are not the culprits—as reform policies that target increased testing, educator quality, and the control of youth assume. Rather, an unjust economy and the policies through which it is maintained create barriers to educational success that no teacher or principal practice, no standardized test, and no "zero tolerance" policy can surmount. It is for this reason that I argue that *macroeconomic mandates continually trump urban educational policy and school reform.*

Policies such as minimum wage statutes that yield poverty wages, affordable housing and transportation policies that segregate low-income workers of color in urban areas and industrial and other job development in far-flung suburbs where public transit does not reach, all maintain poverty in city neighborhoods and therefore the schools. In order to solve the systemic problems of urban education, then, we need not only school reform but the reform of these public policies. If, as I am suggesting, the macroeconomy deeply affects the quality of urban education, then perhaps we should rethink what "counts" as educational policy. Rules and regulations regarding teaching, curriculum, and assessment certainly count; but, perhaps policies that maintain high levels of urban poverty and segregation should be part of the educational policy panoply as well—for these have consequences for urban education at least as profound as curriculum and pedagogy.

We have been attempting educational reform in U.S. cities for over three decades—and there is little significant districtwide improvement that we can point to. As a nation, we have been counting on education to solve the problems of unemployment, joblessness, and poverty for many years. But education did not cause these problems, and education cannot solve them. An economic system that chases profits and casts people aside (especially people of color) is culpable.

How can a successfully reformed urban school benefit a low-income student of color whose graduation will not lead to a job on which to make a living because there are not enough such jobs, and will not lead to the resources for college completion? New curriculum, standardized tests, or even nurturing, democratic small schools do not create living-wage jobs, and do not provide poor students with the funds and supports for enough further education to make a significant difference in their lives. Only government policy can mandate that jobs provide decent wages; and adequate family income or public provision (such as the 1944 GI Bill that paid for the education of 8 million World War II veterans) are necessary to guarantee funds for college degrees to the millions of urban poor who want, and need, them.

I acknowledge that even though economic justice may be a prerequisite for educational justice, more equitable macroeconomic policies will not by themselves create high-quality urban schools. Macroeconomic policy will need to be augmented by educational reform. Providing economic opportunity and realistic hope in urban neighborhoods will be necessary to create the conditions that allow for and support successful urban schools, but these nurturing conditions will have to be supplemented by reforms that prevent racial tracking, low-level curriculum, and poor teaching (for example).

My last book, *Ghetto Schooling,* is sometimes construed as advocating social reform to the exclusion of attention to the schools. In talks that I give, and in classes that I teach, I am sometimes called upon to remind folks that *Ghetto Schooling* ends with a plea to join two kinds of struggles, to connect school reform to campaigns for increased social opportunity. Perhaps a personal example will clarify my position further.

On January 1, 2004, I and colleagues at City University of New York, Rutgers University, and the University of Pennsylvania were awarded $10 million from the National Science Foundation. One purpose of the funding is to research and carry out reform projects in mathematics education in New York, Philadelphia, Newark, and Plainfield, NJ. Another purpose is to organize parents and communities as advocates for college-prep mathematics courses. One strategy under consideration is to engage community organizations active in economic and housing struggles in this educational reform work, thus creating some synergy between the various campaigns. *In this way, educational reform becomes part of the effort to create the conditions that will support it.*

Ghetto Schooling also induces serious depression in some sympathetic readers—those who perceive that I am saying that we need a "revolution" before we can have better schools for poor people. I do not believe that, and I did not argue that in the book. Nor do I argue it here. Despite my serious criticism of public policy as legislated by the political and economic coalitions that govern, I have great faith in the American people. U.S. history demonstrates—and my experience in two social movements confirms for me personally—that the most egregious social policies can be replaced by significantly more equitable ones by the power of a people who are united and organized. From the American Revolution (fought in part against economic policies perceived as unjust) to the labor movements of the 19th and 20th centuries, to the civil rights, women's, bilingual, and disability movements, the most unjust policies have been replaced by liberal and sometimes radical legislation. Today, the Radical Right has weakened many of those mandates, and we need a set of public policies that will protect and support—and provide economic and educational justice for—residents of urban America.

The normal strength of governing political and economic elites—and the power of mass movements to challenge them—does not imply that single individuals have no agency. They do; we each can make a difference wherever we "cast down our buckets," as civil rights leader Ella Baker used to say. But to actually change federal polices that amply benefit the groups that govern, individual agency needs to be compounded by the joint efforts of hundreds of thousands of citizens who are "street-marching mad," and who voice their demands for change together.

Census 2000 revealed that over two-thirds of the poor in large metropolitan areas live in cities and what I will call "urbanized," segregated suburbs. Only about a quarter (26%) of the poor in large metropolitan areas is rural. The concentration of so many poor people in relatively small urban spaces provides fertile soil for insurgency. It naturally offers a potential base for organizing a new social movement. Therefore, I concentrate my analysis on urban areas.

Indeed, I will argue that the disastrous state of the educational systems in urban areas today could provide impetus to organizing a new social movement. Education already has a strong tradition of critical pedagogy and social justice activism to call upon. In U.S. cities, moreover, several active but largely unreported progressive movements are already flourishing: community and education organizing, the living wage movement, progressive labor and faith-based coalitions, and a new and urgent emergence of organized urban youth. People of color are the vast majority of participants in these campaigns, and most of them live in low-income urban neighborhoods. Their children attend underfunded, distressed urban schools. What needs to be accomplished is a convergence of these various movements around a set of issues that all can agree are crucial. I will argue that educational opportunity is one such issue. Economic justice is another. I will also suggest that parent and other educational organizing in cities may have reached the strength to be able to successfully call groups in the other movements to the table to work toward unity. Concerned public school educators would be key in all this work.

The fruits of a social movement for economic justice would not just benefit urban minorities. The many millions of white families who are poor, working class, or even lower middle class would benefit as well. These families are not well served by the 21st century U.S. economy—and would certainly profit from policies (such as a doubling of the minimum wage) that substantially improved the economic milieu in which they—and their black and brown brothers and sisters—struggle to make a living.

I am aware that the presence of just policies does not guarantee equitable implementation or permanent success. As we have seen, civil rights victories such as affirmative action, and even minority voting rights in states like Florida, are not secure. The end of the Vietnam War did not prevent the federal government from waging other unnecessary or unjust wars. Constant vigilance is necessary. *But it is considerably more likely that equitable practice will follow from good policy than from bad.*

Finally, it may be that some readers will feel that in arguing for a new social movement I am indulging in utopian thinking. To that charge, I reply that *the utopian thinking of yesteryear becomes the common sense of today.* Imagine the late 19th century/early 20th century dreams of workers and labor organizers, and know that those utopian schemes for an eight-hour workday, a minimum wage, and some sort of financial assistance when fired, became federal policy in the 1930s, and are accepted as common sense by most Americans today. Millions of black American slaves were legally forced to walk across the South in 1805 to populate and cultivate fields in the new Louisiana Purchase. More black people were displaced during this journey than during the passage from Africa to the shores of the Atlantic (Berlin, 2003, pp. 68, 72). Utopian dreams of freedom must have filled the thoughts of those enslaved men and women. Yet 60 years later, slavery was abolished, and black freedom was inscribed in the U.S. Constitution. I conclude from examples such as these that, far from useless, visionary thinking may be a necessary, prescient prelude to social progress.

PART I

Federal Policy and Urban Education

Analysts typically do not link federal policies to the maintenance of poverty, to the lack of jobs that bedevils American workers, or to the increasingly large portion of employment that pays poverty and near-poverty wages. Yet federal policy is determinative. Congress, to take a blatant example, set the first minimum wage in 1938 at $3.05 (in 2000 dollars); it stands in 2005 at $5.15—a mere two dollars more. (Yearly income at this wage is $10,712.) This sum ensures that full-time year-round minimum-wage work will not raise people out of poverty. Analysis in 2004 found that minimum wage standards directly affect the wages of 8.9% of the workforce (9.9 million workers); and when we include those making one dollar more an hour than the minimum wage, this legislation affects the wages of as much as 18% of the workforce (Economic Policy Institute July, 2004, p. 5).

There are other macroeconomic policies whose consequences concatenate to produce hardship. These especially burden the lives of Blacks and Latinos. Chapters 1, 2, and 3 describe a number of federal policies that have egregious consequences. Among the policies considered (in addition to minimum wage legislation) are job training as a predominant federal anti-poverty policy when there have been too few jobs for graduates; ineffective federal implementation of policies that outlaw racial discrimination in hiring and housing; regressive income taxes that charge wealthy individuals less than half the rate charged during most of the first 60 years of the 20th century, yet substantially raise the payroll taxes paid by the working poor and middle class; and corporate tax policies in recent years that allow 60 percent of large U.S. corporations to pay no federal taxes at all (and in some cases to obtain millions in rebates). The effects of these policies are compounded by harsh union laws and lack of federal protection for labor organizing; Federal Reserve Bank pronouncements that ignore the portion of its mandate to maintain a high level of employment; free trade agreements that send thousands of corporations—and their job opportunities—to other countries; and more.

Also important are policies that would help, but are conspicuous by their absence: for example, regulation of the minimum wage that kept low-paid workers' income at the median of highly paid, unionized workers in the decades after World War II; federal programs for urban youth that would support college completion; a program of job creation in cities; and policies to enforce laws against discrimination in hiring. These and other alternative policy choices are advanced throughout the chapters of Part I.

Chapter 4 closes Part I with an examination of the results of federally induced poverty and low-wage work on urban children and schools. In 2002, 37% of American children (more than 26 million) lived in families that were poor, or low income (in 2004, $18,850 and $37,700 respectively for a family of four). Almost two-thirds (58%) of African-American children lived in poor or low-income families in that year (National Center for Children in Poverty, 2004, 1). Chapter 5 examines empirical research demonstrating ways in which conditions of little or no financial resource can undermine children's educational success. Importantly, however, the chapter also describes hopeful new research documenting that when minority urban low-income families are provided with financial resources and/or better living situations, the job prospects of the adults and the educational achievement of the children typically improve significantly.

PART II

Metropolitan Inequities

While states are defined by geographic and political boundaries, metropolitan areas are shaped by regional markets—for jobs, housing, investment, and production. Metro areas account for over 80% of national output, and drive the economic performance of the nation as a whole. Each metro area is anchored by one or more cities.

Today, metropolitan regions are characterized by population growth, extensive inequality, and segregation. The percentage of racial minorities in large metropolitan areas who live in the suburbs jumped from 19% to 27% during the 1990s. However, a growing share of these families lives in fiscally stressed suburbs, which contain an increasing number of neighborhoods of *concentrated* poverty.

A number of social scientists concerned about poverty have investigated the unequal distributions of public and private investment, production, labor, and housing that characterize U.S. metro areas. They have found the following: Most entry-level jobs for which low-income urban adults are qualified are located in the outlying suburbs; federal and state public transportation systems do not connect these job centers to areas where low-income minorities live, thus preventing poor people from commuting to the jobs there; state-allowed local zoning on the basis of income prevents affordable housing in most suburbs where entry-level jobs are located; failure to enforce antiracial housing discrimination statutes confines most Blacks and Latinos to central cities and segregated suburbs; and federal and state taxes paid by residents throughout metro regions (including inner cities) support development that takes place primarily in the affluent suburbs. These inequitable regional arrangements contribute in important ways to joblessness and poverty in cities and urbanized suburbs, and to the poor quality of services such as public education there.

Chapters 5 and 6 chronicle the new field of metropolitan studies and the consequences it holds for urban education.

8

Metro-area inequities also imply an approach to urban problems that considers regional arrangements as in part determinative of local distress—in both neighborhoods and schools. The spread of concentrated poverty outside the central core also suggests that coalitions between inner cities and urbanized, segregated suburbs would produce powerful political constituencies for education and other reform.

The tendency of federal and regional policies and arrangements to maintain urban poverty and metropolitan inequities suggests that local neighborhoods are not isolated from these forces. Chapter 7 argues that, instead, urban neighborhoods—like urban schools—are extremely vulnerable to federal and regional mandates and practices. The local is not only a product of neighborhood and city cultures, and municipal regulations and policies, but is also shaped by federal and regional decisions both current and historical. Federal policies that sustain urban minority poverty, and metropolitan arrangements that spread resources unequally through regions, have been formative of the problems that plague urban neighborhoods and schools today.

Since the mid-1960s, the federal government has placed hundreds of programs in urban neighborhoods, ostensibly to ameliorate problems of poverty, unemployment, and inadequate housing—with little progress to show for it (although commercial downtowns often thrive). Philanthropic foundations and community-based organizations have also devoted time and energy to improving neighborhoods. There are major disappointments in these latter efforts as well, although there are some interesting successes. Chapter 7 closes Part II with an assessment of the efforts of foundations and community organizations in urban neighborhoods over the years, and finds that most of the successful endeavors arise from local groups that join with others in metrowide coalitions to challenge federal or regional policies that maintain inequities. The results of these coalitions affirm the potential of alliances among inner-city and urbanized suburban educational interests.

Part III

Social Movements, New Public Policy, and Urban Educational Reform

Most books that critique aspects of the social arena end with a list of policy recommendations. I want to go considerably further.

9

I want to provide historically and theoretically based suggestions for ways we could obtain the policies I will recommend.

My reading of U.S. history tells me that social movements have been the most efficacious—if not the only—method of obtaining public policies that offer basic civil and economic rights to African Americans, Latinos, the White working class, and women (for example). Over a century of active political struggle has been necessary to obtain the most fundamental civil rights for Black Americans. Five decades of labor battles were necessary before legislation in 1938 finally provided an 8-hour day, a 40-hour week, a minimum wage, and the legal end to child labor. This decades-long, vociferous, advocacy also culminated in the 1930s in the right to overtime pay, unemployment insurance, social security, and the freedom to organize unions. At least 20 years of activism were required before (White) women were permitted to vote in 1920.

And social movements have changed education. The radical tumult of the Progressive Era opened public schools to the community in many cities, and increased educational opportunity for immigrant families in the form of kindergartens, vacation schools, night schools, social settlement programs, and libraries. As a result of the civil rights movement, Head Start, a radical innovation by activists in Jackson, MS, moved to center stage in federal educational policy; segregation of Blacks in public schools became illegal. Despite later setbacks, integration victories have been significant. Gary Orfield has shown, for example, that "despite the re-segregation of many school districts in the U.S., a Southern black student is 32,700 times more likely to be in a white majority school than a black student in 1954 and fourteen times more likely than his counterpart in 1964" (Orfield, 2001, p. 35). Indeed, the South is presently the only region of the country where Whites typically attend schools with significant numbers of Blacks (ibid., p. 1).

In the 1970s and '80s, the women's, disabilities, and bilingual education movements also had significant impacts on schooling—opening up opportunities previously denied great numbers of students. Lastly, in recent years, a movement of an invigorated and federally expressed political Right has pushed both America and its schools in conservative directions: Education, economic opportunity, and civil rights have all been weakened by the rise of an organized, well-funded political Right (see, for example, Apple, 2001; McGirr, 2002; and Phillips, 2002).

Chapter 8 uses early civil rights activism (between 1900 and 1950) as an example of the historical, but insufficiently acknowledged, relationship between political contention and more equitable public policy. From NAACP Supreme Court victories before 1920, to the outlawing of all-White primaries in 1944, President Truman's Comprehensive Civil Rights Bill in 1946, and the *Brown* decision in 1954, social justice policy followed upon (and indeed, incited increased) public contention and activism by Black Americans.

The South was an extremely dangerous place to publicly protest Jim Crow segregation. What allowed early activists to take on public contestation when it would almost certainly lead to fierce economic and physical reprisals? And later, what allowed Southern sharecroppers, maids, cooks, beauticians, and day laborers—who may have spent entire lives accommodating their resistance—to take part in, no, to build, the massive public rebellions that began in the early 1950s? Chapter 8 attempts to answer these questions by utilizing innovations in social movement theory. This theorizing makes clear that raising people's consciousness about their oppression through reflection and talk is not enough: Physical and emotional support for actual participation in public contention is required.

Chapter 9, *Building a Social Movement*, applies this and other theoretical lessons to the current scene. How can we, in an era as ostensibly conservative as our own, motivate the active involvement of hundreds of thousands of Americans in a movement to change unjust economic and educational policies? How can we make use of the finding that individual and group identities as agents of change develop not primarily because of educators' use of critical pedagogy or other consciousness raising (as crucial as these are), but because of actual participation in situations of political contention? Chapter 9 takes up these questions.

The final chapter puts urban education at the center of attempts to build a politically progressive movement. One theoretically strategic reason for the centrality of urban education is that *inside poverty city schools is the congealed result of economic and other social hardships impinging on urban families.* An enlightened focus on urban education could, therefore, highlight poverty wages, joblessness, and housing injustice as well as the lack of educational opportunities.

Placing education at the center of a unified campaign is also strategic logistically, because concerned city teachers and administrators are well positioned for movement building in poor neighborhoods. They are in close proximity to, and able to have continual contact with, community adults and youth. Educators who have built up trust with these community members are in a perfect position to work with them in planning and implementing social activism.

The main task of Chapter 10, then, is to provide concrete activities that educators in various positions can utilize to make classrooms and schools progressive movement-building spaces. An important goal is to offer ways in which equity-seeking school reform groups (those working to create small schools, for example) and community organizers could join forces. Low-income parents are rarely told about school reforms being planned, and the changes typically have had little community support. If mainstream school reform groups listened, and adapted to, projects that education and other community organizers are engaged in, a synergy could be created that would propel reform outward into the community, and deeper into the school.

Among the most important participants in the process of movement building are urban youth. New research on youth organizations nationwide demonstrates an important consequence of young people's engagement in civic activism: Urban students involved in overt political struggle for their educational and other rights not only improve their schools and communities, but typically end up enhancing their own psychological development and educational achievement in the process. Chapter 10 offers extensive protocols for working with students on progressive issue campaigns and direct political action.

Ghetto schools are often distressing places—toilets and sinks overflow, students are angry and sometimes violent, teachers appear worn down and cynical, computer rooms are full of broken machines, and academic achievement is depressingly low. We understandably want to fix the problems we see—so we police and counsel students, provide staff development for the teachers, create smaller classes and schools, and mount court challenges for increased funding to pay for resources, new programs, and school buildings.

Sometimes these reforms work to make urban schools less stressful, disturbing places—and achievement scores may tick upwards. But if truth be told, these educational improvements rarely affect the material trajectory of most students' lives. A better K–12 education does not increase a child's life chances when there is no decent job the diploma will attract, and no funding that will stay with the graduate through a college degree.

Thus, public policies that concentrate poverty, delimit wages to bare subsistence, and support economic development in unreachable suburban job centers can make a mockery of safer, cleaner, better financed urban schools. The fact that macro-economic and other public policies trump educational policy and urban school reform challenges us to attend to the larger social issues. As advocates for students we need to work for equity-seeking school change, but in order to measurably improve their futures we must enlarge the geographic and policy terrain over which we claim dominion. This means that we need to reconsider what counts as educational policy.

Within our purview should be the elimination of macroeco-nomic mandates that are the building blocks of poverty and that lead to walls of indignation and anger around urban classrooms and schools. These responses to exclusion cannot be remedied by education policy currently conceived. Rather, policies that open up opportunity for urban residents are called for.

This book demonstrates that because of macroeconomic poli-cies (and changes in the U.S. economy they reflect and support) education is no longer the reliable social 'leveler' that it was for individuals and groups who used high school or college to move from urban ghettoes to the middle class. Thus, because of the current political economy and public policy strictures, we must venture outside the realm of education as we know it to pro-vide options for the poor.

The new paradigm of educational policy such a move implies would transform the political and economic environment that currently stymies most student and educator effort in low-income neighborhoods. What *should* count as education policy would include strategies to increase the minimum wage, invest in urban job creation and training, provide funds for college completion to those who cannot afford it, and enforce laws that would end racial segregation in housing and hiring. I return to this theme of an expanded education policy paradigm throughout the book.

While schools may not guarantee opportunity for social mobility, they remain sites of serious struggle for these and other social justice issues. The key now is to make sure we do not confine our modes of contention within current education and public policy choices. Contemplating historically the strategic strength required to put relevant and humane policies in place has led me to argue that a concerted social movement will be necessary to instantiate the economic and educational justice we seek in legislative, judicial, and regulatory decisions. I have written this book to assist in understanding the ways egregious public policy overdetermines the urban educational enterprise, and to support activity that works for fundamental change.

Part I

Federal Policy and Urban Education

1

The Economic Is Political

It is widely acknowledged that one of the most important causes of poorly funded, staffed, and resourced schools is the poverty of the families and neighborhoods in which the schools are located. What is rarely acknowledged, however, is the proactive role of the federal government in maintaining this poverty—and therefore poverty education.

All economies depend on government regulations in order to function. Capitalism would not be capitalism without constitutional and other federal provisions that make legal the private ownership of property, the right of business to charge more for products than the cost of producing them, or the right of corporations to keep those profits rather than sharing them with workers or employees. The 14th Amendment to the Constitution, passed in 1867, turns corporations into "persons" so they will be free from government "interference." Because economies are maintained by rules made by governments, economic institutions are inescapably political; they function according to determinative macroeconomic policies.

This chapter demonstrates that the poverty of U.S. families is considerably more widespread than commonly believed—and is catastrophic in low-income urban neighborhoods of color. I demonstrate that the basic reason people are poor is that there are not enough jobs paying decent wages. In cities, the harsh economic realities of poverty shape the lives of parents of school children, and therefore the lives of their children as well. Neighborhood poverty also impacts the education students receive by contributing to low school funding levels, poorly paid teachers, and a lack of resources.

First, I provide an overview of national poverty as a backdrop to the situation in urban America. I then focus specifically on urban families of color. The chapter that follows describes federal policies that maintain poverty and the paucity of opportunity, and suggests alternatives to ameliorate the situation and thereby buttress the prospects of urban families and schools.

INCOME

Almost three-fourths (70%) of all American employees saw their wages fall between 1973 and 1995 (in constant dollars—that is, adjusted for inflation); even with the boom of the late 1990s, a majority of workers made less in 2000 than they had in 1973. New college graduates earned $1.10 less per hour in 1995 than their counterparts did in 1973. The earnings of the average American family did improve slightly over this period, but only through a dramatic increase in the number of hours worked and the share of families in which both parents worked (Lafer 2002, p. 45; Mishel, Bernstein, and Boushey, 2003, p. 162).

Some of the largest long-term wage declines have been among entry-level workers (those with up to five years' work experience) with a high school education. Average wages for male entry-level high school graduates were 28% lower in 1997 than two decades earlier. The decline for comparable women was 18% (Economic Policy Institute, Feb. 17, 2000, p. 1).

Low wages are an important cause of poverty. Low-wage workers are those whose hourly wage is less than the earnings necessary to lift a family above the official poverty line—in 2004, $15,670 or less for a family of three, and $18,850 for a family of four.

The percentage of people who work full-time, year-round yet are poor is staggering. In 2000, at the height of a booming economy, almost a fifth of all men (19.5%), and almost a third of all women (33.1%) earned poverty-level wages working full-time, year-round. In the same year, over one in four Black men (26.3%), over one in three Black women (36.5%) and Hispanic men (37.6%), and almost half of Hispanic women (49.3%) earned poverty wages working full-time, year-round (Mishel, Bernstein, and Schmitt, 2003, pp. 137–139).

I analyzed figures provided by the Economic Policy Institute to calculate the overall percentage of people who work full-time, year-round, yet make *poverty-zone* wages. Poverty zone is defined here as wages up to 125% of the official poverty threshold needed to support a family of four at the poverty level (ibid., p. 133). The analysis demonstrates that in 1999, during the strong economy, almost half of people at work in the U.S. (41.3%) earned poverty-zone wages—in 1999, $10.24/hour ($21,299/year) or less, working full-time, year-round (ibid., Table 2.10, p. 130). Two years later, in 2001, 38.4% earned poverty-zone wages working full-time, year-round (in 2001, 125% of the poverty line was a $10.88 hourly wage) (ibid., p. 134). These figures indicate that even in "good times" the U.S. pyramid of wages sits squarely on the shoulders of almost half of U.S. employees, who are the working poor.

In 2000, more than half (59.5%) of the working poor were women. Over 60% were White (60.4%). Thirty-five percent were Black or Latino (ibid., p. 353). Over 61.8% had a high school degree or less, while a quarter (24.2%) had some college, and 8% had a bachelor's degree (ibid., p. 353). This last figure indicates that *almost one in ten of the working poor is a college graduate.*

Seventy percent of the working poor had jobs in services or retail trade and 10% worked in manufacturing (ibid., p. 353). The vast majority (93.3%) were not in unions. More than half (57.7%) were under the age of 35 (ibid., 353). It is important to note that these workers are poor by official standards. As we will see below, a more realistic measure of poverty would literally double the amount of income under which people are defined as poor.

Moving up the income scale in the U.S. is more difficult than in other countries. As *Business Week* pointed out several years ago, economic mobility in the U.S. declined after the 1960s. Because most young people earn less than their parents, mobility here is second worst among similar countries recently studied— only Canada is worse (Dreier, Swanstrom, and Mollenkopf, 2001, pp. 18, 47). Low-wage workers in the U.S. are more likely to remain in the low-wage labor market longer than workers in Germany, France, Italy, the UK, Denmark, Finland, Sweden, and Canada (Mishel, Bernstein, and Schmit, 2001, p. 12).

Relatively few U.S. individuals or families make high incomes. In 2000, only 7.8% of women, and 16% of men earned at least three times the official poverty level (Mishel, Bernstein, and

Boushey, 2003, p. 133). In 2001, only 19% of *families* earned more that $94,000, and only 4% made more than $164,000 (in 2001 dollars) (ibid., p. 56).

In the last two decades, income has skyrocketed at the tip of the distributional pyramid. The top one percent of tax filers, the 2.1 million people earning $700,000 a year or more, had after-tax income that jumped 31% in the last few years, while the after-tax income of the bottom 90% of tax filers rose only 3.4% (Mishel, Bernstein, and Schmit, 2001, p. 83).

While employee pay has lagged, CEO pay has skyrocketed. And the ratio of CEO to worker pay has increased dramatically: In the 1960s and '70s, the ratio was between 26% and 37%. In the 1990s, it was between 102% and 310%. By 2001, the ratio had grown to 245% (Mishel, Bernstein, and Boushey, 2003, p. 215). In other words, in 2001, a CEO earned more in one workday (there are 260 in a year) than an average worker earned in 52 weeks (Economic Policy Institute, July 24, 2002, p. 1). In recent years, the average ratio of CEO pay to worker pay in all other advanced countries was considerably lower—18.1 to 1 (Mishel, Bernstein, and Boushey 2003, p. 216).

JOBS

What job opportunities are available for Americans? For two decades, numerous politicians, educators, and corporate spokespeople have been arguing that the U.S. must improve education because people need advanced skills in order to get a job. This is a myth, however. Most job openings in the next 10 years will not require either sophisticated skills or a college degree. Seventy-seven percent of new and projected jobs will be low-paying. Only a quarter of the new and projected jobs are expected to pay over $26,000 a year (Department of Labor, 2002, Chart 9; see also Economic Policy Institute, July 21, 2004).

Most will require on-the-job training only, and will not require a college education; most will be in service and retail, where poverty-zone wages are the norm. Only 12.6% of new jobs will require a bachelor's degree. Of the 20 occupations expected to grow the fastest, only six require college—these six are in computer systems and information technology (Department of Labor, 2002, Chart 8), and there are relatively few of these jobs.

The typical job of the future is not in information technology. Most job openings will be in food preparation and service, and in fast-food restaurants; as telephone customer service representatives, and as cashiers (Dept. of Labor 2002, Chart 9). In the next decade, about 5 million new jobs will be created for food workers, including waiters and waitresses. Another 4 million will be for cashiers and retail salespersons, and 3 million for clerks. Over 2 million will be for packagers, laborers, and truck drivers. Managerial and professional occupations will also need more workers, but their numbers pale compared with openings requiring less education.

Indeed, a typical job of the future is retail sales at Wal-Mart. The average pay at Wal-Mart, which employs over a million people and is the largest private employer in the world, was $20,030 in 2000. According to *Business Week*, half of Wal-Mart's full-time employees are eligible for food stamps (households up to 130% of the official poverty line are eligible) (3/13/00, p. 78).

A main determinant of whether one is poor or not is whether or not one has a decently paying job. The assertion that jobs are plentiful—if only workers were qualified to fill them—has been a central tenet of federal policy for 20 years. In 1982, the Reagan administration eliminated the Comprehensive Employment and Training Administration (CETA), which by 1978 had created almost 2 million full-time jobs, and substituted a major federal job training program (Job Partnership Training Act) (Lafer, 2002, pp. 1–2). Since then, and continuing today, job training has been the centerpiece of federal and state efforts to solve both the unemployment problem and the poverty problem. For almost all of this time, however, the federal government has not collected data on job availability (vacancies). If they had, and if they had consulted studies that had been carried out, they would have found that all the evidence demonstrates that at any given time there are far more unemployed people than there are job openings (ibid., p. 23; see also Pigeon and Wray, 1999, among others). The federal government has spent $85 billion on job training since the Reagan years, claiming all the while that there are jobs for those who want them (ibid., p. 19).

In an exhaustive analysis, labor economist Gordon Lafer demonstrates that "over the period 1984 to 1996—at the height of an alleged labor shortage—the number of people in need of work exceeded the total number of job openings by an average of five to one. In 1996, for example, the country would have needed 14.4 million jobs in order for all low-income people to work their way out of poverty. However, there were at most 2.4 million job openings available to meet this need; of these, only one million were in full-time, non-managerial positions" (Lafer, 2002, 3, pp. 29–44). Thus, "there simply are not enough decently paying jobs for the number of people who need them—no matter how well trained they are"—and therefore job training programs cannot hope to address more than a small fraction of either the unemployment or poverty problems (Lafer, 2002, 3, pp. 88–123; see also Jargowsky, 1998; and Eisenhower Foundation, 1998).

Lafer also demonstrates that throughout the 1984 to 1996 period, the total number of vacancies in jobs that paid above poverty wage was never more than one-seventh the number of people who needed those jobs, and "the gap between jobs needed and decently paying jobs available was never less than 16 million" (2002, pp. 34–35).

In the last 15 years or so, corporate pronouncements and federal economic policies (regarding expansion of visas for foreign workers, for example) have often been premised on the assumption that there has been a U.S. shortage of highly skilled computer technicians. And employers report that scientific and technical positions are often hard to fill (ibid., p. 54). Large corporations have argued that there are no skilled workers at home as a rationale for transferring computer-based operations to other countries. Although there are some shortages (nursing, for example), the evidence suggests that there is no actual shortage of programmers or systems analysts. "Rather, technology companies have hired lower-wage foreign programmers while thousands of more experienced (and more expensive) American programmers remained unemployed" (Lafer, 2002, p. 54; see also Lardner, 1998).

Even in occupations such as nursing where there have been shortages, most technical professions are quite small as a share of the overall workforce, and therefore the total number of such jobs going begging has never been a significant source of job openings. For example, "the combined total of jobs for mathematicians, computer scientists, computer programmers, numerical control tool programmers, science technicians, electrical and electronic technicians, health technicians, and health assessment and treating occupations amounted to only 4.1% of the total workforce in 1984. After twenty years of unprecedented growth, this share is projected to grow to only 6.4% by the year 2006" (Lafer, 2002, p. 54; see also Galbraith, 1998; and Mishel, Bernstein, and Boushey, 2003).

Furthermore, as the technology has been adapted by business, "computer work" has been highly differentiated, with technical knowledge used by a relatively small group of well-paid specialists, and the vast majority of daily computer operators carrying out tasks in relatively low-wage occupations with few educational requirements (social workers, secretaries, credit card and computer call center operators, etc.) (ibid., p. 56; see also Frenkel, Korczynski, Shire, and Tam, 1999; Galbraith, 1998; and Osterman, 2001).

To make the case for terminating the job-creation programs of CETA in 1982, Ronald Reagan argued that "if you look at the want ads, you see lots of available jobs" (Lafer, 2002, p. 44). As Lafer points out, however, "A look at the want ads in the newspapers shows that there are, indeed jobs, but only for the number of people the ads specify; and this illusion masks a deeper truth, which is that for large numbers of the poor there are NO decently paying jobs, no matter how hard they work or what training programs they enroll in" (2002, p. 44).

A report in the *New York Times* in 1999 offered on-the-ground confirmation of the lack of jobs for workers who need them. Journalist Amy Waldman reported that at the height of the "full economy" in 1999, about 5,000 lined up for a job fair in the Bronx, NY. More than 40 employers were inside the Bronx County Building, trying to fill positions from sales clerk to registered nurse. Many of the people in line, who had been waiting for over three hours, said they had been looking for work, most often entry-level clerical positions, for months. Many of the people in line were on public assistance and were trying to get off it. "There is a huge pool of people with entry-level skills and not enough jobs for them," said Lucy Mayo, an employment specialist. Most of the jobs that were available, she said, offered low pay and no benefits. For example, Barnes and Noble, which was scheduled to open a new bookstore at Bay Plaza in the Bronx, had 50–75 jobs to fill. The jobs pay $7.25 an hour, are part-time with no benefits. Some of the large corporations there, however (Montefiore Medical Centers, and the Correctional Services Corporation), offered benefits after six months. One man, aged 25, said he had left his last manufacturing job in Chatham, NJ [a suburb of New York City], because the transportation was eating up half of his $7 hourly pay. With two children to support, he had been looking for work for six months. . . . There were 2,600 jobs created in the

Bronx last year (1998), mostly in retail and construction. Still, 250,000 Bronx residents work outside the borough (Waldman, 1999).

Compounding the problem for entry-level workers, college-educated persons may be crowding them out. Research by Richard Murnane and Frank Levy shows that controlling for a person's mathematics or reading skill while a high school senior eliminates a substantial portion of the growth in the college-to-high school wage premium in a later period (for women essentially all, and for men about one-third). This suggests that it is basic high school-level skills that are increasingly in demand by employers, who are relying more and more on college completion as a screen to get the people who are more likely to have them (Murnane and Levy, 1996, p. 29; see also Pigeon and Wray, 1999).

That employers hire college-educated workers for jobs that require high school skills helps to explain why a more highly educated workforce does not necessarily earn higher wages. As entry-level employees obtain more education, employers merely ratchet up the requirements (see Galbraith, 1998; and Moss and Tilly, 2001).

POVERTY

One consequence of a predominance of low-wage work and too few jobs in the U.S. is numbers of poor people that approach the figures of 1959—before massive urban poverty became a national issue. Although the percentages are lower now, the numbers are still staggering: There were about as many people officially poor in 1993 (39.2 million) as in 1959 (39.4 million)—three years before Michael Harrington galvanized the nation's conscience, and ultimately a "war on poverty," by demonstrating that upwards of 40 million people were poor (Harrington, 1963, p. 9). (In 2003, almost 36 million—35.8 million—were officially poor.)

Most poverty today is urban poverty. Demographic researcher Myron Orfield analyzed the distribution of poverty populations in the 25 largest metropolitan areas in the U.S. and found (confirmed by the 2000 Census) that about two-thirds of the U.S. poor today live in central cities and "urbanized," financially distressed suburbs.

As has been the case since the mid-1960s, most of the urban poor are Black or Latino. As we will see in later chapters, the concentration of Black and Latino poor in low-income urban areas is due not only to a lack of jobs with decent pay (and insufficient income to support a move out if desired) but to the lack of federal and state implementation of antiracial discrimination laws, the lack of affordable housing outside of urban areas, and state-enabled local zoning exclusions based on social class (income). Part II of this book presents a detailed discussion of this new metropolitan demographic, its causes, and the implications it presents for urban education.

The figures on poverty presented so far in this chapter are based on federal guidelines, and they underestimate the number of people who are actually poor. The federal poverty formula in 1998—during the height of the '90s boom—determined that 13% of U.S. households (families and unattached individuals) were poor. A single mother with two children was officially poor if she earned $13,133 or less in that year. In 2003, a single mother of two children was officially poor if she earned $15,260 or less.

Many social scientists have come to believe that these amounts are too low, and that individuals and families with incomes up to 200% of government thresholds are poor. The official formula for figuring poverty—designed by federal employee Molly Orshansky in 1963 and used in the war on poverty—utilized data collected in the 1950s. The formula Orshansky devised was based on the price of a minimal food budget (as determined by the Department of Agriculture). She multiplied the cost of food by three, to cover housing and health-care costs. This figure, adjusted for family size, was the level below which families and individuals were designated as poor.

Research in the 1950s showed that families spent about a third of their budget on food. Since that time, however, the costs of housing and health care have skyrocketed. Thus, most families today spend only about a fifth of their income on food, and considerably more on housing and health care (Bernstein, Brockt, and Spade-Aguilar, 2000, pp. 12–13; see also Short, Iceland, and Ganer, 1999, and recommendations by the National Research Council, reported in Citro and Michael, 1995).

A recent national assessment of working families concluded that twice the official poverty line is a more realistic measure of those who face critical and serious hardships in the U.S. This research documents that working families with income up to 200% of the poverty line "experience as many hardships" as families who are officially poor (Boushey, Brocht, Gundersen, and Bernstsein, 2001, p. 2).

A calculation of the individuals who earned less than 200% of the poverty level in 2001 demonstrates a much larger percentage of poor employees than is commonly acknowledged: 84.3% of Hispanic workers, 80% of Black workers, and 64.3% of White workers made wages at or under 200% of the official poverty line (Mishel, Bernstein, and Schmitt, 2001, pp. 130–139). A calculation of *families* living with earnings up to 200% of the poverty line reveals that Black and Latino families face the greatest financial hurdles. Over 50% of Black and Latino families earn less than 200% of the poverty level, compared to only 20.3% of White families, even though White families make up the majority (50.5%) of families that fall below 200% of the poverty level (ibid., p. 12).

Families headed by a worker with less than a high school education are the most likely to fall below 200% (68.6%), but over three-fourths of families who fall below are headed by a worker with a high school education or more. An indication of the failure of higher education to secure good wages is the fact that over a third (33.6%) are headed by a worker with some college or a college degree (ibid., p. 13). And an indictment of the failure of full-time work to provide a decent living is the fact that a full half (50.0%) of families falling below 200% of the poverty line have a *full-time, year-round worker* (ibid., p. 15).

The statistics in this chapter relate in a fairly staid manner what is actually a potentially inflammatory political situation. A humane reckoning of poverty reveals that the vast majority of African Americans and Latinos who have jobs, and more than two-thirds of employed Whites, do not earn enough to live on. This outrages me, as the experience must anger those who live it. But the situation is not immutable. Economies are indeed political, regulated by officials elected and appointed who formulate legislation, legal decisions, and other policy. These officials, and their mandates, can be changed—but only if all of us who are incensed by the policies' indecency stand together.

In order for injustice to create an outrage that can ultimately be channeled into public demands, knowledge of the facts is necessary, and an appreciation of the consequences must be clear. I hope this chapter clarifies the situation regarding poverty. It is also extremely important, and will be discussed at length later, that people who are poor come to see their situation not as a result of their own failure but as a result of systemic causes. That is, if governments created enough jobs, and if businesses paid higher wages, workers would not be poor.

And knowledge is crucial to an accurate understanding of what plagues urban education. We must know where the problem lies in order to identify workable solutions. We can win the war against poverty and poor schools only if we know where the poverty originates. The next chapter describes one important source, federal policies that maintain low-wage work and unemployment in urban areas, and ways these can set up failure for the families and schools there.

2

Federal Policies Maintain
Urban Poverty

Americans have long had faith in education to raise the economic prospects of the poor. And the federal government, primarily since the 1981–89 presidency of Ronald Reagan, has relied on the policy that increased education (e.g., college or job training) would put the poor to work, and thereby substantially reduce U.S. poverty. African American, Latino, and White workers now have more education than ever before, as detailed in the sections that follow. However, as the previous chapter demonstrates, wages have been falling across the board for at least two decades. For an increasing number of Americans, but for Blacks and Latinos especially, job training, a two-year associate's degree—or even a bachelor's degree—does not ensure escape from near-poverty or even poverty wages.

I believe it is important for educators, public policy analysts, and practitioners to take hold of the fact that economic policies yield widespread low-wage work even among an increasingly educated workforce. This phenomenon seriously strains the credibility of urban school reform as a solution to the problems of the urban poor. Unless we make some changes in the way the macro-economy works, economic policy will trump not only urban school reform but the individual educational achievement of urban students as well.

FEDERAL POLICIES THAT MAINTAIN LOW-WAGE WORK

Federal policies that conduce to widespread poverty-wage work in the U.S. include (among others) minimum wage legislation, antiunionization laws, federal job training programs without job creation, class-biased regulations of the Federal Reserve Bank, ineffective federal implementation of policies that outlaw racial discrimination in hiring, and free trade agreements that allow thousands of corporations to abandon U.S. workers for less-expensive locations in other countries.

This chapter takes an in-depth look at two of the policies most directly responsible for poverty-wage work: minimum wage legislation and federal policies that prevent union organizing. The chapter also attempts a realistic assessment of the widespread belief that lack of education (rather than macroeconomic policy) is responsible for the low wages of workers, and that sufficient increases in education will ultimately reduce poverty.

Finally, the chapter presents a number of macroeconomic policies that would benefit workers as a class, and several additional macroeconomic strategies that would increase opportunities for urban Black and Latino workers in particular, whose situation differs in important ways from that of Whites.

Minimum Wage Policy

A major determinant of wages for almost one out of five employees in the U.S. is the federal minimum wage statute. Of these employees who earn between $5.15, the federal minimum, and $6.15, half lived in households with annual incomes of less than $25,000; 27% were parents, including over a million single mothers (Economic Policy Institute 2002, p. 4; Mishel, Bernstein, and Boushey 2003, pp. 187–199). The minimum wage is a provision of the Fair Labor Standards Act (FLSA), passed in 1938. This law set a minimum wage and standards for overtime compensation. Minimum wage increases are legislated by Congress as amendments to the FLSA. Thus, increases are based solely on decisions made by Congress.

The minimum wage was higher between 1940 and 1970 than it was in 2000 (all in 2000 dollars). In the 1980s and '90s the minimum wage was allowed to fall, despite four increases in the latter decade. The low minimum wage was a major contributor to the growth in inequality after 1980, and to the increase in poverty-range wages of larger percentages of the workforce (Economic Policy Institute, July 2004, p. 2; Sklar, Mykyta, and Wefald, 2001).

The minimum wage law applies to employees of companies with revenues of at least $500,000 a year, and to employees of smaller firms engaged in interstate commerce or in the production of goods for such commerce. Also covered are employees of federal, state, or local government agencies, hospitals, and schools. The law typically applies to domestic workers. Full-time students, apprentices, and workers with disabilities may be paid less than the minimum under special permission of the Department of Labor. States may require higher minimums.

The number of states with minimum wages above the federal level has gone from 6 to 15 in the past few years, with additional states considering action in 2005. Two states, Washington and Oregon, now index their minimum wage to the Consumer Price Index, to pace it with the rising cost of living. In 2004, the minimum wage in these two states was $7.05 in Oregon, and $7.16 in Washington (Economic Policy Institute, July 2004, 12; see also Chapman, 2003).

A full-time employee (working 2,080 hours a year) earning $5.15 an hour earns $10,712 a year, well below the poverty line for a family of three. An analysis in 1998 revealed that a woman working the average number of hours worked by poor, single mothers (1,164 in that year) would earn $11,714 in 1998 dollars if she earned the minimum wage, received food stamps, and the Earned Income Tax Credit or "refund" (see next chapter). Even with these federal benefits, her income was still below the federal poverty line for a family of three in 1998 ($13,133) (Economic Policy Institute, 2002, p. 3).

Increases in the minimum wage raise the wages of low-income workers in general, not just those below the official poverty line: Sixty-one percent of workers who would benefit from an increase to $7.00 in 2006 are women, and disproportionate shares are African American (15%) and Latinos (19%) (Economic Policy Institute, July 2004, p. 7; Economic Policy Institute, 2002, pp. 2–4; Bernstein, Hartmann, and Schmitt 1999, p. 1). Contrary to the claims of those who oppose raising the minimum wage (that an increase will force employers to fire or hire fewer of those affected by the increase), studies of the 1990–91 and 1996–97 minimum wage increases failed to find any systematic, significant job losses associated with the increases, and found no evidence of negative employment effects on small businesses (Economic Policy Institute, July 2004, p. 7).

One of the main lessons of the minimum wage is that this economic policy, a decision made by Congress, is a crucial determinant of who lives in poverty. And thus being poor while working is very much a result of a federal decision that is political in nature. An additional consequence of widespread poverty wages paid by businesses is that when companies do not pay wages on which workers can support themselves, taxpayers are asked to ante up dollars for public assistance (welfare, food stamps, housing subsidies, etc.). This process effectively subsidizes business, but those taxpayers who complain typically blame workers.

Company executives state that they pay the minimum "because they can"—they know that replacement workers are easy to find (Leonhardt, 2003, p. 1). The fact that there is a pool of unemployed labor in reserve keeps all employees' wages down. As Federal Reserve chairman Alan Greenspan acknowledged, a large number of unemployed or underemployed workers leads to a "heightened sense of job insecurity and, as a consequence, subdued wage gains" (Pollin, 1998, p. 20).

Unions and Wages

Belonging to a union is a strong determinant of increased wages for workers in most major occupations and industries. In 2000, union wages were 28.4% higher than those for unorganized workers. Since union members are far more likely than other workers to win employer-provided pension and medical coverage, the union premium for total compensation is about twice as large as the wage premium by itself (Mishel, Bernstein, and Schmitt, 2001, p. 181; see also Mishel, Bernstein, and Boushey, 2003, p. 191).

Federal policies since the early 1980s that allow businesses to fire and otherwise penalize workers for attempting to organize unions have helped to push union membership down from 25% in 1978 to just under 14% in 2000. The decline in unionization has most hurt blue-collar men aged 25 to 34—precisely that portion of the population that experienced the most severe decline in real (inflation-adjusted) wages since 1980 (Lafer, 2002, p.78; see also Mishel, Bernstein, and Boushey, 2003).

Gordon Lafer argues that for non-college-educated workers, unionization can be much more important than further education: "For nonunion high school dropouts, the advantage of finishing school is an increase of $2.25 per hour, while organizing one's workplace will benefit the worker more than twice as much. Similarly, high school graduates contemplating getting some college training short of a bachelors would actually do three times better to organize than go back to school" (2002, p. 78).

The union differential is important for the urban working poor because the difference in wages is most extreme in jobs many of them hold—service occupations—the very sectors that are projected to provide most of the new jobs for non-college-educated workers. In 2000, the union premium for service occupations was an average 69.4%—with weekly earnings for unions members of $554 and $327 for those not in unions. Although White males hold the highest-paying union jobs, the importance of unionization may be greatest for women and minorities. "In 2000, weekly earnings for males who were union members exceeded those for nonunion men by 19.2%; and women union members earned 30.5% more than their nonunion counterparts. Similarly, the weekly earnings differential was 26.7% for White workers, while it was much higher for Black workers (36.7%), and for Hispanic workers" (54.9%) (ibid., p. 78).

There is a particularly serious implication here for urban high school students who will not, under present policy conditions, have the funds to complete college. Rather than obtain further higher education, they should perhaps become involved in the political contention necessary to organize a union at their place of work. There is a lesson in this for educators, too, as it challenges our notion of the power of further education to boost income for low-income minority students. This challenge is explored in detail below.

EDUCATION AND INCOME

Macroeconomic policy is based on the assumption that increased education of the workforce will alleviate poverty. We have already seen that a lack of jobs undermines this assumption somewhat. But *can* education be used as a remedy for poverty and low-wage work? Or must we change federal policies in order to solve the problem?

A person's education is, of course, an important determinant of one's income. However, it plays less of a role than we typically assume. Indeed, the evidence on the relationship between education and earnings shows that education explains about only a *third* of income levels. Therefore, it cannot serve either as an explanation for Americans' falling income or as a workable strategy for correcting this trend.

There is no question that, on average, individuals with more education earn higher salaries. This is true for both men and women. In 1999, wages of college graduates were 74% higher than those of high school graduates. Average hourly wages in 1999 were $20.58 for those with college degrees and $11.83 for high school graduates (Mishel, Bernstein, and Schmitt, 2001, p. 153). However, many factors can mitigate and even reverse the wage effects of education. For example, gender is an important determinant. Female high school graduates earn *less* than male high school *dropouts*. And women with post bachelor's degrees earn less than men who have just a bachelor's (Lafer, 2002, p. 47; see also Mishel, Bernstein, and Boushey, 2001; and Wolff, 2003). For nonsupervisory workers, the relationship between education and earnings is weakest in traditionally female occupations. Howell and Wolff found that the trend of increasing skill requirements accompanied by falling wages was most pronounced among childcare workers, hairdressers, cashiers, office machine operators, receptionists, and typists—all occupations staffed by women (Howell and Wolff, 1991, p. 495).

In this case, it is the absence of federal (and state) policies that is the problem. There are no effective comparable worth laws to equalize the pay for men and women who do the same kind of work, and the lack of enforcement of federal antidiscrimination law allows employers to assign women to low-wage jobs without government reprisal. One study found that effective pay equity policies would enable up to 40% of poor working women to leave public assistance (Lafer, 2002, p. 84).

In addition, discrimination on the basis of race often renders education irrelevant. For example, in the nation's largest labor market, California, a study of entry-level workers found that Black and Latino youth had improved significantly on every measure of skill, in absolute terms, as well as relative to White workers. Yet their wages were falling further behind those of Whites. The effects of race outweighed those of education, with minority workers at every level of education losing ground to similarly prepared Whites (ibid.). Whenever trials have been carried out in which identically qualified Black and White candidates applied for the same job, a "pattern of discriminatory hiring has been revealed across a wide range of entry-level occupations. . . . It is clear than more vigorous enforcement of anti-discrimination laws is a prerequisite to enabling minority workers to realize any payoff to skills" (Lafer, 2002, p. 84).

Educational attainment, then, is cross-cut by institutional factors of unionization, gender, and race—as well as others not discussed here: free trade that attracts companies to low-wage countries; an increasing use of part-time workers; age; and industry regulation—e.g., industries like clothing and toy manufacturing are unregulated, and employers can—and do—pay the minimum (see Galbraith, 1998, Chapter 3; and Wolff, 2003). Since these institutional factors cut across all levels of education, the ultimate wage that any person earns is determined by the interaction of many of these factors (Lafer, 2002, p. 47; see also Mishel and Tierra, 2000; and Howell, Houston, and Milberg, 1999). A telling statistic regarding the weakening effect of education on income is that by 1996, one out of every six college graduates was in a job that paid *less* than the average salary of high school graduates (Monthly Labor Review, 1998, in Lafer, 2002, p. 47). Thus, while education and wages are indeed related, this relationship is often compromised and can even be reversed by other determinants.

Indeed, over the past 30 years, the real wages (adjusted for inflation) of high school graduates fell by 11.3%, while those of college graduates rose only by 5.7% (ibid., p. 153). Most (60%) of the change in the college premium over these years was due to a worsening situation for high school graduates rather than to increasing wages for college graduates. For male workers the trend is bleak. Since 1973, the gap between wages of college- and high school-educated male workers has increased by $4.06 an hour; nearly two-thirds (70%) of this change is due to the bottom falling out of the high school market, rather than rises in the wages of college workers (Lafer, 2002, p. 60; see also Gottschalk, 1997; and Wolff, 2003). As Lafer argues, "in this light, the rising college premium cannot be interpreted as a growing demand for higher education" (ibid.).

An increasing number of college graduates are making poverty wages. Decades ago, at the beginning of the 1940s, between 1.6% and 1.4% of employed heads of households earned around the minimum wage (50% below the federal minimum wage to 50% above it). The vast majority of employed heads of households made more than this. The percentage of workers making around the minimum wage has increased over the years so that by 1990 between 8.8% and 11% of those with a *bachelor's degree* made around the minimum wage. This means that about one of ten workers with a four-year college degree is now making poverty wages (Levin-Waldman 1999, p. 18).

In the 20 years between 1979 and 1999, the number of college graduates in the labor force grew from 17.9 million to 38.9 million—an increase of over 100%. But, they have not been in great demand. Rather, a significant share of them has been unable to find jobs in occupations that make use of their degrees. By 1990, almost 20% of graduates—almost 6 million (5.7 million) college-educated workers—were not able to find college-level work. This total included "75,000 college graduates working as street vendors or door-to-door salespeople, 166,000 as truck and bus drivers, 83,000 as maids, housemen, janitors, or cleaners, and 688,000 who were unemployed" (Lafer, 2002, p. 61; see also Economic Policy Institute, July 21, 2004, pp. 1–2). These figures are derived from workers' experiences in the 1990s. The Department of Labor predicts that in the first ten years of this century, although the retirement of college-educated baby boomers will create more openings in college jobs, the number of new college graduates will continue to grow more rapidly than the number of jobs that require a bachelor's degree. The college diploma has become increasingly less effective in guaranteeing middle-class wages (ibid.).

Indeed, levels of education in the U.S. have been increasing steadily—yet as we saw in the last chapter, incomes have been falling for the last 30 years. The average education of American workers was 9.2 years in 1940; it is now over 13 years. The percentage of American workers with a high school diploma has also increased over the past three decades. This is true for men, women, and all racial and economic groups. Even the education levels of welfare recipients have improved significantly. The share of welfare recipients who have high school diplomas increased from 42% in 1979 to almost two-thirds (70%) in 1999 (Lafer, 2002, p. 51. See also Burtless, 1995; Loprest, 1999; and U.S. General Accounting Office, 2001).

It is important to note that even though college levels have risen across the board, they are still considerably lower for

African Americans, Latinos, and low-income students of all colors. In 2001, 19% of the U.S. labor force had a bachelor's degree, and 8.9% also had advanced degrees. Of non-Hispanic White employees, 21.7% had a bachelor's degree and 10.9% had advanced degrees. The corresponding figure for employed Blacks is 14.1% with a bachelor's degree and 5.6% with advanced degrees; and for Hispanics (of any race) is 8.3% and 3.0% (Mishel, Bernstein, and Boushey 2003, p. 163). College attainment figures also vary by social class: Although 48% of low-income students *who complete high school* now enroll in a 2- or 4-year college upon graduation, only 7% of *all* lower-income students obtain a B.A. by age 26, compared to 60% of upper-income students (Education Trust, 2004b, p. 5; Ingels, 2002). The maximum federal Pell Grant that low-income students can obtain to pay for college now covers only 42% of the average fixed cost of a public four-year institution, compared to 84% 20 years ago (The Education Trust, 2004, p. 19). The lack of financial assistance, and a reluctance to take on huge loans that they fear they will not be able to repay, is a crucial reason low-income students do not finish college (Bloom, 2005, p. 5; see also Fossey and Bateman, 1998; Gladieux, 2004; and National Center for Public Policy and Higher Education, 2002).

If education held prime responsibility for wages, then a decline in the quality of education would lead wages of skilled workers to rise as they become less common and competition for them raises their wages. Thus, if school quality had deteriorated in the last two decades, we would expect to see income inequality growing faster among workers educated during those decades than among older workers. However, every study to research this question agrees that inequality has risen equally among older workers and younger workers, and therefore "no evidence exists for a deterioration in standards of worker education, however they are measured" (Lafer, 2002, p. 52; see also Levy and Murnane, 1994).

Similarly, if the quality of education has declined, then wages would fall as workers acquired fewer skills or less knowledge. But available evidence suggests that the caliber of education has remained constant or improved slightly over the past 30 years. Although achievement test scores are not in total agreement, they suggest that overall the reading and math proficiency of 17-year-olds has held steady or increased slightly since the early 1970s. During the 1970s, '80s, and '90s, the percentage of White 17-year-old students who read at the "intermediate" level or above increased from 83.7% to 87%, while that of African American students increased from 40.1% to 66%. SAT scores improved for every racial/ethnic group during the 1980s, and average scores for the U.S. as a whole rose somewhat through the year 2000 (U.S. Department of Education, 2000, Tables 113, 123, and 133; for trends over the 1980s, see Howell, 1994, p. 84). Average scores for White, Black, Asian American, Mexican American, American Indian, and Puerto Rican students all improved over the 1980s and 1990s (Bracey 1997; also U.S. Department of Education, 2000, Table 133).

Thus, no evidence exists for the belief that deteriorating education—whether measured as fewer years of school, falling achievement levels, or demographics of the workforce—are the cause of the falling wages of U.S. workers. Rather, the evidence points to macroeconomic policy and resulting employer practice as culpable regarding for the worsening position of U.S. workers.

I take two lessons from this: First, for many students, especially females and students of color, economic policy may trump educational attainment. Second, we cannot expect education to compensate for inequalities wrought by macroeconomic policy. The primacy of federal economic regulations in maintaining poor wages suggests that it is not prudent to rely on the reform of education to increase the economic opportunities of Blacks and Latinos from poor families. A change in macroeconomic policies is also warranted.

POLICIES WE NEED

Fortunately, federal policies that make the economy more responsive to the needs of working-class employees are not without precedent in the United States. For example, during the decades following World War II, federal price and wage guidelines kept prices stable and wages up. During those years, the minimum wage was kept at 50% of the median industrial wage. When unionized, well-paid workers did better, minimum wage workers did better too (Galbraith, 1998, pp. 164–166). The antipathy of recent U.S. economic elites to wage and price controls is so strong that—as an example—the United States is the only major developed nation without price or profit controls on even that most important commodity, medicine (Weiner, 2001, p. 1).

Largely as a result of popular protest and organizing, in the decades following World War II, full employment, trade, and labor unions were all protected by federal policies and legislation. After 1969, full employment and protectionism of jobs by trade restrictions were abandoned as national goals (Galbraith, 1998, p. 166).

The Federal Reserve Bank was created in 1913. Its statutory goals are set out in the Employment Act of 1946, and amended by the Humphreys-Hawkins Full Employment and Balanced Growth Act of 1978. Both laws are very clear: The twin goals of economic policy are to maintain a high level of employment and production, as well as to maintain reasonable price stability. In recent decades, Chairmen Burns, Volker, and Greenspan have concentrated on the stability of prices (Thorbecke, 2000, p. 2). They have, for the most part, ignored the mandate to maintain low unemployment—despite the low unemployment of the late 1990s, which was a function of the booming economy itself. Low unemployment, if it is sustained over several years, generally helps the poor first, and helps the poor the most, as more of them are able to obtain work (Economic Policy Institute, July 9, 2004, pp. 1–2). We observed this in the late 1990s, in the uptick of wages in the retail sector, and in the (albeit slight) rise of employment in many central city neighborhoods.

To reinstate the other half of the federal reserve mandate, we need to implement policies that produce low unemployment: Policies like maintaining low interest rates, increasing government spending on infrastructure and human capital development, and creating demand-side pressure—a need for workers. In addition to the support of full employment policies, we should reinstate price and wage guidelines. The wages corporations pay need to be regulated like they used to be, so that wages in the retail and other low-wage sectors are indexed, like the minimum wage used to be.

Other macroeconomic policies that would be important for workers include the creation of jobs by the federal government for those who need and want them; passage of significantly higher minimum wage laws with health insurance and other benefits; elimination for the working poor of regressive tax policies that fall most heavily on them (payroll taxes, for example, as detailed in the next chapter); and the enactment of policies that protect union organizing.

Moreover, the body of worker protection law that already exists does not extend to the new, large group of working poor.

Laws covering workplace health and safety, protection from discrimination, family and medical leave, wage and hour enforcement, unemployment compensation, workers' compensation, and business-closing notice, all bypass most low-wage workers. A majority of workers in low-wage jobs are employed in small businesses, which are not covered by many worker-protection laws. "In other words, workers who are the most vulnerable to the dictates of employers are left without assistance from the government" (Shulman, 2002, pp. 1–3). Many of these most vulnerable workers are Black and Latino residents of urban areas.

BLACK AND LATINO WORKERS

Following the civil rights movement, during the 1970s, Blacks made substantial economic progress: With mass migration to cities came increased years of education and rising wages; and civil rights laws and affirmative action conjoined to increase Blacks' opportunities (Smith and Welch, 1989, p. 90). Indeed, by the late 1970s, wages of Black and White college graduates were nearly equal, and the wages of Black women surpassed those of White women (Freeman, 1976, p. 519). The numbers of Black managers and professionals—especially in government agencies—increased significantly (Moss and Tilly, 2001, p. 5).

But there remained a large group living in concentrated poverty in America's inner cities. By 1990, there were more people living in concentrated poverty in America's cities than at any time since the 1960s. Prolonged unemployment, underemployment, and detachment from the labor market were prevalent (see Wilson, 1987; Anyon, 1997).

During the 1980s, the wage gap between employed working- and middle-class Blacks and Whites began to increase. Black women were less likely to find work than in the 1970s and early 1980s (Bound and Dresser, 1999, quoted in Moss and Till, 2001, p. 6). During this decade there was also a downward movement out of middle-wage employment for Blacks into very-low-wage employment for many, and relatively higher-wage employment for a few (Lawrence Mishel, Jared Bernstein, and Heather Boushey, 2003, p. 140; see also Bound and Dresser, 1999).

And in the early 1990s, in part because of the recessions of 1990 and 1991, young Black workers suffered further wage and employment setbacks, even though Blacks were obtaining higher levels of education than ever, and had been closing the gap with

Whites in both educational attainment and test scores (Moss and Tilly, 2001, p. 6; see also Bound and Freeman, 1992; and Jencks, 1991). During the 1990s, wages diverged widely between young Black and White male college graduates (Bound and Freeman, 1992, p. 201). Latinos also experienced economic regression in the 1990s (Moss and Tilly, 2001, p. 7; see also Corcoran, Heflin, and Reyes, 1999).

By the mid-1990s it was apparent that a larger divide existed between the wages of people of color and Whites than in the 1980s; and, as I noted in the last chapter, by 2000 almost a third (31.8%) of Black workers were in jobs paying less than poverty-level wages and 40.4% of Hispanic workers were making below poverty level wages (while 20% of White workers made less than poverty level wages in 2000 (Mishel, Bernstein, and Boushey, 2003, pp. 137–140).

What accounts for the deteriorated position of Blacks and Latinos in the labor market when they had been obtaining higher levels of education? I have pointed to several macroeconomic policies that play a role. But the common explanation is that they do not have the skills required by the information/technology economy. The increase in earnings inequality of the last two decades of the 20th century is often laid to an upward shift in skill demands. Thus, it is said that because Blacks and Latinos have less or lower quality education, they are not hired by employers. A corollary to this argument is that the "digital divide" is producing a growing racial divide (ibid., p. 43).

To test these assumptions, Philip Moss and Chris Tilly assessed employers' desires for workers' "hard skills" (literacy, numeracy, computer familiarity, cognitive abilities)—which are said to be the basis of the digital divide—and "soft skills," which refer to interaction (ability to interact with customers, coworkers, and supervisors, including friendliness, teamwork, ability to fit in, and appropriate affect, language use, grooming, and attire), as well as motivation (which refers to enthusiasm, positive work attitudes, commitment, dependability, integrity, and willingness to learn) (2001, pp. 44–45).

Managers in various economic sectors interviewed by Moss and Tilly expressed increased demands for *soft* skills more frequently than for any hard skill but for computer literacy. Except for employers in manufacturing firms where workers needed to program computers or read printouts, "all other employers emphasized the soft skills of interaction with customers and motivation for work as just as important as basic reading and arithmetic skills" (or, to use these researchers' phrase, "attitude trumps technical facility" in a large number of jobs) (p. 61). Indeed, another researcher, Peter Cappelli, has concluded that the alleged "skill shortages" decried by employers in the 1990s referred mainly to issues of worker motivation (1996, in Moss and Tilly, 2001, p. 48). Osterman, as well, found in a large, representative sample, that managers report behavioral traits as one of the two most important job criteria in about 82% of cases, and the top criterion in about half (1995).

What Moss and Tilly also discovered, however, is that managers' definition of, and evaluation of, applicants' soft skills is highly subjective and is context bound. Moreover, employers typically conflate the two, aggregating appearance, ways of talking, and self-presentation with possession of the hard skills. In interviews, managers mixed and entangled comments on inner-city Blacks' and Latinos' hard skills (education, intelligence) with evaluation of soft skills (use of language, dress, and attitudes) (pp. 44, 99). Unfortunately, most employers do not screen applicants for entry-level jobs through formal measures; rather, they rely on the pre-employment interview (pp. 44, 209, 213). Thus, the increased desire by managers for soft skills may make it harder for non-White applicants, because it may increase racial discrimination by employers (p. 45).

The lack of enforcement of federal laws against discrimination in hiring is an important reason, that—despite more years of education—a smaller percentage of African American men are working now than in recent decades. Only 52% of young (aged 16 to 24) noninstitutionalized, out-of-school Black males with high school degrees or less were employed in 2002, compared to 62% 20 years ago. In contrast, the labor force activity of comparable White and Latino males has been steady over the last two decades, and employment among young Black women has increased.

Employment for young Black men even declined fairly continuously between 1989 and 1997, despite the strong economic recovery that occurred after 1992. Labor force *attachment* (which includes searching for work) for young Black men suffered a sharp 14 percentage point decline over the 1980–2000 period. This contrasts sharply with the experience of young, less-educated Latino men, who essentially achieved employment parity with their White counterparts during these decades (Offner and Holzer, 2002, p. 3; see also Mishel, Bernstein, and Boushey, 2003, p. 232).

It is important to understand that the weakening attachment of young, less-educated Black males to the labor force occurred despite the higher educational attainment of the group: A much larger percentage of the group held high school degrees at the end of the period than at the beginning (Offner and Holtz, 2002, p. 4; see also Cherry and Rodgers, 2000; and Freeman, 1991).

Discrimination in hiring because of the emphasis on soft skills may be one reason fewer young African American men are working. It is also the case, however, that high incarceration rates among members of this group contribute to their declining employment. By 2000, 10% of Black males aged 20–24 were incarcerated and, among high-school dropouts, over *one-third* were incarcerated (Mauer, 2003a, p. 4). Research by Holzer and Stoll documented that many employers are reluctant to hire individuals with criminal records. Since substantial numbers of prisoners released everyday in the U.S. return to low-income urban neighborhoods, their joblessness contributes to the low rates of employment in young Black males (Holzer and Stoll, 2001, p. 7; see also Mauer, 2003b).

The reluctance of employers to hire young Black males and workers of color in general—this widespread, illegal discrimination in hiring—has important implications for federal policies to assist them. It suggests that policies that might reduce *overall* unemployment in the U.S. in the hopes of employing significant numbers of Black workers may not assist African American males. During the nearly "full" employment economy of the late 1990s, for example, the employment rate of young Black women who did not finish high school rose by 14 points. However, the percentage of those young Black women who were employed went from 23% to 37%—still very low (Mishel, Bernstein, and Boushey, 2003, p.222). So policies that create jobs—with the federal government as employer of last resort—are indicated.

Moreover, it is crucial that we establish programs to ease the formerly incarcerated into jobs, education, and civic life. Sixteen hundred prisoners are released each day in the U.S., summing to almost 600,000 every year. Nearly two-thirds of the nation's prisoners are African American or Latino. In many states, men and women returning to civilian status are barred for life from receiving even temporary welfare benefits. Without access to jobs and without welfare, there is little they can do to obtain money legally.

Former prisoners also lose access to student loans for higher education. In 2001–2002, 48,000 applicants were denied aid for further education under this provision. And in some states they are barred from living in public housing (in which many of them grew up). In 48 states and Washington, DC, voting rights of convicted felons are restricted. As a result of these laws, almost 5 million (4.7) persons are currently unable to vote, and an estimated 13% of Black men are barred from the voting booth (disenfranchisement figures for women are not available). As Marc Mauer (Mauer, 2003a) notes, the consequence of these policies can be huge:

> Consider the 2000 presidential election in Florida, which was decided by just 537 votes. In that state, an estimated 600,000 former felons were excluded from the ballot box under state law, even though they had completed their sentences. We will never know what impact their votes might have had, but the fact that the narrow margin of victory in Florida put George W. Bush in the White House clearly suggests that a small fraction of that group could have changed the outcome. (pp. 16–17; see also Mauer, 2003b).

As we have seen in this and the previous chapter, most jobs in the U.S. economy do not require college degrees, and a large share of these pay little more than subsistence wages. I also reported that about 80% of Black and Latino persons who are at work fill these unrewarding, sometimes degrading, slots. Urban students know these jobs are their future if they join the mainstream workforce. Many minority students, rather rationally it seems to me, reject what they call "slave" jobs, and take up other, often illegal, activities. If they do not have the funds to see themselves through to college completion, urban school reform did not offer them much at all.

Educators who care deeply about these students must come to grips with the fact that no amount of school reform as presently conceived will make the economy accept minority high school graduates in a more humane manner. Even the latest equity-seeking reform—small, democratic, and personally nurturing high schools where advanced courses are offered to make students college-ready—lacks meaning and consequence when students and their families cannot obtain support for the college years.

We need, therefore, to change the way the macroeconomy receives these students. Federal policies that mandate a living wage for entry-level work, that create urban jobs with advancement possibilities, and that penalize employers who prevent labor organizing or discriminate on the basis of color, would yield a vibrant set of economic opportunities that could give substance and meaning to the potentiality of school reform.

Another policy—to provide public funding for qualified low-income students to complete college—would certainly reward and motivate achievement efforts of urban students and, I suspect, teachers as well. Where there is a way, there is a will. Unless the labor market is made more receptive to low-income students, or until these students have sufficient college support, public macroeconomic policies will continue to trump educational achievement—and probably educational effort, as well.

There are other federal policies that curtail the possibilities for urban students and schools—for example, tax policies that cull the income of the working poor but not of vast corporations—and these are described in the following chapter.

3

Taxing Rich and Poor

Money matters. Family income shapes what parents can offer children, and thus affects children's life chances. I demonstrated in Chapter 2 how federal policies regarding minimum wage and union organizing (among other policies) maintain poverty incomes for many millions of Americans. This chapter reveals that rules set by Congress protect great wealth and the extremes of inequality that characterize the U.S. We will see that inequality of income is directly related to U.S. tax regulations. Regressive payroll and state taxes, historically low taxes charged those of high income, unethical but legal tax dodges for the wealthy, and laws that allow corporations with billions of dollars in profits to pay little or no tax, all support income and wealth inequality.

Tax regulations affect the amount of money available for public services like urban education. The dollars available for such spending are directly related to the federal rules about who pays how much tax for what. The less tax money available for public expenditures, the fewer the services, and the lower their quality. If we are concerned to fully invest in urban schools, job creation, and other policies that would create a more just society, we need to find moneys to pay for these investments. This chapter demonstrates that one viable source of income for these services is the vast untaxed income of very rich individuals and corporations.

INEQUALITY

Income inequality was, in 1999, at its highest level since the U.S. Census began tracking these data in 1947 (Economic Policy Institute, September 30, 1999, p. 1). By 1999, the income gap between rich and poor was so wide that the richest 2.7 million Americans, the top one percent, had as many after-tax dollars to spend as the bottom 100 million Americans (about $620 billion). That ratio more than doubled since 1977, when the top one percent had as much as the bottom 49 million (Johnston, September 5, 1999). The income disparity grew so much that four out of five households, or about 217 million people, were taking home a thinner slice of the economic pie in 1999 than in 1977 (ibid.; see also Johnston, 2003).

These figures understate the income of the richest one percent because they exclude income from stocks, which grew rapidly in the 1990s. By 1998, almost half—48.2%—of all households owned stock directly or indirectly (e.g., through retirement plans). But only 36.3% of all households owned stock worth $5,000 or more. And the top wealthiest one percent of households owned 42% of all stocks; the top five percent of households owned two-thirds of all stock, and the top 10% owned almost 80% of all stock. Thus almost 90% of all stock is owned by the wealthiest 20% of American households (Wolfe, 2002, pp. 28–29; Mishel, Bernstein, and Boushey, 2003, pp. 286–288).

Wealth inequality in the U.S. was at a 70-year high in 1998 (the latest data available), with the top one percent of wealth holders controlling 38% of total household wealth. A more limited focus on financial wealth (net worth minus home equity—i.e., liquidity or that which can readily be turned into cash) reveals that the richest one percent of households owned 47% of the total (Wolff, 2002, p. 8). Virtually all the growth in (marketable) wealth during the 1980s and 1990s went to the top 20% of households, while the bottom 40% of households saw its wealth decline in absolute terms (Wolff, 2002, pp. 8, 67).

During the 1990s, there was an explosion of wealth at the pinnacle: There was a 58% increase in the number of households with net worth equal to or exceeding $1 million (to 4.7 million households), and a 269% increase in the number of households with net worth equal to or exceeding $10 million (to 239,400 households). Most of this growth occurred between 1995 and 1998, and was a result of the surge in stock prices (pp. 15–16;

for other studies documenting the dramatic rise in wealth and income inequality in the last 30 years, see the following, among others: Champernowne and Cowell, 1998; Danziger and Gottschalk, 1995; Hungerford, 1993; Levy, 1999; Newman, 1993; Phillips, 1990 and 2002; and Wolff, 1994).

The Black-White wealth gap is significant. In 1998, the median Black household had a net worth of about $10,000—about 12% of the corresponding figure for Whites (Mishel, Bernstein, and Bloushey, 2003, p. 283; see also Oliver and Shapiro, 1997). In 1998, 27% of Black families reported zero or *negative* net worth, compared to 14% of White families (Wolff, 2002, p. 21). The gap in income between African American and White households was almost identical in 1967 and 1989 (ibid., p. 19).

CONCENTRATION OF WEALTH

The concentration of wealth in America is not a new phenomenon. It has a long, instructive past. This history demonstrates that tax rates on the rich directly affect inequality, and that the wealthy, until the early 1960s and President John F. Kennedy's administration, were taxed at much higher rates than in decades since. The historical record also reveals that the only periods during which the concentration of wealth has been halted or reversed are years following sustained political contestation—i.e., mass social movements.

In Philadelphia in the decade before the Revolution, the wealthiest four percent of city residents owned 56% of all assets in the city (Philips, 2002, p. 6). Tax lists in Boston in the 1770s show that the top five percent of Boston's taxpayers controlled 49% of the city's taxable assets (Nash, 1979, p.60).

The Southern colonies, however, were the wealthiest in North America because of slave ownership (Philips, 2002, p. 8). By 1774, wealth in the South per free person was 137 British pounds, compared to 46 pounds in the middle colonies and 38 in New England. Half of Southern wealth was in slaves—some 600,000 valued at about $120 million by 1780 (Phillips, 2002, p. 11).

In 1800, there was a large gap between rich and poor in major U.S. cities. The share of assets owned by the top 10% in New York, for example, rose from 54% in 1789 to 61% in 1795 (p. 18). During the mid-19th century, concentration of income in some cities increased further. In Boston, the share of the top one percent climbed from 33% in 1833 to 37% in 1848 (p. 23). In

Baltimore, Brooklyn, Milwaukee, and New Orleans, the top one percent held between 44% and 39% of wealth in the mid-19th century (p. 23).

Below the Mason-Dixon line in the 1850s, slave prices were 300% to 400% above 1800 levels, and the South was at its highest postcolonial share of U.S. wealth—roughly 30%. Kevin Philips reports that on the eve of the Civil War, "Dixie's four million slaves were worth between two and four billion dollars" (p. 32). Defeat of the South in the Civil War realigned national wealth and income. The share of U.S. assets held by the antebellum South of 1860, about 30%, fell to 12% in 1870 (p. 33).

In the North, income during the latter half of the 19th century became more concentrated, and major industrialists and financiers such as Carnegie, Rockefeller, and J.P. Morgan amassed personal fortunes. In 1863, the upper one percent of Manhattan residents (1,600 families) owned 61% of the city's wealth, up from 40% in 1845 (p. 41). One analysis in 1890 revealed that over half of the assets in the U.S. were held by one percent of U.S. families (up from almost a third of assets right after the Civil War). In Massachusetts, where the top eight percent owned 83% of the wealth in 1859–61, they had 90% by 1879–81 (p. 43).

Labor, Socialist, and other protests against the "Robber Barons" and massive wealth in the decades surrounding 1900— and the Progressive legislation that resulted—slowed down the amassing of the great U.S. fortunes, and temporarily halted the increase in the gap between rich and poor (p. 54). Policies that halted the increase included the 16th and 17th Amendments to the U.S. Constitution, which (respectively) authorized a federal income tax, and required direct election of U.S. senators instead of their selection by legislators—often on the basis of their connection to wealthy industrialists and other sources of wealth. The top rate of the income tax passed in 1913 was 77%—authorized in order to pay for the First World War.

During the Progressive Era, some antitrust legislation was also passed (p. 53), but was weakened during the "Roaring Twenties" by the Supreme Court. In addition, four tax cuts between 1921 and 1928 lowered the top individual income tax rate from 77% to 25% in 1929 (p. 219). By the end of the 1920s, the top one percent had increased their share of wealth to between 37% and 44% of overall U.S. wealth, depending on the calculation (p. 68).

In the 1930s, a period of mass protest against the resurgence of excess wealth during the 1920s and widespread poverty and unemployment of the Great Depression, tax increases were levied on the rich. Wealth deconcentrated once again. In 1935, during Roosevelt's second term, a so-called Wealth Tax was passed. Several new regulations separated banks and investment companies (the connection that had built the J.P. Morgan fortune), made the Federal Reserve Bank more responsive, and prohibited public utility holding companies (p. 71). Tax and revenue acts between 1935 and 1943 shrank the share of wealth of the top income bracket from 44% in 1929 to 28% in 1944 (p. 78).

By the late 1950s, however, the rich had returned. Tax avoidance was on the rise, made possible by increasing numbers of loopholes in the IRS code; and the share of wealth owned by the top one percent climbed back up to 30% by 1958 (p. 79). Its climb has continued since then, as the federal government has almost continually cut tax rates on the rich, detailed in the following section.

INCOME TAX RATES

As suggested in the preceding sketch of wealth concentration, the level of federal taxation is directly tied to the level of concentration of income and wealth and thus also to social inequality. A history of the income tax in America reveals this relationship clearly.

America's first experience with an income tax was in 1861, when the Union needed extra revenue to fight the Civil War. Based on an individual's ability to pay, a three percent tax on yearly income over $800 was imposed (Lewis and Allison, 2001, p. 7). Taxes were withheld from corporations' dividends and from government employees' salaries. After the Civil War, in 1872, most taxes were repealed, including the income tax itself. Taxes on liquor and tobacco were the main source of government revenue by 1868 and made up nearly 90% of government income from then until 1913, when the income tax became a permanent feature of American life via the 16th Amendment (ibid., p. 7). By 1918, there were 55 income brackets, a maximum individual tax rate of 77%, and a corporate rate of 12%. Still, only the wealthiest five percent of the population paid income tax (p. 8). After the First World War, however, a series of four tax cuts during the

1920s lowered the top individual income tax rate from 77% to 25% (Philips, 2002, p. 219).

During the Great Depression, Franklin Roosevelt and Congress raised the top individual tax brackets, implemented inheritance taxes, and eliminated personal holding companies through which some of the rich had deducted the expenses of their estates. A number of other taxes were implemented as well, including taxes on capital stock and dividend receipts. The Social Security Act of 1935 imposed a wage tax—half paid by employers, half by employees—for a system of federally funded retirement benefits (ibid., p. 9). By 1936, the maximum individual tax rate had jumped back up to 79%, and the concentration of wealth had plummeted.

During the Second World War, Congress dramatically expanded the reach of the income tax. The number of taxpayers grew from 4 million to 43 million between 1939 and 1945. From 1940 to 1944, tax rates were raised from 4% to 19% for the bottom tax bracket, while the rate for those at the top was increased to 88% (p. 11). As noted above, this high tax rate decreased wealth concentration by half by 1944 (pp. 75, 59).

During the post–World War II years of broadly shared prosperity in the U.S., income tax on the rich was high. In 1948, the effective tax rate of the richest one percent of families was 76.9%. During the 1950s, it was 85.5%. But Democrat John F. Kennedy brought tax rates for the rich down in 1963 to 77%, and then the effective tax rate of the top one percent was reduced further, in 1965 (pp. 220).

In the 1980s, Ronald Reagan's administration cut the top income tax bracket from 70% to 28%. By 1989 the portion of the nation's wealth held by the top one percent had jumped to 39%, nearly twice where it was during the New Deal—and almost where it had been in 1929 (pp. 92–93). Since then, tax rates on the rich have plummeted further, and concentrated wealth and income have climbed. Philips describes the so-called Reagan Revolution: "During the 1980s, conservative governments cut taxes, conservatized the judiciary, deregulated the economy, passed punitive labor policy, freed trade for corporations to go abroad, and increased the federal role in bailing out shaky banks, savings and loans, and Latin American debtors" (p. 93). As a consequence, there was a shift from the broad-based prosperity of the post–World War II decades to the prosperity of the financial elite (p. 95; see also Galbraith, 1998).

However, also beginning with Reagan's administration, the effective tax rate of the middle-class (median income) family increased steadily: from 5.3% in 1948, to 24.63% in 1990 (Philips, 2002, p. 96). Payroll taxes (FICA, or Federal Insurance Contributions Act for Social Security and Medicare, for example) paid by middle-class individuals have also risen dramatically: from 6.9% in 1950, to 31.1% in 2000 (ibid., p. 149). Clearly, rich individuals and families have been paying less and less, and the middle class more. Corporations, however, pay a declining share.

The share of the federal tax burden paid by corporations *declined from 40% in the 1940s, to 26.5% in 1950, to 10.2% in 2000* (p. 149). In 2001, the corporate share of total federal taxes paid by corporations was down to 9.2%.

Corporations have also been contributing less and less to the U.S. gross domestic product. During the 1940s, corporate income taxes averaged 4.9% of the gross domestic product (GDP). During the 1950s, they averaged 4.7% of GDP. They have declined further, to where in the 1990s, corporate tax receipts averaged 1.9% of GDP; in 2003, they were only 1.3% of GDP (General Accounting Office, 2004, p. 5; see also Fisher, 2002, p. 3).

State and local taxes paid by corporations have also declined. *In 1957, corporations provided 45% of local property tax revenues in the states,* but by 1987 their share had plummeted to about 16%. By 2002, the corporate share of total state and local taxes paid was only 2.9% (Mishel, Bernstein, and Boushey, 2003, p. 66). Research has shown that the decline in the effective state-local corporate income tax rate is due to changes in state tax law, not to shifts in economic activity toward lower-tax states (Fisher, 2002, p. 4).

Probably the most egregious aspect of the corporate tax situation is the fact mentioned briefly in the Introduction: Sixty percent of the largest and most profitable corporations pay no federal income tax at all (U.S. General Accounting Office, 2004, p. 6). According to the well-regarded organization, Citizens for Tax Justice, low audit rates since Reagan's administration, tax breaks, and "congressional indifference to abusive offshore corporate tax shelters," cost the American taxpayers over $170 billion annually in lost taxes (April l7, 2002, p. 1). Several examples of this type of corporate welfare follow.

Microsoft enjoyed more than $12 billion in total tax breaks between 1996 and 2000. In fact, Microsoft actually paid no tax at all in 1999, despite $12.3 billion in reported U.S. profits. Microsoft's tax rate between 2000 and 2002 was only 1.8% on $21.9 billion in pretax U.S. profits.

General Electric, one of America's most profitable corporations, reported $50.8 billion in U.S. profits between 1996 and 2000, but paid only 11.5% of that in federal income taxes. That low tax rate reflected almost $12 billion in corporate tax welfare for GE.

IBM reported $5.7 billion in U.S. profits in 2000, but paid only 3.4% of that in federal income taxes. In 1997, IBM reported $3.1 billion in U.S. profits, and instead of paying taxes, got a tax rebate. Between 1996 and 2000, IBM enjoyed a total of $4.7 billion in corporate tax welfare.

Colgate-Palmolive paid no taxes at all between 1999 and 2000, despite $1.6 billion in reported U.S. profits. Colgate's total tax rate between 1996 and 2000 was *negative* 1.3%, due to $595 million in corporate tax welfare.

It is certainly fair to say that corporate America does not contribute to U.S. federal, state, or local public expenses commensurate with its ability to pay. This deprives governments at all levels of funds with which to provide for the public good.

TAX POLICY AND THE WORKING POOR

Large business may experience corporate welfare, but—like the middle class—the working poor pay taxes. Poor families in many states face a substantial burden when they file personal income taxes. In 2001, in almost half of states that levy income taxes— 19 out of 42 states—two-parent families of four with incomes below the federal poverty line owed income tax. In 17 of those states, single-parent families of three who are poor also pay income taxes. Moreover, about half of 23 states that do not tax the poor still tax families with incomes just *above* the poverty line, even though as we saw in Chapter 2, such families typically have great difficulty making ends meet. In some states, families at poverty-level incomes are charged income tax bills of several hundred dollars (Johnson et al., 2002, February 26, p. 1).

For instance, a two-parent, two-child family in Kentucky with income at the 2001 poverty line ($18,104 for a family of four) owed $596 in income tax, the highest tax on such a family in the U.S. A single-parent family with two children in Kentucky with income at the poverty level ($14,129 for a family of three) owed $361, second only to the tax on such a family levied in Alabama ($388). These amounts can make a big difference to a financially struggling family. Other states levying tax of $200 or more on families with poverty-level incomes include Arkansas, Hawaii, Indiana, Michigan, Montana, Oklahoma, Oregon, Virginia, and West Virginia (ibid.).

Federal and some state governments recognize the challenges faced by families with incomes slightly above the poverty line and have set eligibility for some assistance programs, such as energy assistance, school lunch subsidies, and in many states health-care subsidies, at 125% of the poverty line or above. Thirty states, however, continue to levy income tax on families with incomes at 125% of the poverty line (pp. 12–13).

The federal Earned Income Tax Credit (EITC), enacted by Congress in 1975, is a tax credit available to working families with incomes well below the federal poverty line to roughly double. At its inception, the credit was relatively small in size, but several expansions in the late 1980s and early 1990s have changed the EITC into the "largest federal aid program targeted to the working poor" (Berube, 2003, p. 2).

The maximum amount of income available to receive the credit is from approximately $7,000 to $13,000 for families with one child, and $10,000 to $13,000 for families with two or more children. After these amounts the credit phases to zero. For example, in tax year 2002, a family with two children and an income of $10,700 would receive a $4,140 tax credit—"the equivalent of an additional $2 per hour for full-time work." For families with two or more children, the credit decreases at about $13,500, and reduces to zero at $33,200 (ibid., p. 3).

In 1999, the Earned Income Tax Credit lifted 4.7 million people above the official poverty line, including 2.5 million children—more than any other federal aid program. Nationally in tax year 2000, about 15% of all individual income tax filers claimed the EITC. In Baltimore, 26% of income tax filers were EITC earners; in New Orleans, 36%—and many who were eligible did not file (ibid., pp. 1–5; see also Sammartino, 2001).

The tax break provided by the EITC is dwarfed, however, by the federal tax breaks provided middle-class and affluent home-owners. Homeowners are allowed five different federal tax breaks that cost the government billions of dollars a year. The best-known of these allows interest paid on mortgages for principal residences and/or vacation homes to be deducted on federal income tax returns. Two-thirds of the benefits go to families with high incomes (over $100,000 in 1995). The National Housing Institute calculated that the mortgage interest deduction cost the U.S. Treasury slightly more than $58 billion in 1995. (In comparison, the entire 1995 budget for the Department of Housing and Urban Development (HUD) was $26 billion that year (Zepezauer and Naiman, 1996, pp. 52–53). In 1999, mortgage and interest payment deductions for homeowners totaled $63 billion, three times the size of HUD's budget that year (Dreier, 2000, p. 40).

Other tax advantages of owning a home include tax-free sale, deduction of state and local property taxes on federal income tax forms, and deduction of the interest paid on home equity loans. These advantages alone cost the government about $38.2 billion a year (Zepezauer and Naiman, 1996, p. 55). These authors estimate that the government "gives" to (mostly wealthy) homeowners a little over $96 billion a year (ibid.).

In addition to state taxes, the working poor are taxed on wages—payroll taxes—which they do not get back. A single woman with one child who is working at a job paying $16,000 a year paid $2,448 in payroll taxes in 2001 (FICA, Social Security, and Medicare, employer and employee contributions combined), none of which is refunded or credited. This does not take into consideration state and local taxes (e.g., sales tax, etc.) (Sawicky and Cherry, 2001, p. 2).

The payroll Social Security tax is extremely regressive—poor workers pay proportionally more than rich ones. Social Security tax is paid on money earned up to a threshold of 6.2% of income—or a limit of $87,900 in 2004. After that amount, income is not taxed for Social Security. Wealthy earners pay only the tiny 1.45% Medicare portion of the payroll tax on their earnings over the limit. As federal income tax has been cut, a larger and larger portion of federal revenues has been coming from payroll taxes. At the end of World War II, the payroll tax provided two percent of federal revenues; in 2002 it provided 37%. This rise is a consequence of the fact that major tax cuts of the past 25 years have been heavily tilted toward the rich, and federal payroll taxes have been increased to compensate. The payroll tax rose substantially in the 1980s, during the years Reagan was cutting income taxes on the rich (Reich, 2002, p. 22).

CORRECTIVE POLICIES

Inequality, the concentration of huge amounts of income and wealth of America in a few hands, and the inequities in who is taxed for what, are not the products of a laissez-faire economic system: They are the product of the same bodies that have set minimum wage laws, appointed conservative judges, deregulated prices and wages, enacted punitive labor policies, passed trade laws that push employers to other countries, and appointed officials who do not enforce antidiscrimination laws.

A wealth tax is one policy that would correct some of the financial inequities and would provide moneys to revitalize urban neighborhoods and schools. According to simulations produced by well-known economist Edward Wolff, even a very modest wealth tax like the Swiss system, with marginal tax rates ranging from 0.05% to .30% of wealth (with household effects, pensions, and annuities excluded) could have raised $38 billion in 1989. In the process, only three percent of families would have seen their federal tax bill rise by more than 10% (Wolff, 2002, p. 53). Imposing the Swedish wealth tax instead, at 1.5% initially, rising to a high of three percent, would have added an additional $328.7 billion to U.S. public coffers in 1989 (p. 59).

Wolff has updated these simulations to 1998, using the modest Swiss wealth tax system where the top bracket (the 0.30% range) begins at $1.66 million. If enacted in the U.S., this wealth tax would have created $52 billion in extra tax revenue in 1998 (and a slightly less modest tax would have produced $55 billion in 2001) (p. 74). The 1998 figure represents one percent of total family income and 7.1% of the total income tax revenue. This compares with actual U.S. personal income tax proceeds in 1998 of $737.5 billion, or 13.8% of total income. Only 16.7% of families would have seen their tax bill rise by more than $100, and only 8.5% by more than $300 (pp. 60–61).

In January 2003, the states faced a collective deficit of $60 billion, in part because of the year's weak tax collections. As a result, state legislatures and governors cut social programs (Katz, 2003, p. 1). A wealth tax like Wolff proposes would just about cover that yearly deficit, and could be used to maintain the social programs. If corporate taxes were actually collected at current rates, or if rates were raised to levels in the 1950s, untold billions would be available for use in job creation and urban schools. Political contention, and perhaps sustained public struggle, would be necessary to pry loose corporate funds for the public good.

There is one more type of federal policy that contributes significantly to inequality, and should be corrected: the elevation of a U.S. financial governing body that is not elected—the Federal Reserve Board. This group of bankers has official authority over the money supply of the nation (Philips, 2002, p. 95). An example of how this can become important has been offered by James Galbraith, economist son of John Kenneth Galbraith.

James Galbraith argues that decades of high interest rates contributed heavily to the dramatic increases in the income of the richest 10% of Americans in the last 25 years. The Federal Reserve Board continually raised interest rates during the 1970s and 1980s, and as a result working-class and middle-class Americans began paying more and more interest on their credit card, mortgage, and other debts (including the national debt). Some of this interest payment went to the relatively affluent—like many professionals—through well-performing pension funds. But most of the interest went to the wealthiest 10% of Americans—because they are the ones who hold major stock in the banks owning the credit cards, mortgages, and other debts. And now, average American credit card, mortgage and other debt is at an all-time high. Galbraith demonstrates that these interest payments became a major component of the incomes of the wealthiest Americans throughout the 1980s and of the increases in inequality during that decade (Galbraith, 1998, p. 214).

Indeed, Galbraith demonstrates that the interest payments Americans paid on their debts became a huge transfer program—*a transfer of money from the working class and the middle class to the rich*. This transfer of money through interest payments to the very wealthy is *almost equal to the entire amount that the government pays out to* those receiving Social Security, Medicare, SSI, unemployment insurance, welfare, and veterans' benefits combined (ibid., pp. 85–86). In 1995, government transfer payments for Social Security and Medicare constituted about 17.5% of income in the U.S., while interest payments by the middle-class and poor to the wealthy constituted 13% of income, only four percent less (pp. 85–86).

During the years of high interest, while Americans were paying these sums to wealthy stockholders, many Americans lost their jobs: Unemployment had been 3.9% in 1969 after a period of low interest rates, and it was 11% in 1982 after almost a decade of higher interest rates (pp. 214, 144). Federal Reserve policy that kept interest rates relatively high is thus one more macroeconomic policy that has contributed to the increased inequality of recent decades and should be corrected.

When governments tax their wealthy citizens at rates of 77% and 80%, the concentration of resources in a few pockets shrinks considerably, and there is more money for spending on public needs. In the United States, high taxes on the rich paid many social expenses during the decades after World War II. Since the mid-1960s, the rich have paid smaller and smaller percentages of their wealth in taxes, and relative social spending has slowed. Today, as I have noted, wealth is almost as highly concentrated as it was in 1929 before the Stock Market crash; and for millions of Americans, the social safety net has been shredded. The more of society's resources the rich accumulate, the less available for investment in education, infrastructure, and other public goods; and the less there is to provide resources for those who are in need.

Poverty in America may be "good for business," as Alan Greenspan implies when he remarks that large numbers of unemployed people keep wages down, but poverty also follows this decline in wages, and has tragic consequences for those who suffer through it (Greenspan's remark, in Pollin, 1998, p. 20, is cited on page 32).

Poverty and extremes of inequality have direct effects on urban students and schools. A detailed look at some of these consequences is the subject of the next chapter.

4

New Hope for Urban Students

Macroeconomic policies that set the minimum wage below poverty levels, that train inner-city hopefuls for jobs that do not exist, that do not extract from the wealthy a fair share of social expenses, and that rarely enforce laws that would decrease substantially the economic discrimination of people of color, all support persistent poverty and near-poverty among minority urban populations. This economic and social distress can prevent children from developing to their full potential. Holding two low-wage jobs to make ends meet can sap the energy of a parent and make it more difficult for her to negotiate the public systems in which her children are enmeshed. Being poor in a rich country can lead to ill-placed shame, pervasive despair, and anger. Living in poverty is to experience daily crises of food, a place to live, and ways to keep your children safe. All this can be debilitating; and can certainly dampen the enthusiasm, effort, and expectations with which urban children and their families approach K–12 education.

Moreover, the low social status and perceived lack of clout often ascribed to those who are poor and Black or Latino may prevent staff in institutions like schools, government agencies, and hospitals from offering respect and proper treatment. It often leads to a lack of accountability on the part of the public institutions themselves—a situation that is rarely, if ever, allowed to occur in affluent suburbs.

While poverty does not prevent educational achievement, it certainly limits opportunities for it. As I will report, a recent national study of young children confirms the potential of impoverished circumstances to prevent students' full cognitive growth before they enroll in kindergarten. Of countervailing power, however, is research demonstrating that when low-income parents obtain better jobs and increased family supports, the educational achievement of the children typically improves significantly. These findings empirically support the argument that for the urban poor, even with the right educational reforms in place, school achievement may await a family's economic access.

The two following sections of this chapter describe the consequences of poverty for urban education and children, and the final section provides hopeful results of efforts to raise the social class status of low-income urban residents.

THE URBAN POLITICAL ECONOMY

It is prudent to remember that federal policies are not only implicated in personal and familial poverty but make significant contributions to the erosion of the property tax base in urban neighborhoods as well. In *Ghetto Schooling*, I examined 20th-century federal policies that provided strong encouragement for business enterprises to move from urban locations to suburbia. Such policies include the following, among others: federal guidelines that forbade bank loans for housing rehabilitation or purchase in city neighborhoods ("redlining," beginning in the 1930s), with the resulting deterioration of housing stock and discouragement of business investment in cities; in the late 1940s and '50s, policies that gave substantial tax deductions to businesses that moved from the city rather than renovate; investment tax credits beginning in 1962 that allowed manufacturers to take credit for new industrial plants and equipment but not renovation of existing ones; relocation tax breaks to large corporations; and, during the suburbanization of the post–World War II periods, federal (as well as state) subsidies and land grants to developers and municipalities to build highways, sewer and electric lines, homes and office buildings in the suburbs but not in the city (see Anyon, 1997, Chapters 4, 5, and 7 for details).

By the mid-1960s, inner cities had lost to the suburbs not only most of their middle-class residents but most of their supermarkets, banks, doctor's offices, department stores, hospitals, pharmacies, theaters, and movie houses. Liquor stores and undertakers remained. Indeed, in old industrial cities like Newark, Baltimore, Boston, Chicago, Cleveland, Detroit, Milwaukee, Philadelphia, Pittsburgh, St. Louis, and Trenton, boards of education had begun complaining in the mid-1930s of a dearth of business "ratables" with which to fund education. The city property tax base (which provided the major funding for education) continued to deteriorate following the Great Depression, and remains low—despite the redevelopment of many "downtowns," and the gentrification of some neighborhoods, from which low-income people are pushed out by higher rents. Indeed, many cities have extremely valuable downtown property (think of the financial centers in New York, Chicago, San Francisco, and Atlanta) but city, state, and federal corporate tax rates on this property are about the lowest on record. As a result, wealthy firms in these downtowns contribute little toward urban education and other city services.

Contrary to the assumptions of education policy analysts who argue that "money doesn't matter" and contradicting federal legislation (e.g., the No Child Left Behind Act) that assumes it does not, low urban property tax receipts and insufficient additional school financing have devastating effects on public education. The lack of a property base to pay for services in cities affects school districts by impoverishing them. Despite 30 years of educational finance litigation, the moneys available to most city school systems have not increased enough to offset the disadvantages wrought by the economy.

The Education Trust, an independent Washington, DC-based group, monitors funding available to city districts and, in a 2001 study, demonstrated cities' continued lack of financial resources. "The Funding Gap: Low-Income and Minority Students Receive Fewer Dollars" reports that in most states, school districts that educate the largest number of poor and minority students have fewer state and local dollars to spend per student than districts with the least number of poor and minority students (p. 1). They found that districts that educate the largest number of poor students receive an average $966 less per student than low-poverty districts (p. 1; see also Education Trust, 2004c).

These individual gaps in funding add up to significant gaps per school. In New York, for example, the state with the largest discrepancy, there is a difference of $2,152 per student between state and local revenues available in high-poverty districts and revenues available in low-poverty districts. "This gap translates

63

into a difference of $860,800 between two elementary schools of 400 students each, enough to compete with elite suburban schools for the most qualified teachers and to provide the kinds of additional instructional time and other resources that research and data show can make a difference" (2001, p. 2). The per-student funding gaps translate into the following schoolwide gaps per year in a typical elementary school of 400 students with classrooms of 25 students: in Illinois, $824,000; in Montana, $614,000; in Pennsylvania, $499,200; and in Michigan, $441,200 (p. 2). These schoolwide income gaps confound the effects of family poverty in urban areas.

URBAN CHILDREN AND SOCIAL CLASS

In Chapter 2, I discussed adult poverty figures at the official threshold, and the alarming increase in numbers when a more realistic assessment is made. The same disparities exist between federal and alternative counts of poor children. Sixteen percent of American children—almost 12 million—lived below the official federal poverty line in 2001. Almost half of those children (44%, or a little over five million) lived in *extreme* poverty (less than half the poverty line, or $7,400 for a family of three in 2001)—including nearly a million African American children. This was a 17% increase in the number of children in extreme poverty from 2000, at the end of the economic "boom." These figures are disturbing (Lu, 2003, pp. 1–2; Cauthen and Lu, 2001, p. 3; Dillon, 2000, p. 3).

When more appropriate criteria are applied, however, the results are certainly tragic: A full 38% of American children are identified as poor—27 million who lived in families with income up to 200% of the official poverty line. These children live in poverty as well—although official statistics do not designate them as such. But as Chapter 2 demonstrates, these families experience hardships that are almost as severe as those who are officially poor (Lu, 2003, p. 1; see also Cauthen and Lu, 2001, p. 3).

This revised measure reveals a national scandal that is no longer central to discussions of American poverty, which generally assume that the majority of minority children are no longer poor. The scandal is that the majority of Black and Latino children still suffer poverty. *By the revised measure—200% of the official poverty cutoff—a full 57% of African American children, 64% of Latino, and 34% of White children were poor in the U.S. in 2001* (Lu, 2003, p. 2; see also Mishel, Bernstein, and Boushey, 2003).

Federal policy may not define these low-income families as poor, but some federal regulations acknowledge that they are: The criterion used for reduced price or free lunch for school children, for example, includes almost 40% (39.9%) of U.S. students (and 69.8% of Black, 71.4% of Latino, and 22.7% of White students). The cutoff for reduced price lunch is 185% of the official poverty line and for free lunch is 130% (U.S. Department of Education, 2004, p. 114).

We have long known that social class, or socioeconomic status (SES), is highly correlated with educational achievement: Generally, the higher the resource background of the child's family, the higher the achievement (see Coleman, 1993; Ginsburg, 1999, and Lee and Burkam, 2002; among others). Demographer and independent scholar David Rusk, for example, measured the correlation between SES and educational success by identifying school percentages of low-income students. He found that in communities across the U.S., a full 65% to 85% of school variation in standardized test scores is explained by variations in the school's percentage of low-income students (1999, p. 91; see also Kahlenberg, 2003; and National Center for Educational Statistics, 2003).

Many researchers have documented the specific effects of poverty environments on children's development. For example, poverty has been found to have consistently negative effects on children's cognitive growth. Longitudinal studies demonstrate that family income consistently predicts children's academic and cognitive performance, even when other family characteristics are taken into account. Persistent and extreme poverty has been shown to be more detrimental to children than temporary poverty. Family income may influence children through both lack of resources and parental emotional stress. Finally, poor children have more health and behavior difficulties than those from more affluent families, which mitigates against educational success (see, among others, Bolger and Patterson, 1995; Duncan and Brooks-Gunn, 1997; Houser, Brown, and Prosser, 1997; Korenman and Miller, 1997; McLoyd, 1998; McLoyd, Jayartne, Ceballo, and Borquez, 1994; and Sugland et al., 1995).

Confirming and refining this literature is a recent national assessment of cognitive development and socioeconomic status by Valerie Lee and David Burkham (2002). The authors used data from the U.S. Department of Education's early childhood longitudinal kindergarten cohort, which is a comprehensive data set that provides a nationally representative portrait of kindergarten students. They explored differences in young children's achievement scores in literacy and mathematics by race, ethnicity, and socioeconomic status as they began kindergarten. They also analyzed differences by social background in an array of children's homes and family activities (ibid., p. 1).

The study found that by age 5, the average cognitive scores of children in the highest SES group are 60% above the scores of the lowest SES group (p. 2). The cognitive deficits are significantly *less* closely related to race/ethnicity after accounting for social class. That is, after taking race differences into account, children from different SES groups achieve at different levels (p. 2). Moreover, the effect on the cognitive skill of family structure (e.g., being in a single-parent family) is much smaller than either race or SES. Social class accounts for more of the variation in cognitive scores than any other factor by far.

Lee and Burkham also found that not only do disadvantaged children enter kindergarten with significantly lower cognitive skills than do their advantaged peers, but low-SES children begin school in systematically lower-quality elementary schools than their more advantaged counterparts. "However school quality is defined—in terms of higher student achievement, more school resources, more qualified teachers, more positive teacher attitudes, better neighborhood or school conditions, private vs. public schools—the least advantaged U.S. children begin their formal schooling in consistently lower-quality schools. This reinforces the inequalities that develop even before children reach school age" (p. 3; see also Entwistle et al., 1997; Jencks and Phillips, 1998; Phillips, Brooks-Gunn, Duncan, Klevanov, and Crane, 1998; Phillips, Crouse, and Ralth, 1998; Stipic and Ryan, 1997; and White, 1982).

Taken together, studies of poverty, socioeconomic status, cognitive development, and educational achievement suggest that programs to raise the incomes of poor families would enhance the cognitive development of children and improve their chances of success in education, and later, in the economy.

INCOME SUPPORTS AND EDUCATIONAL ACHIEVEMENT

There is both indirect and direct evidence that increased familial resources raise educational achievement. Indirect evidence is present in a longitudinal study completed in 2003 that found that improving family income reduces the negative (aggressive) social behavior of children, which in turn is likely to lead to better school behavior and performance. For eight years, researchers studied a representative population sample of 1,420 children ages 9 to 13 in rural North Carolina. A quarter of the children were from a Cherokee reservation. Psychological tests were given at the start of the study and repeated each year (Costello, Compton, Keeler, and Angold, 2003, pp. 1–2; see also O'Connor, 2003).

When the study began, 68% of the children were living below the official poverty line. On average, the poorer children exhibited more vandalism, stealing, bullying, stubbornness, and outbursts of anger than those who were not poor. But halfway through the study, a local casino began distributing a percentage of its profits to tribal families. Given to each tribal member over 18, and put in a trust fund for younger members, the payment increased slightly each year, reaching about $6,000 per person for the year 2001. Psychiatric tests administered by researchers for the four years that the funds were being distributed demonstrated that the negative behaviors of children in families who were no longer poor dropped to the same levels found among children whose families had never been poor (decreasing by 40%). Parents who moved out of poverty reported having more time to spend with their children, and researchers identified better parenting behavior. Researchers also identified as important to both parents and children the psychological benefits of not being poor. Poverty puts stress on families, which can increase the likelihood of children developing behavioral problems. One parent in the study told researchers that "the jobs [produced by the casino] give people the chance to pull themselves up by their bootstraps and get out of poverty. That carries over into less juvenile crime, less domestic violence, and an overall better living experience for families" (O'Connor, 2003, p. 2).

Direct evidence that income supports improved educational achievement is also available. In March 2001, for example, the Manpower Development Research Corporation (MDRC) published a synthesis of research on how welfare and work policies affect the children of single mothers (Morris, Huston, Duncan, Crosby, and Bos, 2001). This synthesis reviewed data from evaluations of five programs that provided income supplements to poverty-wage workers (Florida's Family Transition Program; the Minnesota Family Investment Program; the National Evaluation of Welfare-to-Work Strategies; the New Hope program; and the Self-Sufficiency Project). These programs offered supports of differing kinds to poverty-wage workers—income supplements, earnings disregards (rules that allow working welfare recipients to keep more of their income when they go to work), subsidized health care, employment services, counseling, supervised after-school activities for children and youth, and informal get-togethers with project staff.

MDRC's review of the studies found that even relatively small income supplements to working parents—(amounting to about $4,000 per year) improved children's elementary school achievement by about 10% to 15% of the average variation in the control groups (p. 20). These improvements were seen on test scores as well as ratings by parents and/or teachers. The earning supplements had "consistently positive impacts on children's [school] achievement" (p. 63). The positive effects were small, but were statistically significant (pp. 21–22).

Longitudinal studies have found that the achievement and behavior problems of young children can have important implications for their well-being in adolescence and adulthood (e.g., Caspi, Wright, Moffit, and Silva, 1998; Masten and Cosworth, 1995). Moreover, even small differences between children in school achievement early on can translate into larger differences later (Entwistle, 1998). Therefore, as the authors of the research synthesis state, "a program's effects on children, even if the effects are small, may continue to have implications over the course of their lives" (p. 25).

The earning supplements provided by four of these programs did not bring the families above the poverty level. The improvements in children's school achievement and behavior from even these relatively meager cash supplements for working families suggest that if we were to increase family resources substantially, we could probably improve educational and social outcomes for children substantially.

One of these programs did provide an earning supplement that brought the families above poverty level, and showed particularly impressive results for children's behavior and achievement. New Hope for Families and Children was run between 1994 and 1998 in two inner-city areas in Milwaukee. Candidates had to live in one of two targeted areas, be 18 or older, be willing and able to work at least 30 hours per week, and have a household income at or below 150% of the federal poverty level (Huston, Miller, Richburg, Hayes, Duncan, and Eldred, 2001, p. 1). Almost 90% of the adults in the sample were single or separated mothers with children when they entered the study, and 80% were receiving public assistance. The program was conceived by a nonprofit community-based organization and provided several benefits: the earnings supplement, subsidized health insurance, and subsidized child care (p. 1). The program offered help in obtaining a job, and provided a community service job (for up to one year) for those not able to find work elsewhere (p. 1). Advice and support of project staff were made available. The annual cost of providing these benefits was $5,300 per family (p. 5).

New Hope was evaluated at two-year and five-year intervals using a random assignment research design. After conducting outreach in the communities to identify eligible people, the study enrolled over 1,300 low-income adults. Half the applicants were randomly assigned to a program group that received New Hope's benefits, and the other half were randomly assigned to a control group that was not eligible for the benefits.

Evaluations at both time periods showed positive results (Bos, Huston, Duncan, Brock, and McLoyd, 1996; and Huston et al., 1999).The program had positive effects on parents' well-being and coping skills.

> Parents in the New Hope group were more aware of available sources of assistance and support in the community, such as where to find assistance with energy costs or housing problems. More of them also knew about the EITC and its support. A significant number of program families intentionally used the Earned Income Tax Credits as a savings plan for making major purchases, reducing debt, and stabilizing rent and other payments. Parents in New Hope also reported better physical health and fewer symptoms associated with depression than did parents in the control group. Ethnographic data revealed that many parents had children with disabilities or behavioral difficulties, and New Hope helped the parents achieve a difficult balance among work, services, and parenting. The New Hope parents reported fewer problems controlling their children, and parents of adolescents reported more effective management (better control and less need for punishment) (ibid., p. 9).

New Hope improved children's school performance. "At both the two-year and the five-year points, children in the program performed better than control group children on several measures of academic achievement, particularly on reading and literacy tests.

After five years, they scored higher on a standardized test of reading skills, and their parents reported that they got higher grades in reading skills" (p. 13). These effects were slightly more pronounced for boys than for girls. Compared with their control group counterparts, boys in New Hope also received higher ratings of academic performance from their teachers and were more likely to expect to attend college at both the two-year and the five-year assessments. "New Hope adolescents reported more engagement with schools, feelings of efficacy, and expectations to finish college than did their control group counterparts" (pp. 13–14).

New Hope's effects are consistent with results of other programs that have improved children's outcomes by providing wage supplements and subsidized child care (Morris and Michalopoulos, 2000; Michalopoulos, Tattri, Miller, and Robbins, 2002). Indeed, New Hope findings are in line with the increased educational achievement of students that has been identified in large-scale programs that assist families by helping them move from inner-city neighborhoods to more affluent and/or less segregated metropolitan areas. The first of these "mobility programs" was the Gatraux program in the Chicago metropolitan area. The latest is the Hope VI relocation efforts of the federal government. Mobility programs such as these are an important strategy for redressing metropolitanwide inequities in particular, and are therefore discussed in Part II, where the focus is on regional policies and arrangements that affect urban education.

The fact that school achievement improves as family resources increase makes sense: Parents with sufficient time and money are more likely to nurture their children's development with private tutoring, lessons, sports and arts programs, and educationally useful visits to museums and concerts. These parents will typically transmit positive expectations of college acceptance and labor market preparation. And they will have, or be able to procure, the funds for these. Sociologist Annette Lareau has dubbed this kind of child rearing the "concerted cultivation" by middle- and upper-middle-class parents of the skills, talents, and futures of their children (2003, Chapter 1). Lareau found this kind of activity typical of the affluent African American as well as Caucasian families she studied.

There is firm logic in the attention of these parents to developing the capacities and cultural capital of their children: The social class resources purchased by affluence (such as developed cultural capital) are certainly the educational "basics." They are demanded by curriculum and pedagogy, and rewarded by colleges and the labor market.

I believe that in the long run we would do better to enhance the access of the urban poor to economic resources so they, too, can afford the time, money, and inclination to prepare their children for school success. As it is, we depend on schools to create the economic resources and cultural capital that school success already requires; we depend on public schools to create equitable opportunities for urban graduates in a society that hoards economic resources from the minority poor. We are putting the cart before the horse.

Rather, we should—alongside equity-seeking educational reform—provide the financial base of support to urban families and communities that will in itself lay the basis for fuller child development and better resourced families and schools, as in more affluent neighborhoods and towns. The educational success of affluent districts demonstrates to me that economic strength is the engine of systemic school reform.

In this and previous chapters, I have delineated federal policies that undermine systemic school reform by maintaining large poverty populations in city neighborhoods. I have provided evidence that this poverty works against the full development of urban students, and thus dwarfs the effects of curricular, pedagogic, and administrative changes. I have also briefly reprised the political economy of urban history and reminded us of federal decisions over the years that depleted the tax and other political economic resource sources of city governments (and therefore districts) long ago. Importantly, however, we have also seen that even modest financial and other supports for poor families allow the parents better jobs and the children higher school achievement.

Before we can delve into ways to reorder federal policy priorities, I want to examine the effects of metropolitan dynamics on urban populations and schools. For metro-area arrangements exacerbate the inequitable consequences of federal macroeconomic policies. We will see, however, that regional coalitions of community-based groups challenging the federal and regional rules of the game have been making gains in the redistribution of resources in several U.S. metro areas. These groups provide an example of what can be accomplished when we unite groups of people around a common goal and organize for more just public policies.

Part II

Metropolitan Inequities

5

Jobs and Public Transit Mismatches

If we were to make a list of the strategies typically called upon to improve education in impoverished urban communities, policies intended to improve curriculum, assessment, and pedagogy would all appear. Policies that would place jobs in urban communities would *not* appear. And transportation policies that established bus and train routes from cities to outlying suburbs where entry-level jobs exist would also be left off our list.

Yet the availability of jobs locally or transportation to places of work elsewhere, are fundamental to the well-being of urban residents—and therefore to their communities and schools—just as in more affluent communities.

This chapter demonstrates that the location of businesses and public transit routes in a metropolitan area are crucial determinants of where poverty is concentrated in the region—and important therefore to where in the metro area private and public funds are available for families and for public schools. Inserting urban neighborhoods back into regional economies by locating metro-area relevant business there, and providing bus and rail lines so low-income urban residents (most of whom lack auto transport) can reach outlying suburban job centers are fundamentally important to the amelioration of urban poverty and the support of city schooling. It is in this sense that equitable metro-area job location and public transportation policies become covert education policies—and thus worthy of the support and active advocacy of those concerned about urban educational reform.

The arrangements and policies by which employment and public transit (and affordable housing and municipal tax receipts, discussed in the next chapter) are dispersed throughout the cities and towns of a metropolitan area not only have direct effects on resources available for individuals and schools in metro area neighborhoods. They support and in some cases exacerbate the deleterious effects of the federal policies described in previous chapters. The reform of metro-area inequities needs to be among the solutions we seek to urban poverty and poverty schools. Indeed, this and the next chapter will argue that *foundational education reforms would be regional job, transportation, housing, and municipal tax reform*. First, let me briefly define metro areas.

METRO AREAS

The United States today is a nation of regions. Over 80% of Americans live in one of 300 metropolitan areas. Almost half the population lives in the 25 largest regions (Orfield, 2002, p. 1). Metro areas are shaped by regional markets for investment, jobs, and housing (ibid.; see also United States Conference of Mayors, 2002, pp. 1–2).

The Boston metropolitan area, for example, includes the city itself (with about 600,000 residents) in a region encompassing five counties, 129 municipalities, and almost 3.2 million people. The metropolitan economy constitutes about two-thirds of the state economy. The city of Boston has less than 10% of the state's population, but provides 16% of its employment, produces 24% of its goods and services, 21% of total earned income, and 18% of state tax revenues. It is the largest city and the economic and cultural hub of the New England region and its 13.2 million people (Pastor, Jr., Dreier, Grigsby, and Lopez-Garza, 2000, p. 144).

Recent exacerbation of the phenomenon of metropolitan "sprawl" has given impetus to studies of regional problems—as development takes over more and more open land causing traffic congestion, long commutes to work, air pollution, and rising suburban tax rates and housing costs. The phenomenon of suburban sprawl has reinvigorated an interest in regionalism that began over a hundred years ago.

At the end of the 19th century, New York, Chicago, and many other cities moved to annex or consolidate adjacent territory to include land that could be developed. The formation of Greater New York from New York City, Brooklyn, the towns of Queens

County, the Bronx, and Staten Island in 1898 was one of the first successful experiments in metropolitan consolidation (Dreier, Swanstrom, and Mollenkopf, 2001, p. 177; Barnes and Ledebur, 1998).

Attempts to foster administrative efficiency in regions motivated early regional planners. Later, in the 1960s, regionalists began to be concerned about environmental protection, sustainable development, and "smart growth." Development and freeway construction in the 1960s and '70s increased suburban traffic congestion to high levels. By 1974, demands were being made to regulate new developments. Since then, a "new urbanism" has emerged among architects and city planners who argue for denser, more pedestrian-friendly and transit-oriented forms of development (ibid., p. 179).

Regional scholar Myron Orfield analyzed the 25 largest regions in the U.S., with 43% of the U.S. population, in order to determine the distribution of various income and racial groups among cities and suburbs. (Examples of the largest metropolitan areas are the regions surrounding Atlanta, Chicago, Denver, Minneapolis-St. Paul, New York, and San Francisco.) The analysis, according to tax capacity (ability to raise revenue) and municipal costs, describes a new demography of cities and suburbs in the U.S. (Orfield, 2002, Chapter 2; Berube and Frey, 2002).

THE DISTRIBUTION OF PEOPLE IN METROPOLITAN REGIONS

Orfield's studies demonstrate a new demographic of importance to strategies for reforming urban education: Low-income minorities are no longer concentrated in inner cities, but in various segregated, fiscally stressed suburbs, as well. So when we speak of "urban" and "urban schools," we mean not just central cities, but substantial numbers of suburbs that share the characteristics of the inner city. This demographic lays the basis for important political coalitions for educational and other reform between center city and nearby low-income minority suburbs.

Central Cities (e.g., New York City, Queens, Brooklyn, and Bronx, New York; Oakland and parts of San Francisco city; downtown Denver, Minneapolis-St. Paul, and Atlanta, etc.) have 28% of the metropolitan population. At-risk (i.e., fiscally stressed) segregated suburbs (mostly inner-ring suburbs) have 8% of the metropolitan population and are almost entirely Black and Latino. At-risk old suburbs have 6% of the metropolitan population (and are almost all White working class or lower middle class). Adding these together demonstrates that 42% of metropolitan populations live in at-risk municipalities. At-risk, low-density suburbs farther out (formerly rural areas) have 26% of the metropolitan population. Summing these figures reveals that a majority—68%—of the metropolitan population lives in financially stressed, at-risk communities. Less than a third of the population in the 25 largest metropolitan areas lives in relatively stress-free communities (in terms of tax capacity to meet residents' and the community's needs).

The Distribution of Poverty

The central cities have 49% of the poverty population of the metropolitan areas (in almost all cities, this population is Black and/or Latino). At-risk segregated suburbs have 12% of the metropolitan poverty population (Black/Latino). At-risk older suburbs (White working class, lower middle class) have 3% of the metropolitan poverty population. Adding these poverty figures reveals that *two-thirds—64%—of the metropolitan poverty population lives in these urbanized, at-risk suburbs and central cities.* Thus, two-thirds of metropolitan poverty is urban; only about 26% is rural.

As we will see, this new distribution of urban poverty—central city and urbanized suburban—provides the basis for political coalitions between cities and these suburbs. Such coalitions could offer serious challenges to regional educational (and other) inequities.

Distribution of Middle-class and Affluent Suburbs

About 26% of the metropolitan population (and 10% of the poverty population) lives in what Orfield calls "bedroom-developing" suburbs—very fast growing, mostly White, mostly middle class.

Only about seven percent of the population (and two percent of the poverty population) lives in affluent and very affluent suburbs and job centers (what Joel Garreau called "edge cities")— such as Stamford-Greenwich, CT; Pleasanton-Dublin, CA; Dover, MA; Loudon, VA; and Belleview and Redmond, WA (Orfield, 2002, p. 47; also Garreau, 1992).

Orfield concludes, "Overall, inner suburbs tend to fall into the at-risk segregated or at-risk older categories. The middle ring of suburbs usually contains a mix of bedroom-developing and affluent job centers. Most outermost areas contain a mix of at-risk and bedroom-developing suburbs" (2002, p. 48).

Residential Segregation

The 2000 U.S. Census corroborates Orfield's findings that increasing racial diversity in the suburbs is accompanied by a high degree of residential segregation. As an example, while Black and Latino homebuyers in metropolitan Boston are making inroads into the suburban housing market, they are concentrated in seven out of 126 communities (Stuart, 2000, p. 1). Others have pointed out similar patterns in Fairfax County, VA; suburban Chicago; and suburban Maryland (Orfield, 2001, p. 6; see also McArdle and Stuart, 2002; and Stuart, 2002). The 2000 Census also revealed that 54% of all U.S. Latinos now reside in mostly segregated suburbs; the Latino suburban population grew 71% in the 1990s. At 12.5% of the population in 2000, they are the largest racial/ethnic group in the country, barely edging out African Americans at 12.3% (Suro and Singer, 2002, p. 2).

Persistent residential segregation still prevents large numbers of Blacks and Hispanics from moving to better neighborhoods. In many metro areas, minorities with incomes over $60,000 live in *less* advantaged neighborhoods than Whites earning under $30,000 (Logan, 2002, p. 11).

The average White person in metropolitan America lives in a neighborhood that is 80% White (down from 88% in 1980) and only seven percent Black, eight percent Latino, and four percent Asian. A typical Black individual lives in a neighborhood that is only 33% White, 11% Latino, and three percent Asian and as much as 51% Black (in the Northeast and Midwestern cities, and in some Southern cities, Blacks live in neighborhoods where they are absolute majorities). A typical Latino lives in a neighborhood that is 46% Latino, 37% White, 11% Black, and five percent Asian. Whites, then, live in neighborhoods with few minorities, while minorities live in neighborhoods with high minority representation (Logan, 2001, pp. 1–2, 12).

Latinos and Asians are considerably less segregated than African Americans, but now live in more isolated settings than they did in 1980, with a smaller proportion of White residents in their neighborhoods (ibid., p. 1).

Metropolitan Educational Segregation

One consequence of residential segregation in metropolitan areas is, of course, educational segregation: Minority children are enrolled in schools with much higher levels of poverty, as indicated by eligibility for free and reduced-price school lunches (p. 1).

Between 1998–2000 in the U.S., 42% of schools had nine-tenths or more White students, and eight percent of schools had nine-tenths or more Black and/or Latino students. While only 17% of the White schools had greater than 50% low-income enrollments, 88% of the segregated minority schools were characterized by concentrated poverty ("intense segregation"). In other words, "segregated white neighborhood schools were very likely to have middle-class student bodies, but the opposite was the case for Black and Latino schools. In fact, nine times out of ten, segregated minority schools had concentrated poverty" (Orfield, July 2001, p. 40).

Intense segregation for Blacks is still 28 points below its 1969 level, but it has actually grown 13.5 points for Latinos. In 1968, only a little more than 20% of Latino students were enrolled in intensely segregated schools; in 1998, more than one-third of Latino students attended intensely segregated schools (ibid., p. 2).

Central City Poverty

It is important to point out that the new distribution of poverty does not mean that inner-city poverty has lessened significantly. Despite the prevalence of poverty in urbanized suburbs, most cities are in worse shape. The 2000 Census found that the official poverty rate is twice as high in the cities as in the suburbs taken in the aggregate: 18.2% versus 8.6%, remaining unchanged since 1990. Unemployment is significantly higher in cities than in suburbs. In 2000, cities had over a third more unemployment (8% versus 5%) (Logan, 2002, p. 1). The employment rate of young less-educated Black males is much lower in cities than in suburbs, and dropped by over four times as much in cities (9 percentage points) over the course of the 1990s as in suburbs (2 percentage points) (Offner and Holzer, 2002, pp. 1, 7).

Just as suburbs are not monolithic, cities differ as well. Some cities are less stressed—e.g., Denver, Minneapolis-St. Paul, Phoenix, Portland, San Diego, San Francisco, Seattle, and Tampa—with about 50% of children eligible for free-lunch programs and below 10% of the population living in high-poverty census tracts. Other cities are severely stressed—Chicago, Cleveland, Detroit, Miami, New York, Newark, Oakland, and St. Louis—with between 70% and 95% of children eligible for free-lunch programs and from 13% to 24% of the population living in high-poverty tracts (Orfield 2002, pp. 23–25).

Despite the move of some low-income families to urbanized suburbs, 77% of African Americans and 50% of Latinos who are poor live in central cities in census tracts of at least 20% poverty. And many reside in neighborhoods where poverty is more highly concentrated. From 1970 to 1990, the number of people living in central city neighborhoods of "extreme" poverty (40% or more) nearly doubled from 4.1 million to 8 million (Katz, 2000, pp. 5).

But by 2000, the share of the metropolitan poor who lived in extreme poverty neighborhoods had decreased to 6.7 million (Kingsley and Pettit 2002, pp. 1–2). It is likely that many moved to city neighborhoods of only slightly less concentrated poverty: A larger share of city poor were living in tracts with poverty rates of 20% to 30%, and these neighborhoods increased their share of poor families from 18% to 21%. Increases in tracts of around 10% to 20% poverty were from 27% to 29% (ibid., p. 2). An important point here is that although urban poverty has indeed deconcentrated somewhat since the early 1990s to neighborhoods of somewhat less poverty, the two kinds of neighborhoods present highly similar characteristics. For example, census tracts with 30% poor persons have scores on most indicators of social and economic distress that are extremely similar to those in neighborhoods where 40% of persons are poor (share of adults without a high school degree, joblessness, single-parent families, etc.) (p. 2).

By 2000, another change in metropolitan poverty had occurred: an increasing share of census tracts with 30% or more poverty are located in the suburbs of the largest 100 metropolitan areas (15% in 2000, up from 11% in 1980). But central cities of those metros still retain a dominant share of high poverty tracts—62% of them, down from 67% in 1980 (p. 1).

City-Suburban Interdependence

Despite the spread of families and businesses farther and farther from the central city (sprawl), many regionalists argue that the well-being of the suburbs depends to a great extent on the health of the cities, and that the finances of the two are intimately related

81

(Dreier, Swanstrom, and Mollenkopf, 2001, p. 63). The incomes of city residents and those of suburban residents are highly correlated: When suburban incomes go up, inner-city incomes do as well, although by a much smaller amount and from a much lower base (see Ledebur and Barnes, 1993; Savitch et al., 1993; Voith, 1992; and Voith, 1998).

Interdependence theorists point out that despite the many suburban office complexes and shopping malls, central business districts have continued their importance as sites of banking, legal, accounting, and other corporate firms and organizations; they are sites of concentration of supportive services such as communications centers, graphics, and advertising (see Sassen, 2001; and Dreier, Swanstrom, and Mollenkopf, 2001). Indeed, suburban income and property values depend in important ways on the availability of jobs in the central city. Firms in outlying suburbs typically rely on corporate services located in city centers. A study of 5,000 large firms found that 92% of the professional services purchased in the region were purchased from central city companies (Dreier, Swanstrom, and Mollenkopf, 2001, p. 64). These authors argue: "Although dynamic business clusters can exist in the suburbs, cities generally foster higher levels of density and dynamism. It is difficult to imagine cutting-edge clusters in fashion, theatre, art, advertising, investment banking, or design prospering in low-density suburbs. . . . The 'edge cities' described by Joel Garreau are not autonomous from the regional economic network in which the central city still plays an anchoring, crucial role"(ibid., p. 65; see also Barnes and Ledepur, 1998).

Tax rates can be interrelated, as well. In Essex County, NJ, for example, home to both rich and poor municipalities, the decline in land values in Newark over the 1990s shifted an increasing share of county taxes onto affluent Essex County property owners (Alloway and Gebeloff, 2002, p. 2).

SPATIAL MISMATCHES

While metropolitan areas exhibit problems of sprawl, traffic gridlock, long commutes, environmental degradation, and rising housing costs, the problems of concern here are those that work to maintain individual and institutional poverty in central cities and segregated, urbanized suburbs: spatial mismatches within regions of jobs and public transportation networks. These are determinative in important ways of the poverty of urban families, and (as a result) of their neighborhoods and schools, as well.

Jobs

For the last quarter century, a spatial mismatch of entry-level jobs and prospective workers has characterized metropolitan regions: Most workers with low to moderate education levels live in central cities (and low-income inner-ring urban suburbs), and most jobs for which they qualify are located in outlying suburbs. Two-thirds of all new jobs have located in these suburbs. Entry-level jobs such as routine manufacturing, retail, call centers, and data entry have declined in central cities while growing on the urban fringe (Dreier, Swanstrom, and Mollenkopf, 2001, p. 58; see also Glaeser, Kahn, and Chu, 2001; and Allard, 2001).

A study of 92 metropolitan areas found only 17 places where city job growth outpaced suburban job growth during the middle of the 1990s. The bulk of the cities did gain jobs but at a slower pace than their suburban neighbors. For example, from 1994 to 1997, the central business districts in Ohio's seven major cities had a net increase of only 636 jobs. Their suburbs, by contrast, gained 186,410 new jobs (Katz, 2000, p. 3).

During 2002, New York City residents lost 57,700 jobs while residents of the city's six closest counties gained 38,800 jobs (Suffolk, Nassau, Westchester, Rockland, Dutchess, and Putnam). During the same period of time, the city's unemployment rate went up from 7.8% to 9.2% while the unemployment rate in the six suburban counties declined from 4.3% to 3.8% (Bowles, 2003, p. 5).

Exclusionary zoning (state or local regulations regarding land lot size, for example) limit the construction of affordable housing in the suburbs, and thereby prevent people who need the entry-level jobs from moving closer to them. The number of highly skilled professional jobs, such as lawyers and management consultants, has increased in central business districts, yet those who hold them often live in the suburbs (Dreier, Swanstrom, and Mollenkopf, 2001, p. 59).

Few low-income city residents have cars or public transportation available to travel to outlying jobs (Congressional Hearings on Reauthorization of Transportation Bill, 1998; see below). Moreover, their location far from suburban employers means that they are not part of personal networks that apprise job seekers and employers of each other. Studies have found that most entry-level jobs are located through friends and relatives, not through want ads. In a study carried out in the Chicago region, for example, more than 40% of Chicago firms reported that they did not advertise their entry-level openings in newspapers. Rather, they relied on informal means, such as referrals from present workers, which they felt ensured a better-quality worker (Holzer, 1996, p. 82; see also Moss and Tilly, 2001). Yet, as William Julius Wilson has shown for this same city, residents of low-income neighborhoods are not only physically distant from those networks, they are less likely than others to have friends who are employed (Wilson, 1997).

The spatial mismatch between jobs and people has a racial character. Two-thirds of all Whites (including 55% of *poor* Whites) now live in suburbs outside central cities where more than 80% of new job creation has occurred (including most low-skilled job creation). And many poor Whites live in economically mixed, more middle-class areas. On the other hand as noted above, despite the movement of Blacks and Latinos to suburban areas, half of poor Latinos and more than three-fourths of poor Blacks still live in low-income inner-city neighborhoods (Rusk, 1999, pp. 10, 71).

There are a number of policies the implementation of which would connect urban job seekers with employment in regional economies: training programs that make explicit connections between workers in urban centers and suburban employers; transportation reforms that provide public bus or train routes between the city and outlying job centers; the placement of businesses already successful in the regional market within central-city neighborhoods; mobility programs to move families who want to relocate to higher income, less segregated areas; and affordable housing in more affluent areas so entry-level workers could reside closer to job centers.

As one example, innovative job training programs in a number of metropolitan areas have sought to link inner-city job seekers with suburban jobs through collaborations between community-based organizations, businesses, and educational institutions. One of the most successful is Project Quest in San Antonio, TX. Two community organizations that are part of the Industrial Areas Foundation network—Communities Organized for Public Service (COPS) based in Catholic congregations in Mexican American neighborhoods, and Metro Alliance, based in Protestant churches in African American neighborhoods—joined together to create Project Quest. In the early 1990s, they learned that the San Antonio area had added about 19,000 jobs in health care, office work, education, and mechanical repair—with most of them long distances from urban neighborhoods. With the assistance of several local corporations, Project Quest identified occupations and sectors with growth potential and career ladders, and worked with businesses to design curriculum to train prospective employees. They put community pressure on elected politicians to provide $6 million in local, state, and federal funds. Between its inception in 1993 and the end of 1995, Project Quest placed more than 800 trainees in a "comprehensive . . . package of supports, including child care, transportation assistance, medical care, tutoring, modest cash assistance for incidentals, and tuition to community colleges" (Dreier, Swanstrom, and Mollenkopf, 2001, p. 199; see also Moss and Tilly, 2001; and Osterman and Lautsch, 1996). For these programs to succeed, however, transportation between cities and outlying jobs is essential.

Transportation

An ethnographic report in the *New Yorker Magazine* by MacArthur Award winner Katherine Boo describes efforts of two African American women living in a low-income neighborhood in Oklahoma City to obtain jobs and commute to work without a car. The only source of jobs for people in this low-income neighborhood was a distant shopping mall. The city provided no direct transit lines between the two places, so the women were forced to ride buses up to five hours a day to get to the mall and back. At one point for one of the women, the only available job at the mall was during the shift that ended at 9:00 p.m.; but the city buses on the routes she needed stopped running at 7:00 p.m. (2003, p. 4). Her dilemma is not unusual. In 1998, testimony before Congress in preparation for amendments of the Federal Transit Act, documented the following: Even in metropolitan areas with excellent public transit systems, less than half the jobs are accessible by public transit; 94% of very low-income families do not own cars; most workers with annual incomes below $10,000 do not commute to work by car; many of the two million Americans who were scheduled to have their TANF grants terminated in 2002 were unable to get to jobs they could otherwise hold because there was no transportation available (Federal Transit Act of 1998, Congressional Findings).

In 1956, federal politicians promoted the Interstate Highway and Defense Act, which would depend on tax dollars, by arguing that it would defend Americans against the Soviet Union (Rusk, 2000, p. 79). This act established the Highway Trust Fund, which built 41,000 miles of highways around cities and out, to the developing suburbs. By the end of the 1990s, the Highway Trust Fund was spending gas taxes and other state and federal funds in the amount of $20 billion a year. Between 1975 and the mid-'90s, the U.S. spent $1.15 trillion for roads and highways, but only $187 billion for mass transit and $13 billion for intercity train transit [Amtrak]) (Dreier, Swanstrom, and Mollenkopf, 2001, p. 105). Even though more and more entry-level jobs have located in outlying areas, mass transit lines have never been built to connect them to cities—travel by automobile has been the only route (see Jackson, 1995 and 2000).

Indeed, in many states, cities and metro areas pay more in transportation taxes than they get back in services. In Colorado, for instance, the Denver metro area is allocated only 69 cents in revenues for each dollar of tax revenue it contributes. In the state of Washington, Seattle metro area raises 51% of the state's total revenues but is provided only 39% in return. Moreover, metropolitan areas now control only about 10 cents of every tax dollar they generate for transportation spending (Katz, Puentes, and Bernstein, 2003, p. 4).

Transportation is now the second largest tax expense for most U.S. households, utilizing an average 18 cents out of every dollar. Only housing takes a larger amount (19 cents), with food third (13 cents). Low-income households spend a much larger share of their income on transportation: Households earning between $12,000 and $23,000 spend 27 cents of every dollar they earn on transportation. For the very poor (households earning less than $12,000) the transportation burden rises to 36 cents per dollar (ibid., p. 6).

In 1990, a number of transportation reform advocates created a national coalition to advocate for a new course in U.S. transportation policy. This coalition, the Surface Transportation Policy Project (STPP) was an alliance of environmentalists, social equity activists, transit supporters, community groups, and others. The coalition hoped to influence federal transportation law that was to be reauthorized in 1991; they wanted to increase funding for links between inner cities and suburban job centers. STPP crafted and successfully advocated for the new law—titled the Inter-modal Surface Transportation Efficiency Act of 1991 (ISTEA)—which increased funding for public transit, and gave states and regions the discretion to transfer even more of their highway dollars to routes between inner-city and outlying job centers. ISTEA also included requirements for public involvement in regional transportation planning (Chen and Jakowitsch, 2000, p. 4). However, only four states and the District of Columbia (California, Massachusetts, New York, and Oregon) transferred more than one-third of available funds to public transit allowable under ISTEA (Katz, Puentes, and Bernstein 2003, p. 5).

In 1998, the Clinton administration was successful in obtaining passage of a transportation bill that for the first time provided the possibility of federal subsidies to metro areas to support the development of new bus routes, vanpools, shuttles, and mass transit connections between low-income urban and rural locations and suburban employment centers (potential funding for programs such as Bridges to Work, Access to Jobs, and Reverse Commute) (U.S. Department of Transportation Office of Small and Disadvantaged Business Utilization Press Release, June 6, 1998). Localities had to compete for grants from $42 billion in federal funds allocated and, beginning in 1999, match them fifty-fifty with local funds. To date, only a few states or municipalities have taken advantage of opportunities for federal funds under this act to build transit connections between inner cities and far-flung suburban job centers; most of those that did obtain grants built pedestrian-friendly walkways, or light rail systems for suburban commuters (Katz, Puentes, and Bernstein, 2003, p. 5). In 2003, during reauthorization hearings for transportation funding, the Senate cut 16% of the "reverse commute" program, in order to provide more money for suburban commuter rails. The transportation bill, which was the first to establish a regional approach to public transportation that would benefit urban job seekers, is up for reauthorization, and its future is not certain.

In a number of states, grassroots groups have organized around transportation issues. In North Carolina, a coalition called Democracy South worked with local media "to unmask an illicit quid-pro-quo system in which major state campaign contributors (mostly developers and contractors) were rewarded with a seat on the state Department of Transportation's powerful Board of Transportation—the body responsible for highway routing, construction priorities, and other factors that affect where transportation money is spent" (Chen and Jakowitsch, 2000, p. 4).

In East St. Louis, IL, the Emerson Park Development Corporation convinced its regional transit authority to reroute a new rail transit line so that it came to their neighborhood. This generated economic development opportunities and better accessibility to outlying jobs for community residents (p. 50). In Chicago, the Lake Street El Coalition—a collaboration of civil rights, community development, and environmental groups— prevented the Chicago Transit Authority from closing the transit station in low-income Lake Tree. The coalition convinced the authority to reinvest in the station. This would encourage businesses to open near the stop and provide an anchor for neighborhood economic development (p. 5). (Developers more typically build apartments and stores at commuter train stations in affluent suburbs [Holusha, 2003]).

Without available transportation, residents of low-income neighborhoods cannot reach distant job centers and, since there are fewer entry-level jobs in the cities, many urban residents who could otherwise earn incomes and support families remain unemployed and in poverty.

Connecting Urban Neighborhoods to Regional Economies

Most neighborhoods in central cities and urbanized low-income suburbs have bodegas, "deli's" and other small businesses—and relatively few jobs, compared to the number that are needed. One method of increasing the number of jobs in economically depressed urban areas is to reconnect neighborhood economies to regional markets and firms by locating businesses that are successful parts of the larger regional economies in inner-city neighborhoods. Michael E. Porter of the Harvard Business School and main advocate of this approach, argued in 1995: "Long term opportunities for inner cities lie in capitalizing on nearby regional clusters of firms and industries—unique concentrations of competitive companies in related fields. The ability to access competitive clusters is much more far reaching in its economic implications than simple proximity to the city. Building on local clusters involves tapping powerful external economies and leveraging private and public investments in skills, technology, and infrastructure . . . . [For example] Boston is home to a world-class healthcare cluster that abuts the inner city. There are opportunities to link inner-city companies to this cluster as well as to develop focused programs for training and the development of job opportunities for inner-city residents" (1995b, p. 3).

In the late 1990s, a Boston business group, The Initiative for A Competitive Inner City (ICIC), estimated that inner-city consumers constitute $85 billion in annual potential retail buying power—far more than the entire country of Mexico (ICIC, 1998, p. 18; see also Porter, 1995a and 1995b; and Pawasarat and Quinn, 2001). This figure does not include unrecorded income, which could add another $15 billion (Wells Fargo Bank, 1996, p. 11).

A study by Shorebank Corporation, the nation's premier Community Development Bank Holding Company, and Social Compact, a leading organization committed to expanding private business investment in lower-income neighborhoods, confirmed the retail sales potential of inner-city neighborhoods. Findings of their research, undertaken in Chicago, are as follows.

Primarily as a result of the high concentration of residents, low-income neighborhoods like South Shore in Chicago have more buying power than wealthier suburbs. For example, while South Shore's median family income is only $22,000, compared with $124,000 in the affluent suburban of Kenilworth, South Shore packs $69,000 of retail spending power per acre, nearly twice that of Kenilworth ($38,000).

Individuals reporting income under $10,000 make expenditures equaling about 250% of their income (Weissbourd, 1999, pp. 2–4). A major reason for this discrepancy is a large and growing unreported or parallel economy. The unrecorded economy of inner cities comprises some illegal activities, but the far greater part of it (about 80%) comes from legal but unrecorded activities, from nannies and tutors to home contractors and small businesses (Wells Fargo Bank, 1996, p. 11). Although the size of the unrecorded economy cannot be confirmed empirically, the most reliable estimates place it at about $1 trillion annually, or approximately 20% of gross national product (ibid., p. 11).

Given this amount, and given the large number of low-income individuals in the U.S., it is not surprising to learn that individuals with reported incomes under $30,000 make almost a third of all consumer expenditures in the United States. This amounts to

$920 billion annually (Weissbourd, 1999, p. 3). However, the lack of business in inner-city markets drives residents to make a large proportion of their expenditures outside their own neighborhoods. Chicago consumers living in South Shore, and Little Village, one a low- and the other a moderate-income neighborhood, make about 70% and 62% of their expenditures outside their own neighborhoods, respectively. Recent analysis found that local residents in another low-income community in Chicago spend $98.2 million—a stunning 72% of spending on groceries—in other communities. In more affluent Chicago neighborhoods, the expenditure leakage is only about 37%. Known as the "float," expenditure leakage to stores outside low-income neighborhoods signifies a market opportunity for businesses to provide competitively priced goods and services to inner-city consumers, and jobs for local residents (p. 5).

[handwritten margin note: dangerous argument]

Michael Porter's researchers studied inner-city businesses in cities across the country. Their analysis of supermarkets revealed that inner-city markets can generate average grocery sales per square foot up to 40% higher than the regional average, and in some cities the grocers average twice the regional average of sales.

Pathmark stores in high-poverty Bedford Stuyvesant (in Brooklyn, NY) and Newark's central ward, were two of the highest sales generators in the 144-store chain (Porter, 1995b, p. 6). Neighborhood community-based organizations can share ownership of the stores: New Community Corporation, in Newark, NJ, has a majority equity stake in a Pathmark supermarket in Newark's central ward with sales per square foot twice the national average (ibid.).

Porter cites many examples of community-based corporations that are successfully collaborating with businesses. For example, in Boston, the Dorchester Bay Economic Development Corporation was responsible for rehabilitating a building for use by America's Food Basket supermarket. The supermarket operates successfully there and has helped revitalize the (Uphams Corner) shopping district in which it is located (p. 7). Also in Boston, the Super Stop and Shop located at the South Bay Center in Boston's inner city was *the* highest grossing store in the entire 186-store chain (p. 5).

Porter's researchers discovered that many retailers who locate in the inner city have found that building ties within the community and hiring local people are essential to profitability (p. 16). Hiring and training local residents has proved crucial not only to overall profitability but also to the control of "shrink," or theft (p. 16).

Porter estimates that fulfilling the unmet inner-city retail demands could create 300,000 new jobs in these communities. In Harlem, NY, alone, unmet retail demand could create up to 8,000 jobs (p. 17). If employers paid local workers a living wage, these chains could make a dent in inner-city poverty.

Basing retail chains in inner-city neighborhoods creates jobs; and recruitment and training of local workers should be tied specifically to those opportunities. Studies have shown that generic education and training programs—that is, those not connected to specific jobs—generally do not succeed (see Freeman and Gottschalk, 1998; and Timothy Bartik, 2001, among others). Training programs are most effective when they are offered at no cost to prospective employers as part of a locational incentive package. For example, Rosabeth Moss Kanter points out that customized training programs have been instrumental in bringing major job generators to former economically depressed areas of the South. The BMW automobile plant in Spartanburg, SC, and the Mercedes-Benz plant in Vance, AL, are examples. For individuals participating in the training programs attached to these companies, the job placement rates are as high as 99% (2000, p. 161).

In addition, if we are going to support bringing large businesses into urban centers, then we must also insure that local, neighborhood entrepreneurs get access to tax write-offs—say, for renovation and expansion—like the large chains. Otherwise, inner-city neighborhoods will become dominated by large corporations and local stores will be forced to close.

If one cannot find a job near one's home, or obtain travel to a job that is available elsewhere, one is quite effectively rendered jobless and poor. The spatial mismatches delineated in this chapter between urban populations, jobs in outlying areas, and public transit routes are thus important causes of the poverty in urban families and neighborhoods and, thus, urban schools.

The next chapter demonstrates how these employment and transportation inequities are compounded by the maldistribution of affordable housing and municipal resources. These latter inequities exacerbate macroeconomic policies and regional mismatches by concentrating affordable housing in areas where there are few if any jobs, and by channeling funds for investment to towns that are already affluent.

6

Regional Housing Reform
as Education Reform

One of the most egregious social phenomena, one that undermines urban school reform continually, is the housing concentration of low-income students into central cities and urbanized suburban neighborhoods in metropolitan areas across the country. This housing segregation produces the educational segregation of urban Blacks and Latinos into schools where the vast majority of students are poor. Such schools are notoriously underresourced and unsuccessful in promoting high achievement.

Yet housing policies that could lead to the deconcentration of urban minorities from low-income schools are not in the panoply of strategies we typically entertain as solutions to urban school reform. Again and again we attempt to integrate school children by busing, magnet programs, and other court-ordered plans. Yet the underlying cause of school segregation is housing segregation. One of the tasks of this chapter is to lay the foundation for the idea that one of the most important education reforms may be housing policy reform.

The historical balkanization of U.S. metro areas into discrete and unequally resourced municipalities that rely on property tax for education is an important reason for the underfinancing of schools in most urban areas. This metropolitan balkanization exacerbates the problems for urban districts that result from federal macroeconomic and tax policies already discussed. Some states spread tax dollars from more affluent suburbs to cities to increase educational funding in cities, and this is an important step. This statewide educational funding, in fact, is an extant quasiregional model that could be used for other kinds of revenue sharing among metro-area municipalities.

HOUSING

There is a critical shortage of affordable housing throughout metropolitan regions, and in central cities, where most low-income housing is already located. As in the spatial mismatch of jobs, the problem of affordable housing in metropolitan areas has a racial dimension (Powell and Graham, 2002; and Powell, 2000). As I noted in chapter 5, three out of four poor Whites live in middle-class, often suburban neighborhoods, thereby coming into contact with opportunities for better housing, jobs, and education, while most poor Latinos and Blacks live in low-income, inner-city neighborhoods where at least 20% of the residents are poor, housing and education are poor, and jobs are lacking.

David Rusk argued in 1999 that a major reason overall White poverty rates (less than eight percent that year) are so much lower than Latino and Black poverty rates (24% and 28%, respectively, that year) is this "mainstreaming" of most poor White households in more middle-class communities. He argued that mainstreaming more low-income minorities in middle-class areas would lead to lower poverty rates among Blacks and Hispanics as well, as they would be nearer better schools and job opportunities (1999, p. 327).

Although early-20th-century government housing built for low-income people was often racially mixed, federal housing policies since the 1950s have promoted economic and racial segregation by locating public housing in areas of already concentrated poverty (ibid., 1999, pp. 250, 252; see also Massey and Denton, 1993; and Powell and Graham, 2002).

In 1996, public housing projects provided shelter for 1.3 million extremely low-income households. Between 1997 and 1999, more than 200,000 of these units were closed. This loss brought the total number of units affordable to the poorest households to just 1.2 million. With 4.5 million renters extremely poor—earning less than 30% of their area's median income—the shortfall now stands at 3.3 million units. These numbers actually understate the shortage, because higher-income households occupy a full 65% of the units affordable to extremely low-income households (Joint Center for Housing Studies of Harvard University, 2001, p. 24).

The federal government provides rental assistance to about 4.6 million extremely and very low-income renters. Roughly 1.3 million are tenants in public housing, 1.9 million live in privately owned buildings with subsidies tied to the properties, and 1.4 million receive "Section 8" vouchers to rent units in the private market from landlords who agree to rent to them. These programs do not meet the need. More than twice as many extremely and very low-income renter households (9.7 million) receive no federal housing assistance at all.

EFFECTS OF RESIDENTIAL SEGREGATION ON EDUCATION

Confining low-income people of color to housing in poor urban neighborhoods and low-income minority suburbs also produces segregated, low-income schools—neighborhood elementary schools as well as high schools—since most city Black and Latino high school students attend large, comprehensive high schools where the enrollments are almost all low-income students of color. The following characteristics of low-income urban schools are extremely well documented: insufficient school funding; few if any advanced courses; too few qualified teachers; undemanding pedagogy; low academic achievement on the part of most of the students; buildings in disrepair and unprepared for technology; too few classroom computers and computer-prepared teachers; large classes; and all-too-often, unchallenging academic content. All of this contributes to fewer opportunities to learn, lower graduation rates, ultimately very low college graduation rates, and fewer labor market possibilities (Anyon, 1995, 1996, and 1997; Consortium on Chicago School Research, 1996; Darling-Hammond, 2001; and Mickelson, 2001a, 2001b, and 2003, for example).

Thus, federal housing policies that concentrate low-income residents in urban neighborhoods contribute to effects on education that prove in many cases to be overwhelming barriers to high quality schools—and indeed, to urban school reform (Anyon, 1997; Henig et al. 2001; and Lipman, 1998, among others).

There are several kinds of housing policies that would desegregate urban residential areas: mobility programs that relocate urban families who want to move to less segregated and/or higher income areas in the region; construction of more affordable housing not only in central cities but in medium- and high-income areas of the region; and enforcement of federal policies that render illegal the widespread discrimination in housing rental and sales.

MOBILITY PROGRAMS AND EDUCATIONAL ACHIEVEMENT

Experience in Albuquerque, NM, demonstrates that the integration of the poor into working-class and middle-class neighborhoods works to the benefit of poor children. Albuquerque, the nation's twenty-fifth largest district, is one of only five metrowide school systems. There is a high degree of uniformity in the distribution of school resources. And there is an unusually high number of public housing children living in middle-class neighborhoods and attending middle-class neighborhood schools. With 80% of the metro area's population, Albuquerque is a near-metropolitan city. Its housing projects and rental subsidies are widely scattered throughout the city (Rusk, 1999, p. 121).

David Rusk and researchers at the Urban Institute studied the test results of pupils from public housing families in the Albuquerque public schools. They found that for every percentage point decrease in poverty among a public housing project child's classmates, that child's test scores improved .22 of a percentile. In other words, attending a middle-class neighborhood school with 20% poor children rather than a high-poverty neighborhood school with 80% poor children meant a 13% point improvement in an average public housing child's test scores. They also looked at the schools' average test performance and results were even more positive. For every percentile increase in a *school's* average test scores, the public housing child's scores improved .53 of a percentile point. Attending a school whose students ranked on average in the 80th percentile in the national tests as opposed to a school whose students were in the 20th percentile meant a *32 percentile improvement* in the average public housing child's test scores.

The positive educational results in Albuquerque of mixing children of different social classes point to the importance of housing policies for education. In most urban regions, where a child lives largely determines the quality of his or her school experience. The child's school performance is heavily influenced by the socioeconomic status of the child's family and classmates. Thus, one of *the most effective education reforms for improving poor children's school performance would be housing policies that integrate poor families into middle-class neighborhoods and middle-class schools.*

Indeed, there is now substantial evidence that families who move to less segregated and/or higher income areas from their inner-city homes typically improve educational outcomes for their children and economic opportunities for themselves. The oldest of these mobility projects is the Gatraux Program in Chicago. As a result of a victorious lawsuit charging the Chicago housing authority with segregation in public housing, the court ordered the housing authority to move families who wanted to move to less segregated areas of the city and suburbs. The Gautraux program moved over 7,000 families to higher income areas of the Chicago metropolitan region between 1976 and 1998. By 1984, the program was in such demand that on the day that families could enroll in that year, almost 10,000 called in (Rubinowitz and Rosenbaum, 2002, p. *x*).

Although at first a disproportionate number of children who moved were placed in classes for the learning disabled by their suburban schools, the students were ultimately significantly more likely than their urban counterparts to be in college high school tracts, in four-year colleges, and were more likely subsequently to be employed in jobs with higher pay and with benefits than children who stayed in the city (ibid., pp. 127–160, 174–176).

The success of the Gatraux program led to over 50 other mobility programs, including the "Moving To Opportunity" program (MTO), begun by HUD in 1994. The Housing and Community Development Act of 1992 authorized HUD to "assist very low-income families with children who reside in public housing . . . to move out of areas with high concentrations of persons living in poverty [40% or more] to areas with low concentrations of such persons [less than 10% poverty]" (Goering and Feins, 2003, p. 6). Moving to Opportunity projects were carried out in five cities: Baltimore, Boston, Chicago, Los Angeles, and New York.

Congress stipulated that HUD conduct evaluations of the program to determine its effects. The evaluators divided a sample of 4,608 families into three groups: the MTO treatment, or experimental group, which received Section 8 certificates or vouchers that could only be used in areas where 10% or less of the residents lived below official poverty levels, and assistance in finding private rental units. A second group was given Section 8 certificates with no special restrictions on where they were to move, and no counseling. An in-place control group continued to receive housing project assistance in the inner-city neighborhoods where they lived. The families in all three groups of the MTO program tended to be young single mothers (under 35 years of age), African American, with a median income of $8,200. Most stated that their main reason for wanting to move was fear of gangs and violence in the neighborhoods in which they lived (pp. 6, 7, 13).

Research was conducted in all five cities, using HUD data, baseline surveys, follow-up surveys of families, qualitative interviews, and data on juvenile crime, labor market outcomes, and school performance. Among the findings are the following. One to three years after the families in the experimental (treatment) group moved, they lived in significantly more affluent and more racially mixed communities than either of the other groups. In addition, their median incomes were 73% higher than median incomes in the control group neighborhoods and 53% higher than in Section 8-only group locations. In 1997, three years after the program began, the MTO experimental group families in all five metropolitan areas lived in less-segregated neighborhoods than either of the other two groups (p. 26).

Studies of adults in the experimental group in New York and Boston reported significantly better health and emotional well-being than either of the other groups in those cities. Mothers in the experimental groups were much less likely to report being depressed or stressed. The parents had the resources to provide more structure for their children's activities, and used less restrictive parenting styles. By the third year, 10% fewer of the experimental group in New York City were receiving welfare. In Boston, public assistance by MTO families dropped by half, and employment in all MTO sites increased from 27% at the beginning of the program to 43% three years later. Employment of the Boston adults increased by more than one-half (pp. 28, 30).

The outcomes for children in the experimental groups were also encouraging. They attended schools that had higher pass rates, more affluent student bodies, and more resources compared with the schools attended by control group children (p. 117). Young children in the experimental and Section 8 groups "achieved higher test scores than the controls, and experienced fewer arrests for violent criminal behavior" (p. 164).

The authors report in some detail assessments of Hope VI in Baltimore, and state that they are "largely consistent with evidence from the other MTO sites" (p. 163). Young children in the Baltimore experimental and Section 8 groups had standardized reading scores that were on average six to seven percentile points higher than those who stayed in the inner city. "This large effect is equal to around one-quarter of the control group mean of 25 percentile points and one quarter of a standard deviation in the national CTBS math distribution" (p. 165). Children in the experimental group also raised their standardized math scores about the same amount, and their pass rates on the standardized reading test were almost double those in the inner-city schools. High school students in the Baltimore experimental group had a more difficult transition. At least in the first three years of MTO, they had higher rates of grade retention, disciplinary action, and school dropout. The authors suggest that these differences may be due to the enforcement of higher behavioral and/or educational standards in more affluent schools. However, the move by teens from high- to low-poverty neighborhoods did result in fewer arrests for them. It reduced the proportion of juveniles who were arrested for a violent offense and the number of arrests per 100 juveniles by around half (pp. 165–167).

These results of the Moving To Opportunity program research are in general agreement with evaluations of other mobility programs—which have generally led to substantial improvements in neighborhood and housing conditions, mental and physical health and safety, behavior and educational outcomes of children, and adult labor market outcomes (Johnson, Ladd, and Ludwig, 2002, p. 135).

I have argued thus far that programs providing financial and other resources to low-income minority families, or that relocate them to areas of less segregation or higher income, improve the educational opportunities and performance of students. These strategies not only improve the lives of the families who move, but by deconcentrating district poverty can benefit urban schools as well. The construction of affordable housing in less segregated and higher income areas of metro regions, and the reform of state-enabled zoning that excludes poor people, are strategies that hold similar promise.

FAIR SHARE AFFORDABLE HOUSING

Discrimination against individuals of color who want to rent or buy a home is illegal. The 1968 Civil Rights Act outlawed racial discrimination in both publicly assisted and private housing. Indications are that this act, its legislative strengthening in 1989, and mechanisms such as fair housing laws have reduced some forms of housing discrimination against Black and Latino prospective home buyers. However, two recent national studies point to continuing problems. These assessments analyzed indicators of discrimination across the United States: one study in 23 housing markets, and the other of 331 municipalities. These reports identify three problems that have increased dramatically since 1989: geographic steering of prospective home buyers to some neighborhoods and not others, difficulty in obtaining financing information from realtors, and discrimination in the subprime lending market (Turner, 2000, p. 1; Bradford, 2002, p. 1; see also Dawkins, 2004; and Squires, 2003). These studies suggest that much racial exclusion in metropolitan housing markets still exists.

While racial discrimination in housing is illegal, discrimination on the basis of class is not. Federal, state, and local laws generally do not bar communities from housing discrimination on the basis of income. "Local governments are largely free to regulate land use and building requirements in ways that add to the cost of housing and exclude potential residents based on their income. Moreover private housing providers are generally free to discriminate against purchasers or renters based on their income" (Rubinowitz and Rosenbaum, 2002, pp. 4–5). Class-based exclusionary zoning is clearly an area that needs policy and behavioral change. Only a few states have managed to provide places for low-income families to live outside the central city and its inner ring of distressed, low-income suburbs—in most cases by legislating what are called Fair Share Housing laws. These laws mandate that all municipalities in a region build their fair share of low-income and moderate-income housing.

The Massachusetts Fair Share housing program, for example, reduces barriers to affordable housing in all cities of the state and allows an appeals board to override local zoning codes when less than 10% of a community's housing stock is for low- or moderate-income residents. In the past 30 years, more than 25,000 units of housing have been built as a result of this legislation (Orfield, 2002, p. 124). In New Jersey, litigation against so-called snob-zoning led to a State Supreme Court ruling in 1975 ("The Mount Laurel Decision") that required that each community construct a fair share of the metro area's need for affordable housing. Despite some affluent towns' reluctance—which led to state legislative compromises weakening the original decision— over 26,000 units have been built (Jackson, 2000, p. 213; Newman, 2002, p. 1; see also Kirp, Dwyer, and Rosenthal, 1995).

An equitable distribution of affordable housing throughout a metropolitan area could have important effects on urban schools. It would deconcentrate poor students from central cities and low-income suburbs, and place them with their middle- and upper-middle-class peers where, as research demonstrates, poor students are able to achieve at higher levels. Indeed, a spread of poor families in municipalities throughout a region would also help to deconcentrate affluence, and contribute to the diminution of extreme financial inequities that characterize U.S. metro areas, as described below.

METRO-AREA FINANCE INEQUITIES

In terms of financial capacity, almost all the cities in the 25 largest metropolitan areas that Myron Orfield studied are worse off than the vast majority of their suburbs. During the boom decades of the 1980's and '90's, the condition of cities and city schools actually worsened—with a higher percent of students on free lunch and a higher percent of poverty census tracks; the schools grew poorer and more segregated; growth in cities' tax capacity lagged behind their metropolitan averages; and tax capacity became more unequal between city and suburb (Orfield, 2002, pp. 24–25, 26, 28). One cause of their financial difficulties is that a city's revenue-raising capabilities are based primarily on what taxes the state legislature permits it to collect. For the most part, mayors and city councils can set tax rates only within narrow, legislatively prescribed limits (ibid., p. 17).

The federal government provides funds to both cities and suburbs. However, these monies typically have different mandates in the two kinds of places: wealth generation in the suburbs, and services and income, in the cities. A spatial analysis of federal funds in metropolitan Chicago, for example, found that although there was more money spent per capita in cities than in the newer suburbs, the funds in cities went primarily to income support, and in suburbs to wealth creation.

101

Wealth-building programs add to a municipality's future capacity to produce income. For example, home ownership subsidies add to the flow of tax income in the long run. Similarly, federal subsidies for local infrastructure allow an area to produce income in the future. These programs are investments in the area's capital stock. On the other hand, those federal programs that subsidize current consumption in urban areas through income support have few if any long-term consequences (Persky and Kurban, 2001, p. 2).

Politically, cities do not have sufficient numbers of residents to wield the clout in state legislatures necessary to obtain tax policies that would benefit them (Swanstrom and Sauerzkopf, 1993, in Pastor, Dreier, Grigsby and Lopez-Garza, 2000, p. 193). U.S. cities have never had much power in state legislatures, primarily because former rural elites held chairships of powerful committees (which are now typically held by suburban representatives) (Anyon, 1997, Chapter 7). And the share of the cities' vote in national elections has declined in recent decades. During World War II, 32 major cities cast 27% of the national vote for U.S. president. By 1992, their share had declined to 14%. In 2000, residents of cities with population over 500,000 cast only 9% of the vote (Dreier, Swanstrom and Mollenkopf, 2001, p. 235; see also Swanstrom and Sauerkopf, 1993). A study of 12 large cities found that they cast 21.8% of the national vote in 1948 but only 6.3% in 2000 (Dreier, Swanstrom and Mollenkopf, 2001, p. 35).

An additional cause of most cities' low tax base is that they have lost manufacturing companies. A hundred years ago, most manufacturing was located in cities, and was a major source of local revenue. But in all cities over 100,000 population, industry began moving out to the suburbs beginning in the 1920s (Anyon, 1997, Chapter 3). This trend has continued. Now, high-end office space is the major source of revenue for municipalities (Orfield, 2002, p. 35).

Most of the high-end office space is located in wealthy suburbs. The affluent 7% of the population in the 25 regions that Myron Orfield identified has more than four times the office space per household than any other group of suburbs *or* the central cities. They have a disproportionate share of the high-quality office space, too, as 60% to 70% of their office space is rated A or B. Central cities have 51% of office space, but most of it is old, and including wealthy financial centers, only 52% of it is rated A or B. At-risk older segregated suburbs *together* have only 7% of metropolitan office space, with about half (53.5%) rated highly (ibid., p. 36).

When federal and state aid is added to the revenues of large cities, their financial capacity on average is actually 12% higher than that of their suburban counterparts. However, this is more than offset by the cities' higher costs. Poverty, which is typically higher in cities than in the suburbs, dramatically raises the cost of providing local public services (Ladd and Yinger, 1989, p. 10; see also Pack, 1995). And higher density in cities also outweighs the greater comparative revenue capacity in 28 of 30 metropolitan areas studied by Orfield (2002, p. 28). State aid (not including education aid) does increase most central cities' revenue capacity (in 21 of 27 cities studied)—but by an average of only 32% (ibid., p. 58).

An additional source of financial inequality among municipalities in regions is racial segregation of low-income minorities in cities and financially distressed suburbs. Tax base inequality among municipalities in metro regions is highly correlated with racial segregation: The more segregated an area, the more unequal the tax base. Thus, there is a very strong tendency for more segregated metropolitan areas to show greater than average degrees of inequality in tax capacities among municipalities (ibid., p. 59).

Also increasing metropolitan inequality in financial capacity is the fact that since the 1970s, geographic separation of the affluent has increased—and fewer of their tax dollars are available for cities' use. In 1970, the typical affluent person lived in a neighborhood that was only 39% affluent. By 1990, that had increased to 52% affluent. Many families with more money have chosen to flee the cities and older suburbs (Jackson 2000, p. 186; see also McKenzie, 1994).

EDUCATIONAL FINANCE INEQUITIES

Regional financial inequities have serious consequences for urban education since schools are financed by municipal and state funds. Federal education spending—even in urban schools—has never amounted to more than 10% of district spending; currently the national average is around 7%. In most districts, the amount of money that local residents and businesses pay is typically the major determinant of the amount that is spent on schools.

All regions have municipalities that are affluent. I would argue, therefore, that sufficient tax resources exist in metro areas—were they distributed equitably—to fund quality schools for the vast majority of the students. But federal and state policies, regional zoning, and various "gentlemen's agreements" that segregate low-income families in fiscally stressed urban areas condemn them, in essence, to underfunded education.

The racial discrepancies in school funding identified by the Education Trust and reported in Chapter 4 are actually exacerbated by a majority of states, as they send a disproportionate amount of state money to their *lowest-minority* districts (2001, pp. 6, 7). For example, of 47 states studied, 22 send substantially *less* money (that is, a difference of $100 or more) per student to districts educating the greatest numbers of minority students. New York, for example, sends an additional $1,339 per student in state revenue to the districts educating the fewest minority students as compared to those districts educating the greatest number. When this is added to the disparity in *local* revenue, New York's highest-minority school districts have $2,034 less per student than the districts educating the fewest minority students. In Kansas, differences in locally raised revenue leave the highest-minority districts with $204 less than the lowest minority districts, but when you add state revenue the funding gap jumps to $1,403 per student (ibid., p. 7).

Legal challenges to state funding inequities can make a difference. The *Abbott v. Burke* victories in New Jersey, for instance, have resulted in that state targeting its high poverty districts more heavily than any other state (rank of 1 at 252% more). This is true even though New Jersey ranks toward the bottom on the percent of state revenues making up its overall education funding (40%) (p. 8). Other states that target state funds heavily toward poorer districts include Connecticut, Massachusetts, Wyoming, Pennsylvania, Rhode Island, and Virginia (in descending order) (p. 9).

POLICIES TO ALLEVIATE EDUCATIONAL AND OTHER REGIONAL FISCAL INEQUITIES

One method of reducing fiscal disparities between municipalities in metropolitan environments is to implement regional revenue sharing. "Vertical" intergovernmental revenue sharing is widespread: Throughout the United States, federal and state governments provide more than one-third of all local government revenues. Of $721 billion in local government revenues (fiscal 1994), direct federal grants-in-aid totaled about $30 billion; state aid (including pass-through federal funds) totaled about $212 billion (Bureau of the Census, 1997, Tables 478, 482; in Rusk, 1999, p. 220). But "horizontal" revenue sharing between local governments is far less prevalent, and multi-jurisdictional revenue sharing is very rare.

Since the tax on local property is the primary source of municipal government revenues, certain types of development—office buildings, corporate headquarters, upscale housing—are attractive because they almost always generate more revenue than it costs local government to provide services to them. *However, all taxpayers in the region pay state and federal taxes toward the state and federal funds that subsidize development in affluent areas, and therefore all municipalities in the region should be permitted to share in the tax returns that accrue.*

Revenue Sharing

The primary example of revenue sharing is the Twin Cities metropolitan area in Minnesota. The Twin Cities region is one economy. Commercial-industrial developments concentrate in only a few locations, drawing workers and customers from the regional market that extends beyond the city itself. Access to these firms, primarily state and federal highways, is a major determinant of where these developments locate. Cities in the metro area with such access are the ones most likely to attract commercial-industrial development (Rusk, 1999, p. 240).

In 1975, the Minnesota legislature began to implement a tax-base sharing plan. State legislation required that all taxing jurisdictions in the Twin Cities metropolitan area (seven counties, 186 cities, villages, and townships, 48 school districts, and about 60 other taxing bodies) contribute 40% of the increase in assessed value of commercial-industrial property into a common pool. The pool is taxed at a common rate, and revenues are redistributed among all local governments on the basis of each jurisdiction's population and its tax capacity— the per capita market value of commercial and industrial property—in relation to the tax capacity of the region as a whole. A municipality with below-average tax capacity receives a relatively larger distribution from the regional fund, and a jurisdiction with above-average tax capacity receives less (ibid., pp. 239–240).

By 1998, the annual fiscal disparities pool had reached $410 million, about 30% of the region's total commercial-industrial property tax receipts. Of the region's municipal governments, 137 were recipients, and 49 were contributors. Over the years, the contributors have been the Twin Cities' wealthiest suburbs, and the major recipients were St. Paul, inner-ring suburbs, and the financially stressed outlying towns and villages (p. 240).

Myron Orfield ran a series of simulations that demonstrates that tax-base sharing is a much more cost-effective means of reducing tax-base inequity than existing state aid programs. He found that, "On average tax-base sharing reduces inequities by a greater amount than current state aid programs with a pool of money that is less than one third the amount of current aid. Tax-base sharing reduces disparities by two percentage points for each percentage point of shared revenues, while current aid programs reduce disparities by just half of a percentage point for each percentage point of aid" (p. 108).

As in the Twin Cities, the political battles for regional changes such as tax-base sharing need to be fought in state legislatures because state representatives and senators make the rules for local governments' land use (that is, sprawl controls, local zoning powers, and intergovernmental agreements).

Minneapolis-St. Paul and New Jersey's Hackensack Meadowlands are the only places in which municipal tax-base sharing has been tried successfully. However, Portland, OR—which has the nation's only directly elected regional government—has been practicing regional land use planning for a quarter century (Rusk, 2000, p. 98). The democratically elected regional authority, "Portland Metro," covers three counties and 24 municipalities, and represents 1.5 million people. It created regulations that stopped regional sprawl in 1997 by setting a growth boundary beyond which no developments could be built. One result of this boundary was to "turn new private investment back inward to existing neighborhoods and retail areas" (ibid., p. 98). The metro council also attempted to institute mandatory inclusionary zoning, but developers beat back the effort at the state level (p. 99).

MORE EQUITABLE EDUCATION FUNDING

I will argue now that good models already exist on which to base regional revenue sharing to support urban schools. State education funding and state-distributed federal transportation money are already spread throughout metropolitan areas, and their equalizing possibilities could be greatly expanded. Recent experience in Michigan, Washington, Illinois, and Vermont demonstrates that state initiatives to reform educational spending can achieve many of the same equities sought by metropolitan tax sharing. Most of the educational financing reforms in these states have shifted school funding from local property taxes to broadly based taxes collected by the state (Yaro, 2000, p. 71).

Indeed, advice from a regionalist would be that states assume the entire cost of public elementary and secondary education from taxes collected at the state level rather than by locally collected funds. Education expenses represent more than two-thirds of most municipal budgets; shifting education finance to broad-based, state-collected taxes paid into a common pool, for example, could eliminate inequities that arise out of municipal property and other tax-base differences (New York's Third Regional Plan, put forward in 1989 by the states' prestigious Regional Plan Association, advocated just that).

Currently, education in the United States is administered by 14,229 school districts (U.S. Department of Education, National Center for Education Statistics, 2003). If these were consolidated and added to the statewide education administrative functions that already exist, both financial disparities and racial/economic segregation could be reduced. Moreover, metrowide districts should be established. Metropolitan districts (such as Albuquerque, described above) are among the least segregated (Orfield, 1996, p. 832; see also Orfield, 2002). Small, all-minority districts like Hartford, CT (19 square miles) and Newark (23 square miles)—if blended into their surrounding counties—could be desegregated and their funding merged into much larger systems.

Regional districts would allow for economies of scale, and would foster the implementation of important equalizing policies like the provision in the federal "Leave No Child Behind," which allows children in failing schools to enroll in successful district schools. In current city districts, successful schools to which to transfer are few and far between, and in those there are few if any seats available (Gross, 2003, p. 1; Banchero and Olszewski, 2003, p. 1).

As I will elaborate in the final chapter of this book, in order to advocate for equalizing educational policies, central cities and urbanized suburbs need to form political coalitions. The potential clout of such coalitions resides in the already noted fact that almost two-thirds of metropolitan poverty populations live in these urbanized, at-risk suburbs and central cities.

I believe there is ample evidence for the utility of metropolitan housing and finance reform as strategies to improve urban school systems. Affordable housing to which lower income urban families could move would alleviate the concentrated poverty that typically overwhelms urban schools. And policies that would spread more equitably the considerable resources of some to the benefit of all municipalities in a region would increase the ability of urban districts to pay for high-quality programs, personnel, and facilities.

But when we think about the financial distress of urban school systems, we generally do not see a direct link between their poverty and the wealth of affluent suburban districts; we generally believe that the money affluent earners make is theirs to keep, does not flow from the labors of the urban working class, and should not necessarily be shared to educate "other people's children." We tend to blame the poverty of poor districts on city or state politicians, district mismanagement or graft, or on the families who live there.

Yet as I have shown, federal economic policies are culpable, and create a link between suburban wealth and urban poverty. Suburban business owners and other shareholders of companies operating in cities take home profits and dividends that accrue in part from low wages paid to the workers in those companies. General Electric, for instance, with $15.13 billion in U.S. profits in 2002, figures that it made about $45,000 in profit per worker.

Business professionals, executives, and well-paid managers also derive salaries from monies that are available because of company profits. The tenacity with which owners of small businesses fight attempts to raise the minimum wage, and with which executives of large corporations seek sources of cheaper workers across the globe, testify to the link between low wages, higher profits, and therefore better salaries and dividends.

Moreover, as we have seen, wealth produced in both urban and suburban businesses has long depended on infrastructure supported by taxes paid by residents living throughout the metropolitan region. Indeed, urban residents continue to contribute to affluent suburbs through taxes used for further development in outlying municipalities, as well as through tax income lost at all government levels because of corporate write-offs and relocation incentives. We must remember that it is federal tax dollars—paid by city residents as well as others—that have provided the billions funding telecommunications, electronic, aerospace, medical and other research labs, most of which have located in affluent suburban job centers (federal subsidy that developed the computer and Internet industries—beginning in suburban Palo Alto—is just one of many examples).

It seems only fair, then, that metropolitan tax-base sharing be more widely instituted. Distributing tax resources equitably throughout a region would return to low-income municipalities a portion of their past and continuing contributions to suburban affluence—and would better finance urban schools and neighborhoods. When we think, therefore, about where to obtain funding for urban school systems, we should remember that wealthy suburbs are, and have been at least in part, dependent on profits earned in the cities and on city residents' tax dollars. I would argue, therefore, that parents in poverty urban schools have a right to financial recompense from the coffers of America's Scarsdales, Shaker Heights, and Beverly Hills.

SOCIAL MOVEMENTS AND NEW POLICIES

The policies I have promoted so far in this book are not likely to be popular with political and economic elites or, indeed, with many in America's middle class. Public policy theorist Theda Skocpol has argued that broad popular support of social policies—especially by the middle class—is necessary for their adoption and survival. One of the examples she uses is social security, which is beloved by the middle classes, she argues, and therefore secure as national policy (1991, p. 420).

It may be true that middle-class support is necessary for the passage and survival of a social policy. But it is also the case that most, if not all, legislation that has favored the middle class, the poor, the working class, and minority communities—including social security and Medicare—was adopted in large part because of popular protest and public demand—or in response to social crisis and the contention which threatened to follow. In the early years of the 20ᵗʰ century, for example, after massive protest beginning in the 1870s, the 12-hour workday became a federal maximum. Later, in the 1930s, after tumultuous organizing by a plethora of groups, legislation creating long-term mortgage loans for those without sufficient cash to purchase homes, public housing programs, and various worker protections—as well as social security—was passed. (Medicare was included in the 1960s, following concerted political organizing by seniors.) Only as a result of the assassination of Martin Luther King, Jr., was the nation's first Fair Housing law passed (Massey and Denton, 1993, p. 194). Billions of dollars were provided to cities only after a decade of civil rights mass mobilizations and riots in over 100 American cities. The whole host of civil rights legislation—not only the 1964 Civil Rights and 1965 Voting Acts, but the programs of the Great Society and War on Poverty (Model Cities, Elementary and Secondary Education Act, Head Start)—and federal aid for community development in the 1970s were only adopted after decades of political struggle by civil rights activists, community residents, and supporters.

Even the more recent passage of Empowerment Zone legislation to assist urban neighborhood economic development was approved in response to the riots following the trial that acquitted the officers who beat African American Rodney King in Los Angeles. The legislation had been proposed in the early 1980s, but only after the riots in Los Angeles was it passed in 1993 (see Lemann, 1994; and Davis, 1994).

Thus, public contestation certainly seems necessary if we are going to fulfill the redistributive potential of American democracy and U.S. education. The challenges and possibilities of protest and a new social movement, which could enable us to adopt both federal and regional leveling strategies such as those promoted here, are subjects that occupy the entirety of Part III. First, however, it is prudent to see what we can learn from efforts that have already been made to improve cities and their neighborhoods.

7

Local Challenges to Federal and Regional Mandates

The local is not only a product of neighborhood and city cultures and municipal regulations and policies but is also shaped by federal and regional decisions both current and historical. As preceding chapters make clear, federal policies that sustain urban minority poverty, and metropolitan arrangements that spread resources unequally throughout regions have circumscribed the life chances of residents in urban neighborhoods today.

A central argument of this book has been that we need to significantly improve economic opportunities and conditions in low-income urban neighborhoods in order to provide infrastructural support that will nurture systemic, long-term school reform. In *Ghetto Schooling*, I argued that "if we do not resuscitate our cities, we face an impossible situation regarding school reform: Attempting to fix inner-city schools without fixing the city in which they are embedded is like trying to clean the air on one side of a screen door" (1997, p. 168).

If we accept the premise that strong neighborhoods are important for school reform to take hold, then we must ask how we can accomplish urban rejuvenation. By what methods can we improve low-income neighborhoods and the lives of residents?

This has been a question many have tried to answer. The present chapter critiques strategies of the main long-term players: Federal efforts since the 1960s, and efforts by philanthropic foundations and Community Development Corporations (CDCs) over the same decades. These efforts have failed to revitalize urban

111

neighborhoods largely because they have tried to change localities and individual residents *without challenging the underlying federal and regional rules of the game.*

In addition to CDCs, grassroot community-based organizations have a long history of attempting to solve the problems faced by residents of urban neighborhoods, and they have not been particularly successful, either. There have been some significant recent successes, however. These successes result from coalitions of political, labor, and religious groups that combine—across the municipalities of a metropolitan area—to systematically challenge federal and regional policies and arrangements that build barriers to economic opportunity.

This chapter describes some of these coalitions, and argues that they offer a working model that school reformers could emulate. Regional coalitions demonstrate, in the long tradition of political protest in America, that organized public contestation is necessary if we are to build a strong foundation in cities—not only to lessen poverty but to ensure that curricular, pedagogical, and equity-seeking school reform can take hold and have meaningful consequences for student futures.

FEDERAL PROGRAMS

Since 1960, hundreds of federal programs—announced with much fanfare and promise—and ostensibly geared to elimination of neighborhood poverty, unemployment, and dilapidated housing, have been implemented to varying degrees in cities. Such programs include (among others) Model Cities, Urban Renewal, Job Training Partnerships, Empowerment Zones, Enterprise Communities, and the recent Hope VI (a HUD program advertised as replacing high-rise public housing with mixed-income communities—but see below).

Numerous scholars have argued that these and other federal urban efforts of the last 40 years have kept assistance to relatively superficial "quick fixes," and have confined treatments to the area within a neighborhood's boundaries—limiting remedies to what regionalists call *in-place* or *place-based* strategies. We now know that these programs have not been able to stem the federally supported flow of resources outward to the suburbs (Dreier, Swanstrom, and Mollenkopf, 2001, p. 103; see also Downs, 1994 and 1999; Jargowsky, 1997; Lemann, 1994; Orfield, 2002; Rusk, 1993 and 1999; and Weir, 1999).

I would argue that another reason the federal urban programs have failed is that they left unaltered the basic macroeconomic policies and regional arrangements that define the underlying rules maintaining poverty and scarcity. This is not to say that there have been no federal programs addressing urban problems that have been worthwhile. Several, if fully implemented, would prove extremely useful: For example, the Community Reinvestment Act of 1977, intended to outlaw redlining by banks and realtors; the Federal Fair Housing Law, passed in 1968 (and its stronger iteration of 1989), which made a wide range of discriminatory practices in real estate rental and sales illegal; or the federal Transportation Efficiency Act-21, which reformed federal transit by (in part) providing options for states to establish regional reverse-commute approaches to public transportation between inner-city workers and suburban jobs, and to give communities input into where these rail lines should be placed.

We saw in Chapters 5 and 6 that the equity potential of federal transportation and housing antidiscrimination programs has been severely curtailed by nonimplementation. And reliable studies document that the Community Reinvestment Act is not being fully implemented either. Assessment in nine cities by the National Training and Information Center found that 15 of the top 25 lenders (60%) in the U.S. are not strictly regulated by the act; only one percent of the loans made by the top 25 lenders in 2001 went to low- and moderate-income borrowers in low- and moderate-income census tracts; and only three percent of the loans made by the top 25 lenders in the U.S. in 2001 went to African Americans (Parson 2003, p. 2).

In addition, the federal Hope VI Public Housing Demolition program, begun in 1992 to replace high-rise ghetto housing built in the 1950s and 1960s with improved mixed income housing, has destroyed public housing primarily in areas that appear amenable to attracting private retail investment and high-end redevelopment—like a project just half a block from Boston Harbor, now deemed a prime real estate location. Only seven of the first 35 Hope VI redevelopment awards were for sites that in fact had high-rise housing (Anders, 2002, pp. 11, 4). According to data generated by HUD itself, during the fiscal year 2001, Hope VI redevelopment awards "resulted in the displacement of an estimated 6,046 families—95% of whom were people of color, and 79% of whom were African American families" (ibid., p. 39; but see Popkin et al., 2004 for cities where Hope VI seems to be working better). Clearly, good policy is not enough; public pressure must be continually brought to bear to achieve just implementation.

Although commercial downtowns in many cities have rebounded with the help of federal and other rehabilitation programs, conditions in most urban neighborhoods have improved only slightly, if at all. (And increasingly, gentrification of neighborhoods is pushing low-income residents out, as they can no longer afford to live there.) As I noted in Chapter 5, concentrated poverty still marks many city neighborhoods and has begun to characterize some suburbs, as well. As in the poorest neighborhoods during the 1960s (e.g., Harlem in New York; South Central in Los Angeles; and Roxbury–North Dorcester in Boston) poverty rates of 50%, and labor force participation rates of *under* 50% continue to characterize these neighborhoods (Wallin, Schill, and Daniels, 2003, pp. 2, 274; Gittell and Gardner, 1997, p. 10).

During the last four decades, various groups have attempted to fill the void left by inadequate federal programs. Philanthropic foundations, CDCs, and a variety of grassroots, neighborhood-based organizations (NBOs) have been active in low-income neighborhoods over the years. The following sections assess these efforts and highlight not only the pitfalls of local efforts but some of their promising strategies.

PHILANTHROPIC FOUNDATIONS

Over the years, much hope has been placed in foundations to improve city neighborhoods. The nation has more than 56,000 grant-making foundations. Combined, these organizations gave about $27.6 billion in 2000 and $29 billion in 2001—about three times as much as in 1975 (The Foundation Center, 2002, pp. 1, 3). Relatively few philanthropic foundations fund urban community development organizations and projects: Ford, Rockefeller, Surdna, North Star, Charles Stewart Mott, William and Flora Hewlett, Hyams, Stern, Hazen, Edna McConnell Clark, Pew Charitable Trusts, Annie E. Casey, John D. and Catherine T. Macarthur, Joyce, and Unitarian Universalist Veatch Program at Shelter Rock, are the best known (Shuman, 1998, p. 1).

At their worst, foundations fund discrete, categorically determined projects unconnected to others, for a short amount of time, dropping them to fund the next "flavor of the month." One year, for example, welfare reform is in, and criminal justice is out; domestic AIDS is out, and global AIDS is in (Berkshire, 2003, pp. 1–5).

At their best, foundations fund comprehensive, longer-term programs with a regional focus that have as a goal to foster responsiveness in urban and rural government agencies. To date, there are very few exemplars: the five-city Neighborhood Jobs Initiative of the Rockefeller Foundation, the federal-state endowment of California Works for Better Health Initiative, and the Annie E. Casey Foundation's Jobs Initiative (JI) (Policy Link, 2001, p. 36).

The Annie E. Casey Foundation's Jobs Initiative is comprehensive, long-term, culturally sensitive, and has as a goal to influence systemic regional workforce development changes. Started in 1995, this eight-year, $30 million initiative was an attempt to achieve ambitious changes in workforce development in six cities (Denver, Milwaukee, New Orleans, Philadelphia, St. Louis, and Seattle). The foundation commissioned technical experts to guide them on how to analyze regions for workforce development (ibid., p. 23). They hired intermediary organizations such as government agencies and faith-based community organizations to connect low-income, mostly inner-city neighborhoods with the larger metro economies. These intermediaries created innovative programs to connect under- and unemployed urban persons to area businesses, community colleges, employment networks, CDC programs, and labor union training. One example is the Wisconsin Regional Training Partnership that prepares workers for the 50,000-job-strong metal industry in the region (p. 10). The Jobs Initiative funded remedial education, soft skills training, family support, transportation and child care, job search and retention support, and counseling for thousands of people.

Project evaluation by ABT Associates and The New School University, as well as ethnographic research with project participants, found that the involved families' lives improved significantly as a result of the program: Employees were placed in quality jobs with better pay ($9.15/hour), medical benefits, and career ladders; and children experienced more material goods and new, safer neighborhoods. In some cases, children were retrieved from foster care and enrolled in services that corrected developmental delays. Parents' "new career pathways increased both skills and wages which, in turn, instilled pride, increased self-esteem, brought additional supports into their lives, and increased their ability to negotiate systems and institutions" (Workforce

Development Policy and the AECF Jobs Initiative, 2002, pp. 2–5; Fleischer, 2001, pp. 5, 19, 21).

As Annie E. Casey material acknowledges, however, even with their improved wages, many of the participants were still living in poverty (Fleisher, 2001, p. 23). This poverty suggests that even an initiative as comprehensive and successful as JI cannot move workers out of poverty until employers agree to upgrade wages. And this will most likely not occur without federal or state mandates.

Perhaps it is unrealistic to expect philanthropic foundations to fund progressive social programs. Kim Klein, co-publisher of the *Grassroots Fundraising Journal* and author of *Fundraising for Social Change*, believes organizing for social change will never get significant funding from foundations. "The big foundations [the five percent of them that give away 90 percent of the money] come from excess wealth. They were set up to protect the interests of the founders. The idea that they are going to address the unfair distribution of wealth [in society] is ludicrous" (2000, pp. 1–3).

Indeed, liberal foundations give only a tiny piece of their budgets to building social movements. J. Craig Jenkins and Abigail Halli studied foundation funding of progressive social movements. They discovered that foundations commit only 1.1% of all their grants to such movements. Only 1/6 of these foundation grants (0.2% of *all* foundation grants) go to indigenous social movement (e.g., grassroots) organizations (1999, p. 3).

Even if liberal foundations gave considerably more, their monies would not counter the effects of federal policies. In the last decade, for example, foundations have spent hundreds of millions of dollars on job training and on trying to place people in jobs in cities. But in the last decade, the federal government has spent $300 billion (and over a trillion dollars in the last 40 years) on roadways and bridges—all of which, as I pointed out in Chapter 6, bypass neighborhoods where job seekers live and have little or no public transportation to suburban job centers.

The state of philanthropy in urban neighborhoods in the early 21st century is that many CDCs and grassroots organizations compete for a very small pot of money to carry out projects that are important for people in the neighborhood. This provides an extremely important service, filling a void left by governments. But funding by philanthropies is not going to save city neighborhoods.

COMMUNITY DEVELOPMENT CORPORATIONS

After the elections of Nixon and Reagan, governments largely abandoned inner-city neighborhoods to the care of community and faith-based organizations. CDCs (some faith-based, some not) have worked hard to provide residents with housing and jobs. There are approximately 3,600 CDCs nationwide (National Congress of Community Economic Development, 1998, p. 1). About half of those serve urban areas, with the other half split equally between suburban and rural areas. Most CDCs today are small, with 60% of them employing 10 or fewer staff members, and they continue to serve a predominantly poor population (CDCs at the Crossroads? 2002, p. 8). Housing is the most common activity, with between 80% and 90% involved in the development or financing of affordable homes. However, commercial real estate development and business enterprises are increasingly common activities (ibid.). Many are also involved in education, child care, and workforce development (job training and placement) (Gittell and Vidal, 1998, p. 34; Gittel, 1997, p. 25).

The great majority of CDCs produce housing at a very modest rate, with half of those involved in the activity producing or sponsoring fewer than 10 housing units a year (Gittell and Vidal, 1998, p. 34). The largest 10% of CDCs produce more than 50 units a year—which is, however, twice the low-income housing produced annually by the small, independent for-profit developers who constitute more than 75% of U.S. homebuilders (p. 35; see also Vidal, 1992; and Walker, p. 1993). The most generous estimates indicate that Community Development Corporations produced about 30,000 to 40,000 housing units a year during the 1990s—a far cry from what is needed (Drier, 1999, p. 182). As one long-time organizer observed, "in two years, a nonprofit developer might build 200 units of housing, while around him 500 units are lost through abandonment or high rents," i.e., gentrification (ibid.).

In order to obtain grants from foundations and government entities, CDCs—as nonprofits—are restricted by IRS 501c(3) regulations from engaging in politically partisan activity. CDCs are increasingly dominated by professionals with a technical orientation, have narrow membership bases, and avoid the social activism which characterized their work in the 1960s and early 1970s. CDCs in minority low-income neighborhoods are increasingly staffed by middle-class Whites (Gittell, 1994, p. 11; and

1997). Competition between CDCs for funds is intense. Foundations seem to be giving larger amounts of money to fewer organizations, and to those that can demonstrate results. CDCs must often have the data and statistics to prove performance (CDCs at the Crossroads? 2002, p. 19).

And CDCs have not changed the fact that the neighborhoods they operate in are extremely poor. For example, Newark NJ's New Community Corporation, begun after the city's riots in 1968, is the largest and most comprehensive CDC in the country. It is widely regarded as a model organization, employs 2,000 people (the vast majority of them Newark residents) and houses more than 7,000 people in 3,000 units of low-income housing. It has numerous programs, which, according to its Web site, "touch the lives of 50,000 people every day" (http://www.newcommunity.org).

Yet the neighborhood is still (as it was in the 1960s) one of the poorest in Newark—and, therefore, in the nation. The median family income in the CDC's census tracts in 1960 was $29,668 (in 2002 dollars); in 2000 the median family income was less— $25,335 (in 2002 dollars). The median per capita income in the neighborhood in 2000 was $10,617, lower than the city average (which was $13,009) (my calculations).

Another well-known CDC is The Dudley Street Neighborhood Initiative in Boston—brought to fame by Peter Medoff and Holly Sklar in 1994 in their book, *Streets of Hope*. Residents of the Dudley Street neighborhood accomplished what no other CDC has been able to do: They acquired the abandoned land within their neighborhood boundaries by eminent domain, and developed it. The Dudley St. Neighborhood Initiative has grown into a collaborative effort of over 2,700 resident members, businesses, nonprofits, and religious institutions concerned with revitalizing the area where 24,000 people live. Yet, it remains one of the poorest neighborhoods in Boston. The per capita income of $7,600 compares to nearly $16,000 for Boston city. The median family income for the area is $20,848—with 32% of the area's population falling below the official poverty level (all in 2000 dollars) (http://dsni.org, "2002 Highlights," 2003, February 20).

In 1999, David Rusk carried out an analysis of 34 CDCs that were the longest-lasting, largest, and considered by two national support organizations at the core of the CDC movement to be "exemplary" (including Newark's New Community Corporation)

(Rusk 1999, p. 48). He found that in every case, the target neighborhoods' poverty levels increased between 1970 and 1990, as they did in the vast majority of low-income urban neighborhoods in the U.S. (see also Jargowsky, 1997). He found as well that the median household incomes in the target areas declined over the years, and fell further behind regional income levels (ibid., p. 49).

The continuing poverty in neighborhoods where CDCs have been active does not deny that the physical attributes of local streets and buildings may be in better condition and more attractive than in the 1960s. It is not to deny that many people's lives have been improved by the services CDCs provide. What the persistent poverty does point out is the power of federal policies and regional arrangements to thwart the potential of CDC programs. In the many cases where job training and placement is a CDC priority, persistent neighborhood poverty demonstrates that as long as jobs available to men and women trained by the CDC's pay poverty wages, and as long as public transportation routes bypass outlying job centers or business investment is withheld from urban neighborhoods, residents will remain poor.

The ability of CDCs to eliminate poverty in urban areas is not only delimited by federal and regional systems. Many CDCs have become clients in their city's patronage system of political spoils, and no longer challenge the basic rules of the game as they did in the 1960s and '70s (Weir, 1999, 186–187). Veteran political activist and scholar Peter Dreier argues that CDCs have failed in their larger mission to revitalize urban neighborhoods because they are isolated and unconnected to large social constituencies: "[T]he vast majority . . . are not part of a network. . . . They are politically isolated in their own communities, unable to work simultaneously on local, state, and federal issues. . . . They are not, in other words, part of a movement" (ibid., p. 186).

GRASSROOTS ORGANIZATIONS

There are millions of grassroots organizations that could be instrumental in challenging federal and metro-area rules of the game. According to grassroots scholar David Horton Smith, the U.S. has 7.5 million grassroots associations (in addition to 2 million nonprofits with paid staff) (Bothwell, 2003, p. 3). Poor urban neighborhoods are home to many of these associations. Researchers in one lower-income Chicago neighborhood, for example, found over 150 associations; among them were such groups as the Dickens Block Club, Act Now, Amistad Spanish Speaking Youth, and Damen Ave. Revitalization Effort (Kretzmann and McNight, 1997, pp. 111–112). Urban housing projects are home to citizen associations, as well. In the Cabrini-Green public housing project in Chicago, for example—which journalists and politicians have long described as devoid of community—researchers identified extensive social networks and neighborhood institutions, many organized and run by residents. A selected list of community-based groups includes four religious congregations, a legal services group, youth sports organizations, tutoring and college preparation, preschool, day care, a newspaper, counseling, and job training (Bennett and Reed, 2000, p. 131).

The existence of active resident organizations in poverty neighborhoods belies the stereotype of a passive, unconcerned population. Citizen participation in organizations is present; what is missing, however, is the coordination of these groups across neighborhoods of the city and the region.

MODELS OF LOCAL—REGIONAL COLLABORATION

In some metro areas, community organizations have joined with labor, religious, and political groups to confront foundations, governments, and corporations on regional and statewide levels. These coalitions challenge metropolitan and federal policies that determine local problems. These groups no longer let politicians off the hook, demanding that governments at varying levels carry out their responsibilities to residents, as they do in more affluent municipalities.

One example is the Campaign for Sustainable Milwaukee, a long-term, broad-based advocacy coalition composed of over 200 community, religious, labor, and business organizations. The coalition was formed to address a number of interrelated issues affecting the city and region that were beyond the capacity of any one organization to address. The coalition's success stems from its strategy of campaigning for specific issues that were identified by members as meaningful to a broad base of people. The issues also had to address the quality of life of the entire region, especially Milwaukee's inner city. Since 1996, Sustainable Milwaukee has focused on higher wages in area jobs, workforce training, and transit reform for job access. Sustainable Milwaukee was instrumental in pressing for the passage of the city's Living Wage

Ordinance (which mandated that employers pay workers higher than the federal minimum wage). During the effort, the Living Wage Campaign task force found that just over 50% of the local jobs paid less than $20,000 annually. The ordinance passed both the city and the county of Milwaukee as well as the school district, and stipulates a minimum wage of $7.70 per hour plus benefits (http://www.policylink.org/ress_milwaukee.html).

In addition, the Central City Transit Task Force of this group led efforts to redirect federal transportation funds to better serve the needs of Milwaukee's central-city workers to access suburban employment opportunities. The Task Force advocated for the construction of light rail to link central-city neighborhoods to suburban employment centers. They also developed an alternate bus and light rail proposal that won the support of the Milwaukee and Waukesha County boards. Unfortunately, the plan was rejected by the state, which decided to cut the light rail and extra bus and car pool lanes from the state transportation plan. In response, the coalition filed a civil rights lawsuit against the transportation department on the basis that the allocation of transportation funding violates the civil rights of inner-city minority communities (Policy Link, 2000, pp. 14–16).

A second example of a regional coalition of community-based groups challenging federal and metro-area policies is Jobs With Justice (JWJ), a campaign for workers' rights. This coalition of labor, community, religious, and other nongovernmental groups organizes in urban areas and across regions, and in the last few years has spread to a number of states. It was founded in Miami in 1987 by several unions that realized that unless they worked together they would be defeated. JWJ was founded during the anger and frustration resulting from President Reagan's firing of the striking air traffic controllers in 1982, and the subsequent efforts by Eastern Airlines to squash the machinists and flight attendants unions (Center for Community Change, 1998, p. 3).

The Massachusetts JWJ has 70 member organizations, two-thirds of which are unions. The coalition includes Association of Community Organizations for Reform Now (ACORN), local tenants organizations, a local Women's Alliance, as well as religious, political, and immigrant groups. In 1998 they began an ultimately successful Right to Organize campaign involving members of the Haitian community, which makes up a large portion of health care employees in the metro area (ibid., p. 3).

The Buffalo, NY, Jobs With Justice has been involved in a number of hard-fought efforts to protect workers from layoffs and poor working conditions. When the Service Employees International Union (SEIU) attempted to organize janitors for better wages at the Marine Midland Bank building in Buffalo, JWJ organized support from a range of community-based organizations. The protests culminated in a series of high-profile events, including an announcement by the Buffalo Area Metropolitan Ministries that it would withdraw its accounts at Marine Midland to support the campaign. The action that finally broke the bank's refusal to raise wages was a prayer vigil and fast the JWJ held on the front steps of the location of a party the bank held for its officers and big clients to celebrate its purchase of rights to the city's hockey arena. The public pressure and embarrassment forced them to give in (p. 4).

Campaign for a Sustainable Milwaukee and Jobs With Justice are two of perhaps 20 such coalitions of local groups joining with others across regions and states. Their organizing strategies flow from the understanding that most local problems have been created by policies and decisions made far from the borders of the neighborhood.

REGIONAL CAMPAIGNS AND SCHOOL REFORM

The efforts of regional and state coalitions have not solved the problems of low-income urban residents in Milwaukee, Buffalo, or Massachusetts. Much more certainly needs to be accomplished. The existing coalitions are internally fragile, not connected to one another, and nationally few in number. But they have won wage, transportation, and labor union victories that demand our attention. I believe their method might be usefully employed by those concerned with urban educational reform.

Even though it may not appear to be the case when one is in the classrooms and corridors of a poverty urban school, very few educational problems originate in local schools or neighborhoods. As I have argued in Parts I and II, macroeconomic decisions taken at the federal level, arrangements made among metro-area developers and other power brokers, and public policies promulgated by state and city politicians create conditions in urban areas that practically preclude high-quality public schooling. Local remedies therefore rarely suffice—at least not in the long run. Thus, it behooves us to pay attention to the larger collection of forces pressing on urban teachers and students, and to attempt to lift that weight from their shoulders. Building coalitions of groups across neighborhoods of a city, across inner city and segregated suburb, and throughout metropolitan regions should become a priority. And these campaigns ought to be aimed at unjust metro-area, state, and federal barriers to effective urban school systems, as well as at school and class size, and pedagogy.

Equity-seeking educational reform groups like New Visions and small-school advocates in cities nationwide should join with community-based groups that have recently been active in parent and other education organizing in cities across the country. The two kinds of campaigns have much in common, and much to learn from each other. Chapters in Part III describe the surge of education organizing in urban communities, and provide methods for cooperation between these groups and mainstream school reformers.

During the last few decades, mainstream urban school reforms have had little, if any, public constituency. Rarely has a neighborhood or resident group advocated for the reforms being implemented by big city school systems. There are, of course, a couple of important exceptions to this, most notably the demand for local educational control in late 1980s Chicago. In other cities, if any "constituency" existed for urban school reform, it was the funder or publisher of programs or tests, the researchers or consultants who designed the products, or the corporate and government groups designating what should be done to urban schools.

But neighborhood constituencies are forming in cities across the nation, as educational organizers embolden and conjoin parents and other residents to demand equity in funding, district accountability, and pre-college opportunities. It remains to connect this educational struggle to other community campaigns for jobs, housing, and public transportation (for example), so that school reform demands will have the power of a social movement behind them. This is the heart of my argument in Part III.

Part III

Social Movements, New Public Policy, and Urban Educational Reform

8

How Do People Become Involved in Political Contention?

Preceding analyses of federal and metropolitan barriers to the opportunity of urban low-income people of color suggest that, if we are realistic, we will acknowledge the plethora of policy changes that must be accomplished in order to provide meaningful life chances for poor families and neighborhoods. These new opportunities—and their ultimate actualization by residents—will be crucial to the sustainability of urban school reform: Economic access and the improved social standing its fulfillment provides parents, students, and communities will be prerequisites to full funding and other educational opportunities in urban districts. But economic justice, this important precursor of systemic urban school reform, will not be achieved without concerted, sustained political struggle. Although activism for economic opportunity is necessary, educational reform must be a target of sustained contention, as well. As civil rights veteran Bob Moses has argued, urban students and communities will have to demand what many people say they do not want—quality education (2002, p. 20).

How do we carry out the political struggles that are needed? Where can we look for guidance?

My reading of American history, as I have stated throughout, is that social movements are catalysts for the enactment of social justice legislation, progressive court decisions, and other equity policy. In order to think deeply about how we might mobilize a unified force for economic and educational opportunities, I therefore turn to history. We can learn from stories of the past how people developed social movements, and what encouraged actors to get involved. History also reveals relationships between public policy, equity, and contention. In turning to history for assistance, I could have chosen to study the labor movement, women's movement, or other social struggles. Because of my personal involvement in civil rights, I look there.

Recent historiography of African American protest during the first half of the 20th century has led me to two heartening conclusions. First, this early civil rights activity was incredibly important "spade work" that prepared the ground for the mass flowering of protest in the 1950s and '60s. The modern civil rights movement did not spring from untreated soil, as most schoolbooks imply. Rather, it grew slowly, developing roots and branches, over the years.

That this long development proved necessary prompts me to view optimistically our own future activity. Since the mid-1980s, a largely unpublicized building of protest for economic rights has taken place in America's cities. This has already prompted new policies—for example, Living Wage laws in 120 cities and counties (with over 70 more campaigns in progress). Organizing for educational justice in urban neighborhoods has grown, as well. This campaign is also bearing fruit. These burgeoning movements for minority rights will be described in the next chapter, along with three others that have recently illuminated the urban landscape. Civil rights history prompts us to understand these campaigns as the continuation of a long-term project.

The second conclusion I have come to is that even before a mass civil rights movement prompted far-reaching federal legislation like the 1965 Voting Rights Act, the dialectic between social activism and the promulgation of social justice policy was apparent. This, too, inspires confidence. Early protest for Black rights produced new, more equitable policy even in early decades of the 20th century, which led to an increase in activism and, in turn, additional equity policy. There were of course multiple causes of the ascendance of both protest and better policy, but the dialogue between them stands out clearly.

For example, activism by middle-class Black women's civic groups and the newly formed NAACP in the first decades of the 1900s led to the unconstitutionality of the "grandfather clause" as an exemption from literacy tests for voting, and led as well to the end of legal apartheid (legally defined Black and White zones of residence) in the Supreme Court decisions *Guinn v. United*

States in 1915 and *Buchanan v. Warley* in 1917 (Fairclough, 2001, p. 82).

Black veterans returning from World War I angrily transgressed the Jim Crow strictures during the 1920s, and in the decade of the 1930s, public protest was continuous, as the Communist Party organized Black industrial workers in cities of the South and sharecroppers in the rural counties (Kelley, 1990). After numerous voter registration drives by African American civic leagues and radical youth groups like the Southern Negro Youth Congress (SNYC) in this tumultuous decade, as well as three lawsuits by the NAACP, the Supreme Court declared all-White primaries unconstitutional in 1944 in *Smith v. Allright*. As a result of this decision, Southern voter registration drives increased many times over, and by the early 1950s the number of Black voters in the South had gone from a few thousand (in 1940) to about a million (Fairclough, 2001, p. 204). The symbiotic relationship between protest and good policy revealed in this early civil rights history should clarify the efficacy of public contention, and give us hope that our own efforts will yield results.

But how do we get people involved? How did Black Southerners come to the decision to take part in protest—despite frightening White reprisals? What social processes helped them to build a movment? And in our own time, what strategic, conceptual decisions and processes prompt people to engage in movement-building?

To think about these questions, I turn to social movement theory. The rest of this chapter appropriates new developments in the field, and uses examples from civil rights history to illustrate the theoretical constructs I develop. In this, I add my own effort to those of youth and adult organizers and activists who continually develop and utilize theoretical and historical concepts in their work.

Theoretical Constructs

Following the tumultuous 1960s, social movement theorists utilized several major concepts to explain how the social movements of that and other decades originate:

1. Changes in the economy or political system provide resources that can be mobilized to develop social movements.

2. Organizations offer insurgents valuable assistance in mobilization of available resources. A large body of evidence finds that organizational strength is correlated with challengers' ability to wrest concessions from governing elites.

3. Framing, a collective process of interpretation, links opportunity and action. Movements frame grievances within collective action frames that lend dignity to claims, connect them with other struggles, and help to produce a collective identity among participants.

4. Repertoires of contention (strikes, marches, sit-ins) are the means by which people engage in contentious collective action. The forms these actions take are a resource that actors can use to press their claims.

This classical approach yielded a research agenda that produced a large body of empirical evidence correlating the factors listed above with increases in activism (see Gamson 1990; Klandermans, Kriesi, and Tarrow, 1988; McAdam, 1982; Morris, 1984; Snow et al., 1986; and Traugott, 1995).

However, classical social movement theory left individual actors out of the equation—and did not ask the question of how individuals actually get drawn into contentious politics. The role of personal agency remained unexplored: What allowed people who have (for years, perhaps their whole lives) been accommodating in their daily resistance to decide to participate in direct challenges?

Finally, classical theory did not assess interactions between the various factors it identified as leading to social movements, and did not identify component mechanisms and processes that might make up each category of explanation. The theory was a rather static chart of what happened in the various episodes and movements studied.

In 2001, Doug McAdam, Sydney Tarrow, and Charles Tilly published *Dynamics of Contention*, which unpacked the classical concepts of social movement resources and "mobilizing structures." They identified constitutive mechanisms or processes of these and other theoretical constructs, and argued that these interact with one another in any number of ways to produce contentious politics. In this approach, the role of human agency is paramount, and explanations focus on the question of what social and cognitive processes involve people in protest.

I have engaged their theory, changed it some, and use the result in combination with several still relevant categories of the classical approach, to attempt to identify personal and social processes that assist people in producing sustained public contention. I have re-cast one other assumption of social movement theory, as well. Most scholarship on political movements partitions social protest into discrete "waves" of contention: Movements emerge, run their course, and abate. Long periods of quiescence or contention contained within the system follow months or years of overtly transgressive protest. This theoretical chunking captures an obvious truth. However, a different truth also characterizes movements for personal rights in the U.S., and that is their extremely long run. African Americans' political protest against segregation extends over the entire 20th century, and stretches ahead of us now—as do the struggles of Latinos, workers, and women. While various time periods witness more legally contained than socially transgressive activity, both kinds are present in most decades.

This continuity of protest over the long haul demonstrates that social movements do not necessarily die. They change and persist. Civil rights struggle, for example, continues—both quietly in courtrooms (regarding affirmative action, a living wage, urban education funding, immigrant and voting rights) and more noisily in transgressive public protest by community groups, parent and education organizers, faith-based organizations, and progressive labor unionists. Movement activities continue in organizing by the Industrial Areas Foundation and the Association of Community Organizations for Reform Now, in outreach by the New York Center for Immigrant Rights, and in the cross-country freedom ride from California to Washington, DC, sponsored by immigrant-based progressive unions.

The following theoretical constructs attempt to capture personal and social processes and mechanisms by which people come to public protest and movement building.

Attribution of Opportunity

The first process I apply from *Dynamics of Contention* has to do with how people interpret changes in the political economy. For such change to encourage social protest, people must view developments as presenting opportunities for waging struggle (McAdam, Tarrow, and Tilly, 2001, pp. 58–59). The suburbanization of minority poverty, the deterioration of wage and job opportunities and of the rewards for educational attainment, even the 2004 election of George W. Bush, need to be seen as openings through which to push for equity. This cognitive apprehension of new opportunities sometimes helps people see old arrangements in a new light: Situations that were previously understood as oppressive but immutable, can be re–imagined and viewed as useful.

Historical examples of this process include the use of the 19th Amendment, which extended the right to vote to women, to attempt to register Black women in the segregated South in 1920, although it was clear that most Whites did not interpret the suffrage amendment to include Black females. As I noted in the first section of this chapter, protest in each decade led to new policy, and each decision by the Supreme Court or Presidential Proclamation set people to work to take advantage of the new mandate.

There are less obvious examples of the process of attribution of opportunity, as well. In the 1930s and '40s, Blacks were becoming consumers as the cotton economy ailed and more farming families moved to Southern and Northern cities. Many realized that they had new leverage over businesses where they shopped. "Don't Buy Where You Can't Work" campaigns of the 1930s, and sit-ins and boycotts of restaurants and other public facilities by Black college students in the 1940s, as well as 1947 Freedom Rides to test interstate bus segregation—all took advantage of the economic changes affecting African Americans (for descriptions of these activities see Fairclough 1995; Olson, 2001; and Payne, 1995).

Later, the mass boycotts of White-owned businesses and Southern bus companies—whose profits depended on Black ridership—were an opportunistic appreciation of the companies' dependence on Black ridership. Economic pressure on Southern Whites—through boycotts or sit-ins, for example—often brought quicker results than dealing with city politicians, or long, drawn out legal challenges (Payne 1995, pp. 328, 484; Raines 1983, p. 152; see also Fairclough, 2001; and Morris, 1984).

Occasionally governing groups are destabilized by world or domestic events. This weakening of the legitimacy of the government can be appropriated for ways it might enhance the possibilities of social protest. Most U.S. labor history exemplifies such decisions to understand crises as opportunities for mobilization: Workers and allies responded to the economic and social crises produced by industrialization in the late 19th and early 20th centuries—and again during the Great Depression—and successfully organized for new laws that benefited labor, urban education, and women's suffrage.

The converse occurs as well: Concerted protest can foster the destabilization of elites and thereby stimulate change: Think of the movement against the Vietnam War and how this broad-based effort destabilized President Lyndon Johnson's administration, the ruling political and economic coalitions, and increased the pressure to end the war.

Indeed, it is sometimes necessary for social activists to decide they must create a crisis in order to force concessions from governing groups. The following description of civil rights demonstrations in Birmingham in 1963 illustrates this choice:

The strategy of the civil rights campaign in Birmingham was to paralyze the city through massive direct action. The plan was to bring out enough demonstrators and create mass arrests that would fill the jails. "The mobilization and deployment of thousands of protesters was key; without them social order could be maintained and the movement would fail" (Morris and Staggenborg, 2002, p. 38). At a crucial stage, movement leaders were not able to bring out enough demonstrators to fill the jails and the campaign seemed to be in jeopardy. Strategists decided to mobilize thousands of youth to engage in demonstrations. "The children filled the jails, clogged public spaces, and provoked the use of attack dogs, billy clubs and fire hoses, thereby precipitating the crisis needed to win the struggle" (p. 39). Political pressure caused disorder, destabilized the governing regime, and achieved massive social change in Birmingham.

Appropriation of Existing Organizations, Institutions, and Cultural Forms

Closely related to attribution of opportunity is the process whereby people actively appropriate existing organizations, institutions, and cultural forms. In this expression of personal agency, social institutions become more radical; change their function, purpose, and manner of operation; and are useful for transgressive politics. (McAdam, Tarrow, and Tilly, 2001, pp. 47–48).

The Southern Black church during the 1950s and 1960s is a salient instance of this process. Until the 1950s, most Black church leaders in the South (but not all congregants) saw their churches as preparation for salvation, not as a way to change the present. In the 1950s, urban (and then some rural) congregants and pastors appropriated the church and transformed it into a major tool of the civil rights struggle. The extensive committee structure and community activities of women members were appropriated by congregants for civil rights; the format and activities of the Sunday service were altered somewhat by pastors to provide the structure and tone of mass political meetings; extensive, widespread church networks were energized and organized for planning and sharing protest information (see, for example, Morris, 1984).

Cultural forms such as music can be appropriated, as well. In 1946, the African American gospel song, "I'll Overcome Some Day," (the melody of which derives from the older 19th-century spiritual, "No More Auction Block for Me") was sung by several hundred Black employees of the American Tobacco Co. in Charleston, SC, when they were striking. One day a woman on the picket line, Lucille Simmons, changed the pronoun "I" to "We," and the singing continued using the plural. When a group of the strikers visited the Highlander Folk School, Pete Seeger heard them sing the song, and taught it to Guy Carawan and Frank Hamilton, who—almost three decades later—introduced it to the founding convention of the Student Non-Violent Coordinating Committee (SNCC) in North Carolina. The song, "We Shall Overcome," became the familiar anthem of the civil rights movement (Payne, 1995, p. 71; and Candovan and Candovan, 1983.)

These institutions and cultural forms were already part of Blacks' experience. Only minor, but crucial, alterations in focus, purpose, or mode of functioning needed to be made by individuals and groups.

Outsiders and Bicultural Brokers

Exogenous organizations can be appropriated for political mobilization, as well. This personal and social process is exemplified by Black Southerners' early use of the Communist Party. The U.S. Communist Party was an organization that originated outside the South. When it moved into Southern cities and rural areas in the 1930s, it brought resources to Black workers and farmers that they did not have: It provided a place and a forum for discussion, and a framework for understanding the roots of poverty and racism and for placing these in larger perspective. It assisted members in challenging the hegemony of White supremacy and Black elites, and created an atmosphere in which people could analyze, discuss, and criticize their society. The party offered an assurance of support and protection for transgressive activity; the presence of an organization engendered a sense of power (Kelley, 1990, pp. 93–94, 100, 108).

Southern Blacks appropriated the U.S. Communist Party and made it into a "race organization." The party was composed mostly of poor Blacks, rather than Whites from the North. The party and the CIO unions they organized became broad-based movements with a strong civil rights agenda, saturated in Black local culture, paying little heed to national or international Communist Party dicta (ibid., p. 151). Most of the members were semi-literate and devoutly religious, and long before congregants in the 1950s were appropriating aspects of the Black church to the political struggle, Southern Communist Party members were doing so. They developed strategies such as disguising political meetings as church meetings, and keeping minutes by underlining pertinent words or phrases in the Bible (p. 45). They transformed church songs into labor songs. "Give Me That Old-time Religion," for example, became "Give Me That Old Communist Spirit" and later was transformed into a song about the Scottsboro Boys (pp. 94, 105, 107).

In the 1930s, Black college students in the radical Southern Negro Youth Congress (SNYC) and later in the 1960s Student Non-violent Coordinating Committee (SNCC) who traveled into the farm country of the South to organize sharecroppers and tenant farmers were "bicultural brokers" who brought perspectives gained from city living and higher education to the support of local people.

Many important and well-known events in later Southern civil rights history were brokered by bicultural men and women with Northern experience—A. Philip Randolph, SNCC convener Ella Baker, Eleanor Holmes Norton, Bob Moses, James Farmer, Andrew Young, and Martin Luther King, Jr. had all lived in the North.

Aldon Morris and Suzanne Staggenborg make a related point when they argue that outsiders (e.g., African American leaders such as Martin Luther King, Jr.) who were relatively new to a city could be more effective than local leaders in pulling people together because they were not entrenched in any one faction in the city or area (2002, p. 43).

Creation of Regional Organizations

The role of organizations in social movements has been hotly debated. Piven and Cloward, for example, contend that organizations weaken social movements, because political insurgency tends to be abandoned as groups build hierarchy and procedure, and cooperate with government bureaucracies in attempts to further the interests of their members (1997). Aldon Morris, on the other hand, demonstrates that without the strength and reach of the well-organized Southern Christian Leadership Council (SCLC) and its ability to bring local groups together in the South, the civil rights movement might have faltered (1984). Most likely, successful social movements need different kinds of organizations at different times, and even different kinds of organizations contemporaneously. But an umbrella group is crucial. Series of protests do not become a movement without some form of organization to coordinate and create synergy and overall direction.

The analysis in Part II of this book demonstrated the importance of regions in the maintenance of inequity in the U.S. The civil rights movement in the 1950s and '60s in the South was prescient in its regionalism. One of the most important features of the movement in those decades was what Morris calls "movement centers"—civil rights organizations made up of other organizations. These were more than coalitions: They were formally organized but partly autonomous; regional, yet rooted in localities. SCLC, formed in 1957 by groups that had collaborated to guide the Montgomery bus boycott, may be the best example. This regional organization was able to provide strength to local struggles by sending in resources, and acting as a "rudder," as King put it, to the movement. Regional groups connected local problems to state and national issues, and were crucial in creating a national movement (see Fairclough, 1995, pp. 319, 379; also Morris, 1984).

Other regional organizations (Congress of Racial Equality or CORE, SNCC, and the Council of Federated Organizations or COFO, a coalition of all the civil rights groups in Mississippi) were less formally structured than SCLC, but their spread over wide areas gave them a broad reach and allowed them to create a synergy between small groups of civil rights workers.

Leadership Development

The development and role of leadership in social movements is not well theorized (Aminzade, Goldstone, and Perry, 2001; and Morris and Staggenborg, 2002). Scholars debate what kind of leadership works best—individual or group, hierarchical or democratic, indigenous or exogenous, or a mix (Ganz, 2000; Marx and Useem, 1971; an d Morris and Staggenborg, 2002).

But one thing is certain: Civil Rights leaders in the 1950s and'60s did not drop from the sky fully formed. They emerged out of participation in the struggle. Martin Luther King, Jr., for example, emerged as a leader during the Montgomery bus boycott of 1955–56, as the following account of this process makes clear.

E.D. Nixon and fellow civil rights leaders in Montgomery had been examining the backgrounds of people arrested for refusing to give up their seats on city buses for several years, and finally found a perfect candidate in NAACP activist Rosa Parks (Raines, 1983). Until her arrest and the resulting boycott, most Black ministers of Montgomery had shied away from public attempts to fight segregation (Olson, 2001, p. 114). But at Parks' arrest, the riders of Montgomery's buses—mostly women, going to and from their jobs as maids, cooks, beauticians, and cleaning ladies—erupted with fervor, and seemed ready to boycott the buses with leadership from the ministers or without them (ibid., p. 114.)

At Dexter Ave. Baptist Church, newly arrived, 26-year-old Martin Luther King, who had not yet finished his doctoral dissertation, resisted the attempts of his friend Reverend Ralph Abernathy to get involved. King refused, saying he was not ready to take on a commitment to social protest; he wanted to dedicate himself to developing his preaching and prove himself to his well-educated congregation. But he did agree to open his church to a planning meeting (pp. 113–114).

When King and Abernathy arrived at the church for the meeting, they were met with hundreds of women (and some men) who were ready to go ahead with a boycott. In the wake of their enthusiasm, Montgomery's Black leaders formed a new group to develop the boycott (the Montgomery Improvement Association), and Abernathy was astonished when newcomer King accepted the presidency.

The boycott lasted over a year, and would ultimately involve the vast majority of Montgomery's 50,000 citizens—not only maids and cooks but beauticians, janitors, teachers, doctors, and college professors. It was the largest prolonged defiance of racial discrimination in the country's history (pp. 116, 118). And it was from his work during those turbulent days that Martin Luther King, Jr., emerged as a civil rights leader.

King and other well-known leaders who traveled the country generating support for civil rights were dependent on the organizing work of local leaders, most of whom were neighborhood women. The process of establishing links and connections with grassroots organizations provided the mass support for the large protests. The women formed "bridges" between regional and local groups (Collier-Thomas and Franklin, 2001, p. 3; see Barnett, 1993; and Robnett, 1997).

Most of the participants in mass mobilizations in the South were not well educated or middle class. They were working class and poor. As Charles Payne demonstrates, they were sharecroppers, day laborers, laundresses, and cooks. They were "yardmen and maids, cab drivers, beauticians, barbers, custodians and field hands" (1995, p. 133). It was these people who made up the mass of the movement, and from whom local leaders emerged as the struggle progressed.

Over the many decades of civil rights history, participation in Citizenship Schools developed activist leaders. Begun by African American women's groups in the 1920s, utilized by the Communist Party and SNYC in the 1930s and early 1940s, then picked up by Septima Clark and Ella Baker in the '50s, Citizenship—or Freedom Schools, as they came to be known—not only taught civics and literacy for voter registration but discovered and developed local community leadership (Kelley, 1990, p. 213; Collier-Thomas and Franklin, 2001, p. 112). Citizenship Schools were highly successful, and were subsequently developed by CORE, NAACP, and SNCC. Almost 900 of the schools operated in the South between 1961 and 1970 and many women (and a few male) leaders emerged from those schools. Teachers frequently became grassroots leaders, and in many cases they replaced local clergy as community leaders. Andrew Young and *Sweet Honey in the Rock* singer Beatrice Reagon got their start in the movement in this way (Rouse 2001, pp. 113, 115, 117).

Other leaders emerged from their participation in more confrontational protest: Fannie Lou Hamer, for example, a challenger of Lyndon Johnson and leader of the Mississippi Freedom Democratic Party in 1964, had a sharecropping background, and developed leadership skills through immersion in the struggle to develop an alternative political party to the Democrats in Mississippi (ibid., p. 139).

It is entirely possible that without the movement, many local women would not have had a forum through which to develop as community leaders; and it is probably true that without their leadership, the movement would not have developed the mass base that it had. Many experienced activists argued that "[voter] registration drives were more successful to the degree they could be locally organized and staffed, which [the activists] attributed to the importance of 'intimate knowledge of [the] conditions, psychology and people' involved" (quoted in Payne, 1995, p. 247).

Centrality of Youth

A crucial process in the development of the civil rights movement was the active participation of youth. James Farmer and other CORE activists in the 1940s were graduate students in their 20s, as was Martin Luther King, Jr., in 1954. The 400,000 American Blacks who fought in World War I and their descendants in World War II were most likely in their late teens or early 20s (Vincent, 1972, p. 33; Cronon, 1955, p. 28). Most members of SNYC in the 1930s, and SNCC in the '60s were college students. Indeed, throughout the 20th century, sit-ins, boycotts, and "freedom rides" were planned and carried out primarily by students and other youth. High school girls and boys often took part—and sometimes played leadership roles in—civil rights activity in Southern cities and farmlands (see, among others, Chafe, Gavins, and Korstad, 2001; Olson, 2001; and Payne, 1995).

Writing about Greenwood, MS, Bob Moses argued: "We can't count on adults. Very few who 'have the time' and are economically independent of the white man are willing to join the struggle, and are not afraid of the tremendous pressure they will face. This leaves the young people to be the organizers, the agents of social and political change. . . . [I]t is a sign of hope that we have been able to find young people to shoulder the responsibility for carrying out the voting drive. They are the seeds of change" (quoted in Payne, 1995, p. 250).

Student movements in the U.S., France, Italy, Mexico, and Spain in the 1960s, and in Tiananmen Square in 1989 China attest to the importance of youth leadership in the struggle for social justice. Indeed, it is doubtful that social movements would develop at all without central participation of the young. As I will discuss in detail in Chapter 10, the crucial role played by youth is one of the reasons that concerned U.S. educators should be at the center of efforts to build a social movement.

Many educators comment on the widespread anger of urban youth today. Some theorists argue that anger can be politically mobilizing. Social movement scholar Sydney Tarrow, for example, reasons that emotions like anger, love, loyalty, and reverence are clearly more mobilizing than others, such as despair and resignation. Anger can be 'vitalizing' and is more likely to be present in triggering acts of resistance, whereas other emotions, like resignation or depression, are 'devitalizing' (1998, p. 111; Gameson, 1992; Melucci, 1996). Chapter 10 provides concrete suggestions for how we can appropriate the anger of youth to constructive political ends.

Community Organizing

Although the fact is not often acknowledged, one of the most important strategies of civil rights work throughout the 20th century was community organizing (see Payne, 1995, for full development of this theme). Working in neighborhoods, using local networks and contacts to urge residents to participate in resistance activities, was central to civil rights protest both North and South. Barely past her teenage years in 1916, Septima Clark taught and organized rural families on St. John's Island in North Carolina; Ella Baker mentored a Socialist group in 1920s Harlem; Socialist A. Philip Randolph and other union organizers went door to door for the Pullman Porters in 1920s Chicago; the Communist Party organized men, women, and families in communities North and South; SNYC college students registered sharecroppers to vote in the 1930s and organized Southern farm workers; and Robert Moses and other young SNCC workers lived and worked in rural communities in the 1960s. All of these activities were part of the tradition of community organizing.

Experienced community organizers describe the strategies they used to "open up a town" to voting drives. One registration worker "frequently found that the real leaders were not the people in places of position. An elderly woman of no title and with no organizational support might be highly influential simply because she was noted as a kind of personal problem-solver. Sometimes, such a person, because of her effectiveness in small matters and the trust consequently built, could be a key figure in efforts to persuade people to register to vote in a difficult area" (in Payne, 1995, pp. 248–249).

Another community organizer said he would go for the persons who were economically independent of Whites and their reprisal: " . . . the undertaker, the grocers, the preachers. Then he would go to the school principal. . . . Having made contact with these, he would assume that he had discovered the . . . community leaders. . . . He would regard the deacons of the churches . . . as very important to anything he undertook" (Payne, 1995, p. 249).

In other cases, neutralizing Black middle-class leaders was an important first task: "I would do this to neutralize them. They do not usually oppose having the job done—they want it done, but they don't want to be embarrassed if someone else does it and they are left out. After seeing [the middle-class leaders] I would find people prepared to work hard for recognition. Then I'd try to wed the two together and monitor the group" (ibid., p. 250). The process of community organizing, not often thought of as part of civil rights movement-building, was in fact an important strategy throughout.

Social Construction of New Identities through Participation in Transgressive Politics

Re-imagining economic developments, institutions, and cultural forms as potentially oppositional does not by itself bring social change. And developing "critical consciousness" in people through information, readings, and discussion does not by itself induce them to participate in transgressive politics—although it provides a crucial base of understanding. To activate people to create or join a social movement, it is important to actually involve them in protest activity of some kind (McAdam, Tarrow, Tilly, 2001, p. 62; see also Meyer, 2002, and Payne, 1995 among others).

To make this point, the authors of *Dynamics of Contention* argue that people do not "become political" and then take part in contention; rather, participation in contention creates new, politicized identities: "*[I]dentities modify in the course of social interaction*" (p. 126). In other words, shifts in political identity do not so much *motivate* contentious political action, as develop as a logical *consequence* of it (p. 320). One develops a political identity and commitment—a change in consciousness—from talking, walking, marching, singing, attempting to vote, "sitting in," or otherwise demonstrating with others.

Not only do personal identities change as people become involved in protest, but gradually new categories of social actors emerge from the process: Participation by individuals over time in concerted struggle creates new political categories and groups. The rebellions that created the French Revolution also created the "sans-culottes," (who refused to wear the pants of elites as a protest) and ultimately produced the "French citizen" as a class of political actors (pp. 55–63). Indeed, McAdam, Tarrow, and Tilly argue that "contentious politics always involves the social construction of 'politically relevant categories' such as (for example) feminists, civil rights activists, or 'suffragettes' (p. 58).

As Southern sharecroppers began to register to vote, and continued in this politically contentious activity, a new collective identity was constructed by them individually and as a group: They came to see themselves, and they became—individually and as a "class"—a new category: Black citizens who were entitled to representation, entitled to their rights.

Such "signifying work" was evident at the close of the successful Montgomery bus boycott in 1956. As Martin Luther King noted, the courageous, organized, successful actions of the participants in the boycott "had rendered the conventional identities—members of this or that congregation [or] 'our Negroes', for example—inadequate descriptors" of the celebrants (p. 319). After the boycott, King described the "new Negro:" "[W]e walk in a new way. We hold our heads in a new way" (p. 319). The boycott not only changed the laws in Montgomery but helped to create, and became an expression of, "a new collective identity among Southern blacks generally"—a result of mass participation in the 381-day protest (McAdam, Tarrow, and Tilly, 2001, p. 320).

Creation of Innovative Action Repertoires

As people participate in contention, they develop new strategies of action out of everyday activities, routines, and cultural forms. During the French Revolution, for example, barricades—which were originally erected to protect neighborhoods from thieves— were turned into protection from authorities trying to quell the neighborhood rebellions (ibid., p. 41). Sit-down strikes from the labor movement in the 1930s became sit-ins at lunch counters and other public facilities throughout the South in the next decades.

This creative process of turning everyday activity into strategies of rebellion over the centuries has included effigies, boycotts, and nonimportation; petitioning, attacks on a wrongdoer's house, assaults on a miller's grain store, collective use of public space; occupation of buildings; songs, industrial sabotage, legal action, violent encounters, organized public demonstrations, rent strikes, refusal to pay taxes, interstate bus rides and "die-ins" (by gay activists). Clothing has been used as a form of protest—the sans-culottes of the French Revolution, and women's bloomers, for example (ibid.).

Strategic repertoires are often created "on the spot," in the heat of action. They include slogans and symbols that resonate with the protesters' demands, and have powerful connotations. For example, the call for "Black Power" was coined in 1966 during a march to protest the killing of NAACP activist James Meredith in Mississippi. One of the SNCC marchers, Willie Ricks, shouted "power for black people." Shortened to "Black Power," it was picked up and chanted by other marchers, and ultimately made famous by Stokeley Carmichael and the Black Panthers (The Staff of Black Star Publishing, 1970, p. 44).

We see that as political identities emerge from participation in protest, repertoires of action and altered cultural forms develop concurrently, as people take part in contentious politics.

Appropriation of Threat

The infamous Bull Connor—who began his crusade against integration and civil rights activists as Birmingham city commissioner in the late 1930s—was but one of tens of thousands of Southern officials who for many decades attempted to intimidate Blacks and ward off protest with violence (Fairclough, 2001, p. 276). Television transmission of this violence in the 1960s helped to delegitimate such tactics in the mind of the nation. Civil rights demonstrators learned how to make use of the violence by kneeling in a prayerful position in the face of it—not only as a means of protecting themselves but as a way of highlighting a peaceful posture and the unfairness of the officials' behavior. In this strategic mechanism, protestors were appropriating Connor's violence for their own ends.

Nonviolent civil disobedience was a process long used by Black activists. As Adam Fairclough reminds us, "the practice of staging nonviolent protests in the hope that the oppressor would react violently [and thus discredit himself] was fundamental to the Gandhian concept of *satyagraha*, or civil disobedience (2001, p. 277). Martin Luther King, Jr., described this concept and his and the SCLC's use of it in his "Letter from Birmingham City Jail:" "Nonviolent direct action seeks to create . . . a crisis and establish such creative tension that a community that has constantly refused to negotiate is forced to confront the issue" (p. 276). When the SCLC launched demonstrations in Bull Connor's Birmingham in 1963, they were using this tactic, and appropriating official violence. To do this, they needed to attempt to appropriate the media. Andrew Young explained, "We wanted the world to know what was going on in the South. We had to craft a concise and dramatic message that could be explained in just sixty seconds. That was our media strategy" (p. 278). Blatant provocation of violence by the protestors would have destroyed the sympathy of television viewers.

Members of SNCC in 1964 appropriated the social status of White college students from the North in order to obtain federal protection for civil rights workers. SNCC invited 1,000 students from elite colleges to Mississippi to participate in extremely dangerous rural voter registration drives during the summer of 1964 (see Carson, 2001; McAdam, 1988; also Fairclough, 2001; and Payne, 1995). The federal government had not fulfilled the promise of the 1957 Civil Rights Bill to protect civil rights workers, and the murder and beatings of Black civil rights participants continued.

As SNCC executive staff meeting minutes reveal, members knew that the death of a White college student would attract national attention. One staff member argued, "We must bring the reality of our situation to the nation. Bring our blood to the White House door" (Fairclough, 2001, p. 285). The disappearance and ultimate death of three civil rights workers—two of whom were White Northerners—created a national uproar, and forced the FBI into supporting protestors in the South (ibid.).

Appropriation of Social Networks

Doug McAdam analyzed the applications of the Northern college students who applied to be part of Freedom Summer. He found that of the 1,000 applicants accepted into the program, those who came South to participate "were more likely to be members of civil rights (or allied) groups, have friends involved in the movement, and have more extensive histories of civil rights activity prior to the summer . . . in fact nothing distinguish[ed] the two groups more clearly than this contrast [in 'social proximity' to the project]" (1988, p. 65; see also McAdam, Tarrow, and Tilly 2001, 132).

McAdams's analysis suggests that belonging to a social group or network increases the chances that a person will decide to participate in contentious politics; and in this phenomenon we also find important evidence that initial participation makes *further* participation more likely.

In the South, leaders of civil rights groups used local networks to publicize and implement transgressive activity. They found that the best way to spread the word about upcoming demonstrations was to request that ministers announce it at Sunday morning services. During bus boycotts in Baton Rouge in 1953, and later in Montgomery, dense networks of residents provided carpooling for people to get to work (Morris, 1984, p. 58). Later, networks of Black college students in campus NAACP chapters were behind the rapid spread of sit-ins to cities throughout the South in 1960 and '61 (p. 198).

Cross-class and Cross-generation Alliances

Although it is the case that, generally speaking, social groupings make their own movements—workers, the labor movement; middle-class White women, the feminist movement; gays and lesbians—their own sympathizers from other groups are often involved, as well. Civil rights struggles throughout the 20th century have involved the participation, to varying degrees, of Whites and Blacks of all social classes. Consider the African American and Caucasian professionals in the 1900s NAACP and Black women's civic organizations; the middle-class pioneers such as A. Philip Randolph in the 1920s and '30s; middle-class Black college students of the 1930s and '40s, and Black and White college students of the '60s; consider White elites who "defected" to enter the struggle full time (Allard Lowenstein, Anne Braden, Bob Zellner, for example).

Civil rights history was also blessed by a number of family activist traditions. Longtime activist Ella Baker was inspired by her mother's involvement in the Black Baptist women's missionary movement of the early 1900s; 1960s radical Angela Davis learned social justice from her mother, a 1930s SNYC member and teacher who was close to the Communist Party. Malcolm X's father was an admirer of Separatist Marcus Garvey in the 1920s; Martin Luther King, Jr., Septima Clark, and many others had parents who were social activists (Collier-Thomas and Franklin, 2001, p. 44; Kelley, 1990, pp. 203, 234; see also Olson, 2001).

Charles Payne notes that many of the core activists in Mississippi came from families with traditions of overt defiance or activism: James Meredith, Medgar Evers, Fannie Lou Hamer, and Robert Moses (1995, pp. 233–234). Discussing the movement in Greenwood in the 1960s, Payne remarks,

> The people who formed much of the core of the movement ... frequently came from families with similar traditions of social involvement or defiance, subtle or overt. These were the people who joined earliest and often the people who worked hardest. In [some] cases defiance takes the form of explicit political involvement pre-dating [the arrival of civil rights workers]. In other cases, it takes the form of self-conscious attempts to shape the way in which children thought about race and in ways that go beyond the familiar custom of telling children that they were just as good as whites. . . . The common thread is a refusal to see oneself as merely acted upon, as merely victim. (ibid.)

There are certainly many activist families whose history we do not yet know. But these examples suggest that a good deal of political learning and development takes place outside of educational institutions, and is an important resource for movement building.

Communities have memories, as well, and these can be an important source of support. In the 1960s, young Stokely Carmichael and a handful of other SNCC organizers moved into the Black belt Lowndes County where in the 1930s SNYC and the Communist Party had worked. To Carmichael's surprise, poor farmers of all ages, especially older ones, came to the first meetings "enthusiastic and fully armed" (Kelley, 1990, pp. 229–230). Some of the residents had been participants in battles in Lowndes County 30 years before, when SNYC and the Communist Party had organized there. Charles Smith, one of the 1960s Black leaders in Lowndes County, was a former party member active in

1935, and had been a labor organizer on the docks in Mobile. He turned his home into SNCC's living and working quarters and offered sustenance and leadership. As Robin Kelly notes, "The radical thirties were part of the collective memory of the [Lowndes] County's families" and facilitated the protests of the 1960s (ibid.).

Social Contradiction as an Impetus for Radical Action

The ghetto explosions in American cities of the late 1960s were in part a result of dashed expectations of the millions of Southern Blacks who had fled Jim Crow hoping to find freedom and jobs in the North and were dearly disappointed by what they encountered. This profound disappointment is an example of the power of social contradictions to stimulate revolt. Other contradictions have also stimulated activism.

Rising education levels have often been associated with rebellion against social strictures—as, for example, when the preprofessional training that became widely available to women in college courses in the 1960s bumped up against corporate hiring procedures and the "glass ceilings" that well-educated women experienced upon their arrival in business and professional life. This contradiction between their preparation and lack of opportunity motivated many to join the modern women's movement. The influx of Black Southern college students in the 1930s and '40s, emboldened by new knowledge, were motivated to participate more fully in civic and economic protest against a society that would not acknowledge them.

The labor movement, too, has been informed by contradictions: the contrast, for example, between the ideology and practice of democracy in the civil sphere versus the loss of personal rights in the workplace. This has long been a source of frustration, and has certainly motivated workers over the years to take part in labor union organizing.

War, as well, will point up contradictions in American society. In 1919, Du Bois explained the consequences of fighting for the freedom of others when one's own was not assured. He argued that this experience in World War I would change forever the consciousness of the Black soldiers: They would "never be the same again. . . . You need not ask them to go back to what they were before. They cannot, for they are not the same men anymore" (in Bates, 2001, p. 28).

147

The contradiction between U.S. rhetoric of freedom and the reality of brutal oppression of Black citizens in the South haunted U.S. foreign policy during the Cold War that dominated foreign relations by 1947. Federal officials were caught in the contradiction of criticizing the Soviet Union for oppression that was becoming more and more evident at home as protests grew in number. This contrast certainly contributed to the relatively strong support of civil rights by Presidents Truman and Eisenhower (Dubziak, 2000, p. 11).

The Process of Legitimation

As news of the mass mobilizations grew in the 1950s and '60s, and especially as television stations broadcast pictures of Whites beating and hosing Black protesters, a national consensus formed that the goals and values of the protesters were legitimate. The overwhelming size of the 1963 March on Washington for Jobs and Freedom—250,000 strong and the largest demonstration in the nation's history at the time—lent moral backing to the civil rights movement and forced the active support of President Kennedy and other federal officials for congressional civil rights legislation—namely the Civil Rights Act of 1964, the Voting Rights Act of 1965, and, later, the 1968 Fair Housing Act (Williams, 2003, p. 25).

The process of federal government certification of the legitimacy of the civil rights crusade had developed slowly—beginning with Franklin Delano Roosevelt's edict #8802 in 1941, which outlawed the discrimination of Black workers in the military (Bates, 2001, p. 10). The *Brown* decision's rejection of the "separate but equal" doctrine in 1954 put the U.S. government on the side of public integration, and legitimated the intense political struggle for equal educational and other public rights that followed.

An important federal acknowledgment of the movement itself came in the form of the 1957 Civil Rights Act, which made interfering with a person's right to vote illegal. This act empowered the Justice Department to investigate the harassment and murder of activists (although, as we have seen, it was tragically slow to do so) (Fairclough, 2001, p. 240).

Without national consensus, and without certification by a federal authority—and the protection this would provide—White Southern violence and the states' rights that allowed it would probably have escalated to the point where Blacks would have found it difficult if not impossible to maintain the struggle. National consensus and ultimate certification by authorities are important if movements are to reach their national potential (McAdam, Tarrow, and Tilly, 2001, p. 158).

Social movement theory and the history of political movements—in this case civil rights—provide a rich tapestry of possibility. Images of suffering, rebellion, and victory grace the walls of the American past. If we are willing, we can appropriate this brocade, and design the future with it.

Knowledge of history and theory, in other words, should give us hope, and could provide confidence that, with appropriate effort, we can lift economic and educational burdens that oppress the U.S. poor. But, you may respond, we live in a conservative time, with government suspicion of protest heightened, motivated by terrorism and war; the current landscape is not hospitable. History reminds us, however, that rarely does the status quo seem to invite rebellion. It takes the active appropriation of whatever conditions exist to begin transforming the present. The next chapter argues that the present is, in fact, rife with radical possibilities.

9

Building a New Social Movement

I have argued that federal and other public policies severely delimit educational opportunity in urban school systems. I have also argued that even when school reform succeeds it fails—as there are few, if any, positive consequences for students' futures. The analysis suggests that solutions to the problems of city schools should not be limited to reforms addressing class size, standardized testing, and small schools. We need solutions to the problems of urban education that are considerably more comprehensive—that provide foundational support for the schools and their reform. We need policies that deal with the complex causes of the poverty of the schools in which teachers and students, neighborhoods, and families are caught. Joblessness, low wages, and concentrated segregation of poor families all create formidable barriers to urban educational equity and reward.

How are we going to obtain policies that will help us to remove macroeconomic and regional barriers to systemic school change and economic access? We need to double the minimum wage, create decently paying jobs in cities, and provide transportation to where suburban jobs are located. We need to tax great personal and corporate wealth to pay for this public investment and share proceeds among rich and poor municipalities in U.S. metro areas. Most of these programs would threaten America's corporate elites and the politicians dependent on their largesse, and may indeed appear impractical to sympathetic readers.

Critical social scholars on the left usually end their books with a list of policy recommendations, but rarely risk putting forth strategies for the policies' realization. Authors may feel there is too much risk involved in charting a path that may appear incendiary to elites, or unrealistic to others.

I am taking this risk. I have been arguing that to obtain policies that could set the stage for economic and educational justice, we need to apply the pressure that a social movement can provide; this and the final chapter make explicit suggestions for implementing that goal.

Consider that before the civil rights movement, many Southern Whites said that sharecroppers and tenant farmers did not *want* to vote—they were "apathetic"; or they were "content"; and some Black farmers told Robert Moses and other civil rights workers that they had not wanted to get involved in "dat mess" (Moses, 2001, p. 17). Yet sharecroppers and tenant farmers were central to the mass movement that emerged in the 1950s.

Interestingly, the decade of the 1950s was not a radical time. McCarthyism and the prosecution of former radicals certainly must have given would-be activists pause. Yet a mass movement did develop in that decade, and in a little over ten years wiped away the most egregious racist policies and practices. It is true that the civil rights movement did not eliminate all barriers to voting (think of Florida in the 2000 presidential election); and it failed to remove basic determinants of racial injustice such as lack of jobs, poverty wages, segregated housing, and underperforming city schools. But the primary goal of the civil rights movement was voting and citizenship rights, and in that it was, in the main, successful. The movement ultimately changed federal and state laws, American mores of acceptability, many institutional practices, and U.S. culture. To argue that the civil rights movement failed is to trivialize the mass oppression that went before.

It is our turn now, and we can move the task forward. Many millions of African Americans, Latinos, and immigrants continue to suffer from economic and educational injustice. We could certainly increase the radical outcome of this moment in history by working to create a social movement that would force the issue on education, jobs, and housing. Building a social movement is, of course, a monumental task, but I would argue it is no greater a task than that faced by our compatriots in 1950.

Indeed, the beginning years of the 21st century are—at least in regard to civil rights and education—not unlike the 1950s, with both times being ostensibly conservative while at the same time having potentially revolutionary legal structures at the ready. By 1954 and the *Brown* decision that separate public facilities are unconstitutional, over 30 years of effort had resulted in significant Supreme Court and presidential policy providing legal ground for Black citizenship—and an impetus for further activism.

Similarly, the year 2000 brought with it 25 years of legal battles at the state level to remove urban educational inequities. Over 70% of these court cases have been successful and many new state mandates have been written by the courts; more than a few await full funding. The passage of the federal "No Child Left Behind" legislation in 2002 gave further legal grounding to equity demands, despite the many limitations of the act. In regard to jobs and housing there are multiple antidiscrimination laws on the books (most resulting from the civil rights movement), which have not been fully enforced, but the very existence of which could provide important leverage for new demands.

Other similarities between then and now include the fact that in 1950 there was a stable urban Black working class at the same time that a much larger group of Black farming families had been made economically redundant by the industrialization of agriculture, the demise of labor-intensive cotton farming, and the absence of protective federal or state policy. These millions of displaced workers—and their urban working-class peers—formed an important constituency of the mass insurgency. Today we are in an analogous period of the Black political economy: A small group of Blacks are in middle-class positions—one result of the civil rights struggle and resulting progressive policy—while the vast majority have again been economically disenfranchised, this time by policies that regulate the terms of an information economy and remove opportunity from urban communities. These millions, too, could provide a mass base for a new social movement.

It may seem that the despair and sense of futility alleged to characterize America's current urban poor are similar to the fatalism that was said to keep earlier rural Blacks from mass rebellion in the segregated South. Even if this is the case, it is also true that fatalism provides but a fragile dam against the onslaught of a mass social movement. We can, like organizers of earlier decades, mobilize the underlying rage, and channel the energy that is released.

Indeed, there are already a number of existing, smaller, social movements in urban areas—constituted primarily by people of color who live there. There is more activism in 21st-century urban neighborhoods than at any time since the Black Panthers and Young Lords of the 1960s. This chapter will describe five current but not well-known movements, and will then suggest, using lessons from a theorized history, what we could do to build a unified and strengthened movement for social justice. The final chapter puts urban education at the center of this effort.

ALREADY EXISTING SOCIAL MOVEMENTS

We do not have to build a social movement for economic and educational rights from scratch. Five separate but interrelated movements have been growing rapidly since the late 1980s. They are renewed community organizing for economic justice in cities, an increasingly sophisticated movement of education and parent organizers in urban neighborhoods, an active group of progressive labor unions whose members are immigrant and other minority workers, a living wage movement in municipalities across the country, and an emerging movement of organized inner-city youth.

Community Organizing

A good number of the 7.5 million grassroots groups in this country advocate for progressive causes; and most of the 3,000 Community Development Corporations (CDCs) are politically liberal as well. Many grassroots groups and CDCs organize residents in their neighborhoods. But the community organizing movement has been led by two large, well-established progressive groups—the Association of Community Organizations for Reform Now (ACORN) and the Industrial Areas Foundation (IAF). Both of these engage in not only local but regional and state struggles against the underlying "rules of the game." Both have a national presence.

ACORN is the nation's largest organization of low- and moderate-income families, with about 150,000 member families organized into 750 neighborhood chapters in 60 cities across the country (http://www.acorn.org). ACORN has been organizing low- and moderate-income communities for over 30 years around such issues as affordable housing, public safety, predatory lending, living wage, community reinvestment, and most recently, education.

ACORN activists are skilled at public demonstrations that call out parents and community residents in high-profile, media-covered events. The *New York Times* gave extensive coverage to ACORN's successful 2002 effort to organize Brooklyn, NY, parents to vote against privatization of a local school by Edison, Inc. Acorn and the parents then began pressuring the Board of Education to provide increased resources to the school. ACORN has recently launched ambitious political campaigns aimed at state legislatures, including a press for $10 million from the state of Illinois to increase parent engagement in Chicago school reform.

Since 1999, ACORN has been engaged in a major effort to protect urban neighborhoods from predatory lending by companies such as Wells Fargo. Predatory loans are made in concentrated volume in poor and minority neighborhoods where better loans are not readily available. The loss of equity and foreclosure when the loans cannot be repaid at the high interest can devastate already fragile communities. ACORN has been campaigning to stop these abuses by promoting state legislation and federal regulation, putting pressure on particular offenders, and education and outreach in communities.

They have played a leading role in passing city and state legislation to restrict this practice, winning reforms from federal regulators, and waging an ongoing fight to block a bill in Congress aimed at preempting state and local protections. ACORN has organized thousands of victims of predatory loans to tell their stories and to get involved in efforts to keep others from encountering the same problems. These ACORN members have protested at lending company offices and the homes of CEOs, rallied outside legislative sessions, and testified in city, state, and federal hearings. At the same time, neighborhood actions have prevented foreclosures and forced lenders to repair the worst loans, empowering ACORN members to keep pushing for bigger victories.

The other community organizing group with a national presence is the Industrial Areas Foundation (IAF). The IAF is an organization of organizations, primarily of churches in low- and moderate-income neighborhoods. IAF employs about 150 full-time professional organizers. There are about 60 IAF locals in 20 states and Washington, DC. These groups are made up of nearly three thousand congregations and associations and tens of thousands of ministers, pastors, some rabbis, women religious leaders, and state and metropolitan lay and civic leaders. Between three and four million Americans are members (Gecan, 2002, p. 4).

The IAF is descended from the organization of the same name started by Saul Alinksy in 1940 in Chicago. The IAF does not organize around issues until it has organized a neighborhood. They begin by meeting with leaders and members of churches and associations that reflect the racial and religious diversity of a community. They are financially independent: Local leaders and institutions must commit their own dues money of $250,000 for organizing projects before they may pursue foundation money. The IAF trains neighborhood residents and leaders from local congregations in 10-day institutes that develop residents' skills of organizing, writing petitions, negotiating with city hall, and public speaking. The "iron rule" of the IAF is "Don't do for others what they can do for themselves" (p. 10; see also Shirley, 1997 and 2002; and Warren, 2001).

Member congregations of the IAF are organized in a federated regional and state structure that gives them power on a larger level without abandoning the priorities and ultimate authority of local organizations (Warren, 2001, p. 74). State IAF networks cannot dictate to local affiliates. Leaders from local organizations develop state policy, as they meet to build relationships or social capital, bridging across localities and local racial groupings (ibid., p. 75). With its federated structure, the IAF overcomes the limitations of local organizing, and yet does not become a national or regional organization that has no real ties to its local constituents.

The IAF used this strategy with success in Texas in its school reform efforts—the Alliance Schools program. By 1999, the program covered over 100 schools, and had pressured the state legislature to substantially increase the funding, resources, and technical expertise of each school. There has been improvement in test scores. However, the main success of the Alliance Initiative is the development of a culture of engagement, protest, and organization among the parents and communities in which the schools are located. IAF affiliates in Albuquerque, Tucson, Phoenix, and Omaha, in addition to the rest of the Southwest, have joined the IAF in these efforts (ibid., p. 85; see also Shirley, 1997 and 2002). In Brooklyn and Bronx, New York City, IAF founded three public high schools; two are among the highest performing schools in the city (Gecan, 2004, p. 8).

Education Organizing

The second already existing movement, part of and yet distinct from community organizing, is organizing specifically for school reform, or education organizing—which describes the actions of parents and other community residents to change neighborhood schools through an "intentional building of power" (Mediratta and Fruchter, 2001, p. 5). Larger groups doing education organizing are part of the IAF/ACORN universe described above, but many additional groups are involved as well (Brown, 2003, in Lopez, 2003, p. 1). Education organizing aims to create social capital in communities, and to encourage parents and other residents to utilize their collective strength to force system change (Giles, 1998, p. 2). Education organizing attempts to build leadership in parents by providing skill training, mentoring, and opportunity for public actions (Lopez, 2003, p. 4). Parents conduct community and school surveys, speak at rallies, mobilize other parents and community residents, and plan and enact campaigns aimed at school and district personnel and practices (ibid., p. 4; see also Collaborative Communications Group, 2003, p. 17).

Because education organizing gives parents a base outside of school—typically in alliance with other community groups— parents are not dependent on school personnel for approval or legitimacy (Lopez, 2003, p. 2; see also Zachary and Olatoye, 2001). When successful, parent organizing in poor communities yields the clout that parents create among themselves in affluent suburbs, where, with their skills and economic and political influence, they closely monitor the actions of district educators and politicians.

Several studies of parent organizing groups in low-income neighborhoods around the country document their rapid increase in number and influence, especially since the early 1990s (Mediratta, Fruchter, and Lewis, 2002; Gold, Simon, and Brown, 2002; and Collaborative Communications Group, 2003; see also Beam, Eskenzai, and Kamber, 2002). Moreover, 80% of 66 parent organizing groups studied by the Collaborative Communications Group are working not only in local neighborhoods, but in regional or state coalitions formed to improve district or state education policy. One such group is Mississippi-based Southern Echo, which has grassroots community organizations in Tennessee, Arkansas, Louisiana, South Carolina, Kentucky, Florida, North Carolina, and West Virginia (Collaborative Communications Group, 2003, p. 34).

Southern Echo is an exemplar in several ways: It is regional, multigenerational, and led by former civil rights and labor union activists. The group describes itself as a "leadership development, education and training organization working to develop new, grassroots leadership in African American communities in Mississippi and the surrounding region" (p. 27). Until 1992, their work focused on jobs, affordable housing, and rebuilding community organizations. When they shifted their attention to education in the early 1990s, they began to organize around minority rights.

Southern Echo worked to create a force that could put pressure on state education officials. They provided training and technical assistance to help community groups carry out local campaigns, and created residential leadership schools for parents and community members that lasted two days or more; they published training manuals, and delivered hundreds of workshops in communities (p. 29). One result of the work of Southern Echo and an affiliate, Mississippi Education Working Group (MEWG), is that on October 23, 2002, the Mississippi State Board of Education agreed to fully comply with federal requirements for providing services to special education students—for the first time in 35 years. Echo leaders report that this was "the first time the community came together to force legislators, the state board of education, superintendents, special education administrators and curriculum coordinators to sit down together" (p. 33).

A particularly impressive education organizing group in the North is the Logan Square Neighborhood Association (LSNA) in Chicago—founded in the 1960s to work with the variety of problems local residents faced in their community. In 1988, when the Chicago School Reform Law created local schools councils, LSNA began to assist parents and community members to work to improve their schools (Mediratta, Fruchter, and Lewis, 2002, p. 27). Among the accomplishments of LSNA and parents are construction of seven new school buildings, evening community learning centers in six schools, mortgage lender programs to offer incentives for educators to buy housing in the area, parent training as reading tutors and mentors, the establishment of bilingual lending libraries for parents, a new bilingual teacher-training program for neighborhood parents interested in becoming teachers, and collaboration with Chicago State University to offer these courses at the neighborhood school at no cost to participants (p. 28). Mediratta, Fruchter, and Lewis report that the extensive parent engagement and LSNA's other initiatives "have contributed to achievement gains at its member schools. In its six core schools, the percent of students reading at or above the national average in 1990 ranged from 10.9 percent to 22.5 percent. By 2000, the percent of students reading at or above national average ranged from 25.4 to 35.9 percent" (p. 28).

The final example of education organizing comes from South Bronx, NY. This group, Community Collaborative for District 9 (CC9), is an important instance of coalition building—between parents, community-based organizations, the teachers union, and a university partner (Mediratta, Fruchter, and Lewis, 2002, p. 29). Organizational members include ACORN (which has been organizing parents in Districts 7, 9, and 12 for a decade); the New York City American Federation of Teachers (AFT); Citizens Advice Bureau (a local CBO providing educational services to residents for 30 years); Highbridge Community Life Center (a CBO providing job training and educational services since 1979); Mid-Bronx Senior Citizens Council (one of the largest CBOs in the South Bronx); parents from New Settlement Apartments; Northwest Bronx Community and Clergy Coalition (which unites 10 neighborhood housing reform groups); and New York University Institute for Education and Social Policy (which conducts research and evaluation and provides other technical assistance to community and education organizing groups).

The CC9 coalition researched educational best practice to determine what reform they were going to pursue. They decided that stabilizing the teaching force in their low-income schools was critical, and that increased staff development and lead teachers at every grade level in the schools would give teachers skills to be more successful with their students and thus encourage them to remain in district classrooms. The coalition then organized residents, petitioned, demonstrated, and engaged in other direct action campaigns to obtain New York City Department of Education funding to pay for the reforms. At every step, neighborhood parents were in the forefront. In April 2004, New York City provided $1.6 million for the first year of lead teachers and staff development throughout the 10-school district. Efforts are being made to create a coalition of community groups, parents, teachers, and progressive labor unions to push for the lead teacher program in low-income schools throughout the city.

Progressive Labor Unions

The progressive wing of the labor movement is the third of the already existing movements. Overall, U.S. labor unions count a membership of about 16 million (of which 51% are women and minorities) (LeRoy, 2003, p. 11). Although many unions have traditionally maintained an exclusionary stance toward minority workers, it is also true that others have worked strenuously for social justice. Organized labor was instrumental in the passage of major civil rights legislation, the abolition of child labor, the establishment of the 40-hour week and the eight-hour day, the minimum wage, Social Security, occupational safety and health standards, higher wages for industrial and other organized workers, and protection from business abuses that are allowed by federal law.

Minorities are an increasing percentage of the labor force and of unions. Between 1976 and 1988, while the nation's overall labor force grew by 26%, the percentage of Black workers rose by 38%, Asian American workers by 103%, and Latinos by 110%. The concentration of Black workers in public sector jobs partly explains why the unionization rate of African Americans is relatively high (Kelley, 2002, p. 1). The public sector is about 37% unionized (LeRoy, 2002, p. 12).

Unions with large numbers of minority workers, the more progressive unions, have begun collaborating with community organizations in large urban centers, and have experienced a good deal of success. Justice for Janitors, launched in 1985, has become in many cities "a civil rights movement—and a cultural crusade" (Kelley, 2002, p. 17). Justice for Janitors has been deeply committed to mass mobilization through community organizing and civil disobedience (ibid.). Utilizing sit-down strikes, members have waged militant, media-covered campaigns in major cities. In Los Angeles, for example, Justice for Janitors is largely responsible for a stunning increase in unionized custodial employees: The percentage of janitors belonging to unions rose from 10% in 1987 to 90% in 1995 (p. 18). As Robin Kelley remarks, "Justice for Janitors succeeded precisely because it was able to establish links to community leaders, to forge an alliance with Black and Latino organizations, churches, and progressive activists from all over the city. They built a powerful mass movement that went beyond the downtown luxury office buildings and the [local union] headquarters into the streets and boardrooms" (2002, p. 18).

In Washington, DC, the group led the struggle of Local 82 of the Service Employees International Union (SEIU) in their fight against U.S. Service Industries—a private company that used nonunion labor to clean downtown office buildings. In March 1995, Justice for Janitors organized several demonstrations in the city that led to over 200 arrests. The protesters blocked traffic and engaged in other forms of civil disobedience, demanding an end to tax breaks to real estate developers as well as cutbacks in social programs for poor people. In December 1995, the National Labor Relations Board concluded that the janitorial company USSI had "a history of pervasive illegal conduct by threatening, interrogating, and firing employees they deemed unacceptable, especially those committed to union organizing" (ibid.). African American workers, in particular, were the subject of firings. The Board's decision against USSI was a significant victory for SEUI because the company could no longer discriminate against the union (p. 18).

Other progressive unions include the Hotel Employees and Restaurant Employees (HERE), American Federation of State, County, and Municipal Employees (AFSCME), and various locals of other unions.

Living Wage Movement

The fourth already existing movement is the national campaign for a living wage. In 1994, an alliance between labor (led by AFSCME) and IAF religious leaders in Baltimore launched a successful campaign for a local law requiring city service contractors to pay a wage that brought workers above the poverty level. Since that time, community, labor, and religious coalitions have won similar ordinances in over 100 municipalities including St. Louis, Boston, Los Angeles, Tucson, San Jose, Portland, Milwaukee, Detroit, Minneapolis, and Oakland, and in 15 states. Syndicated columnist Robert Kuttner has described the Living Wage Movement as "the most interesting (and underreported) grassroots enterprise to emerge since the civil rights movement . . . signaling a resurgence of local activism around pocketbook issues" (cited on http:// www.acorn.org).

Typically, living wage ordinances cover employees of companies holding large city or county service contracts or who receive substantial financial assistance from the city in the form of grants, loans, bond financing, tax abatements, or other economic development subsidies. As I noted earlier, the concept behind living wage campaigns is that limited public dollars should not subsidize poverty-wage work. When employers receiving tax dollars or tax breaks pay their workers less than a living wage, taxpayers end up funding not only the initial subsidy but then the social services low-wage workers may require to support themselves and their families. Public tax dollars should be reserved for those employers who demonstrate a commitment to providing family-supporting jobs. Increasingly, living wage coalitions are proposing requirements in addition to raised wages—such as health benefits, vacation days, community hiring, public disclosure, community advisory boards, environmental standards, and language that supports union organizing.

Scholarly assessments of the economic impact of living wage laws demonstrate that in many localities where these ordinances were passed, between 40% and 70% of the jobs did not pay enough to support a family of four without subsidies or a single parent and child above the poverty line. In many cases, the raises are small but important (average living wage raise is to $8.74 without health benefits and $9.53 with health benefits, for ordinances passed in 2002). Research has found that raising wages above poverty levels does not increase prices or local unemployment, as employers typically predict (see Bernstein, 2002; Need, Christopher, et al., 1999; Pollin and Luce, 1998; and Weisbrot and Sforza-Roderick, 1998).

An important goal of the Living Wage Movement is that of extending the living wage to all businesses with at least 25 employees—including hotels, shops, fast-food restaurants, and discount stores. Such an ordinance was passed in March 2003 in Santa Fe—the only municipality in the country with this regulation. Business interests are actively attempting to discredit the law, by arguing that it will force them to move, and there is a possibility that the ordinance could be defeated at the polls, as occurred in Santa Monica in 2002 by a narrow margin of voters. This defeat reminds us that as long as there is no federal mandate for decent wages, pay increases are vulnerable to local employer campaigns.

Youth Organizing

Contradicting popular stereotypes of inner-city youth as dangerous and uninterested in education is the last of the existing movements. Increasing numbers of African American, Latino, and Asian teenagers in cities across the country have been organizing for the right to courses that prepare them for college, for better educational funding, and for a resolution of other social justice issues like an end to police violence and mass incarceration of their peers. In the 1990s there was a surge in youth organizing. In 1992 in Chicago, for example, there were no political youth organizations. By 2002, there were 14 large, well-established progressive youth groups in the city, and several in suburbs as well. Over 500 well-established politically progressive youth groups are active in urban areas around the country (Wimsatt, 2002, 3–4).

Brief descriptions of three groups follow. *Boston Area Youth Organizing Project* (BYOP) is an organization of youth led by teens and supported by adults. They are notable for their regional reach. According to their Web site, their goal is "to increase youth power and create positive social change" (http://www.byop.org). To do this, they develop countercultural values, build relationships across differences, train and develop leaders, identify key issues of concern, and take action for justice. BYOP is partnered with an adult group, the Greater Boston Interfaith Organization, which began in inner-city Roxbury in Black churches, and now includes metro-area chapters and at least one synagogue. Among BYOP's successes are the following: They pressured the Boston mayor and City Council to add $1 million for textbooks and to extend students' public transportation passes from 6:00 to 8:00 p.m.; they successfully lobbied for the first legislation in the country to lower the local voting age (this legislation is pending at the state level).

Schools Not Jails, a group based in Los Angeles, is one of the many youth organizations that engage in direct action to support their demands. Here is a short description of one such action: "The train was packed with dozens of high school students who had walked out of classes and jumped onto the BART subway without paying. They came from San Francisco, Oakland, Daly City, San Leandro, Hayward, Richmond, and Pittsburg. Many had never participated in a protest action before, and the level of excitement ran high. They were on their way to Concord, another Bay Area city, to demonstrate against miserable conditions in their schools as well as the statewide attacks on immigrant rights, affirmative action, and now bilingual education" (http://www.schoolsnotjails.com).

The final youth organization, the Student Labor Action Project (SLAP), stands out because of its extensive collaboration with other progressive groups. SLAP links high school youth and college students to economic justice issues. In 1999, unions involved in Jobs with Justice campaigns and the United States Students Association joined together to create the Action Project to support and advise student-labor work that has been emerging in communities across the country. SLAP facilitates networking, training, material-development, and technical assistance for student activists in communities and on campuses.

SLAP along with other youth groups—United Students against Sweatshops and the Prison Moratorium Project—work together to help organize actions on high school and college campuses in support of immigrant workers' rights, living wage jobs and the right to organize, and an end to sweatshops and youth incarceration (http://www.jwj.org/SLAP/slap.htm; for other groups see *What Kids Can Do* (http://www.whatkids cando.org); and *Funders' Collaborative on Youth Organizing* (http://www.fcyo.org).

The five movements described above each have different foci, although their goals are closely related. There is some overlap in personnel, and occasional collaboration. But the five movements are largely distinct and have relatively few members overall. New York University activist/scholar Norm Fruchter, for example, estimates that even though there may be a hundred education organizing groups in New York City, it is likely that only 10% of New York City students are directly affected by their programs and campaigns (personal communication, August 25, 2004).

Given that these movements are small, we need to think about how we could get more people and groups involved. Given that the movements are not conjoined, we need to think about how to unify them into one large force.

LESSONS FROM HISTORY AND THEORY

To consider these strategic problems of movement building, I apply lessons extracted in the theoretical exposition of the last chapter. Initial theorizing yielded a set of categories—Attribution of Opportunity; Appropriation of Existing Organizations, Institutions, and Cultural Forms; etc.—and these constructs should prove useful for thinking about the present. Here I will add my suggestions to those theories of practice already developed by organizing groups in communities across America. Following the application of theory, the last and final chapter of the book will place education—and concerned educators—in the center of attempts to build a movement for social justice.

Attribution of Opportunity

We can view current confluences as presenting multiple opportunities for radical political intervention, even when it may not seem that they do.

The new geography of minority poverty—covering central city and segregated suburbs—is one development that can be utilized strategically. This demographic offers possibilities for cross-place collaboration that potentially involves almost two-thirds of the poor people in large U.S. metropolitan areas. There are already a number of organizing efforts that are regional in scope (see Chapters 5 and 6) but very few that take an explicit city-suburban focus. One that does is the *Gamaliel Foundation*—a multiracial, city-suburban church-based alliance centered in Chicago. Gamaliel is constituted by a network of ministers, professional community organizers, and community groups working to "rebuild urban and older suburban communities" throughout the nation. Their regional networks include over 40 grassroots organizations in 11 states—including every major metropolitan area in the Midwest, western New York and Pennsylvania, and Oakland, CA. They have successfully organized around issues of regional tax equity, land use, transportation, and governance. This organization certainly provides a promising model for regional mobilization (http://www.gamaliel.org).

Urban-suburban coalitions of distressed, segregated school districts could force the issue of equitable funding in metro areas and the many states that have had legal challenges to the constitutionality of existing school finance. Comprehensive state education reforms already on the books (e.g., Kentucky and New Jersey) or in process (e.g., New York and California) demand, for their ultimate success, that urban communities and supporters organize around them and get people "in the streets" to demand passage and full implementation. Lawyers can win legal mandates, but only demonstrations and public outcry can obtain full implementation.

The New Jersey funding equity court case, *Abbott v. Burke,* for instance, which mandates extensive state investments to compensate for economic disadvantage, has not been fully implemented by the state legislature in over 25 years of continual litigation on the part of lawyers for the states' urban school districts. There has been no organized constituency of urban residents to press for full enforcement of the law. In 1991, by contrast, well-organized and highly vocal middle-class and affluent taxpayers massed at the state capital in demonstrations against a proposed tax hike to pay for the court's education mandate. The governor responded by repealing the tax increase (Anyon, 1997, p. 204; see also Dumas and Anyon, 2005).

An economic development that has potentially powerful consequences for progressive organizing is the collapse of the traditional well-paying working-class job. As chapters in Part I document, an increasing percentage of jobs available to low-income workers pay poverty or poverty-zone wages. This development provides a rationale for organizing for better economic policies, as well as for low-income student access to college preparation courses and funds to complete college. The collapse of working-class job opportunities could also provide a basis for organizing for meaningful programs of vocational education for the noncollege-bound student. As I have noted, figures demonstrate that most jobs in the U.S. do not require college, but rather on-the-job training. Public schools could become a meaningful part of the preparation for these positions if they offered programs combining academic study with realistic vocational training and job placement—combined, crucially, with union support for minority workers and better starting salaries. All these could be strategic organizing goals among low-income students and families.

There are technological developments that could also be appropriated for mobilization in urban communities. In late 2002 and early 2003, the Internet-based group, Moveon.org, successfully utilized the Internet to organize demonstrations in cities across the country against the invasion of Iraq. During the 500,000-strong demonstration against the Republican National Convention in New York City in early September 2004, activist groups coordinated over 150 protests using cell phones and text messaging. As other authors have pointed out, Internet access, E-mail, and cell phones have enhanced movement building by increasing the networking and communication capabilities among groups (see Castells, 1996 and 2000; McAdam, Tarrow, and Tilly, 2001; Melucci, 1999, and Rheingold, 2002). The World Wide Web and cell phones are increasingly utilized by urban residents, especially youth, and could be appropriated to political ends.

Appropriation of Existing Organizations, Institutions, and Cultural Forms

As the next chapter illustrates in detail, public educational institutions in the U.S. can be sites of appropriation as movement-building spaces. Education in the U.S. has always had a contradictory nature. On the one hand, schools have been primary agents of social control and the reproduction of class, gender, and racial advantages and disadvantages. However, education also has had—and continues to have—potentially liberatory, egalitarian, and transformative possibilities as well. This contradictory nature of schooling holds out promise that concerned educators can make central contributions to the transformation of society through their work in schools. Many authors have developed extremely important ideas about ways in which teachers can utilize critical pedagogy and create democratically run schools (Ayers, Hunt, and Quin, 1998; Bigelow and Peterson, 2002; Darder, Torres, and Baltodano, 2002; Delpit, 1997, Fine, 1994; Freire and Macedo, 1987; Giroux, 1997; hooks, 1994; Ladson-Billings, 1994; McLaren, 2002; Perry, 2003; Sleeters and McLaren, 1995; and Shor, 1992, among many others). I will add to this rich tradition in Chapter 10 with activities educators can use to engage students in public contestation and political campaigns, thereby increasing the appropriation of classrooms and schools as movement-building spaces.

Outsiders and Cultural Brokers

Residents of urban neighborhoods—low-income youth and beleaguered poverty-wage workers—should not be expected to organize a movement alone. Bicultural, bi-class brokers such as progressive teachers, social workers, and other minority and White professionals concerned with social justice need to take advantage of their own relatively privileged status to provide spaces and opportunities for low-income urban residents to air grievances, discuss and strategize, and—most important—to engage in contentious politics.

Groups can also act as brokers. Groups already active in existing movements can broker relationships, coalitions, and convenings that could get people talking about uniting for social justice. Called intermediaries, such brokers as Local Initiatives Support Corporation in the community development field, Center for Third World Organizing in the community organizing field, and Cross City Campaign for Urban School Reform and Southern Echo in education, could perhaps play these roles. Well-regarded unions like SEIU and HERE, or groups with a national base like IAF and ACORN, could act as intermediaries to call people to conference to discuss a united movement for economic and educational opportunity.

Creation of Regional Organizations

As Chapter 7 suggests—and as the civil rights movement confirms—groups that work on a regional level are more likely to make inroads on injustice than groups that work only in their neighborhood.

And larger, umbrella groups (like the Southern Christian Leadership Conference) that can pull people and organizations together over large geographical regions can reach national audiences. Without an umbrella group, there can be a cacophony of messages and dissipation of effort.

Intermediaries and their representatives could form an umbrella group to assist smaller movements to coalesce and reach scale. An umbrella group should have its own funding: It might obtain money from Hip Hop moguls, progressive unions, church groups, established civil rights organizations, or liberal foundations. Five separate movements would be stronger and more forceful as one.

Leadership Development

As I argued in Chapter 8, leaders emerge from the struggle itself. Those who work with adults and youth need not only to involve them in contentious politics, but should set up situations where leadership can emerge, be nurtured, and developed. Nascent leaders can be identified in neighborhood and church-based organizations and after-school groups. As in the civil rights movement, if we involve current youth in political struggle, and if we support them in opportunities to lead, they will develop leadership abilities, skills, and experience. These acquisitions constitute social *capital* in the best sense of the word: skills and knowledge that will assist people in making changes to society from which they will truly profit.

Centrality of Youth

Urban youth have a powerful critique of education and White society. Hip Hop lyrics express their complaint: The group Dead Prez states that minority youth are urged to stay in school and get a job, but are not told that "the job gonna exploit you every time." Hip Hop icon Tupac Shakur wrote that Whites would *"rather see us locked in chains"* than in school or decent jobs.

Most Hip Hop lyrics are replete with violent epithets, and words and phrases—like nigger and bitch—that many adults find offensive. But until its commodification and spread to White suburban teenagers in the late 1990s, when it lost some of its political edge, this language—that is, Hip Hop discourse—was a form of overt rebellion and transgression against mainstream White and Black middle-class America. It expressed the anger, angst, and frustration of many young people of color (Kitwana, 2002; Dimitriadis, 2001, among others). Hip Hop, however, as Todd Boyd remarks, "is a testament to overcoming the obstacles that American life often imposes on its Black and Latino subjects, and in this, it is a model of what 'we shall overcome' means in the modern world" (2002, p. 152).

The rebellion in Hip Hop also gives the lie to any stereotype of universal fatalism among young people in cities. The lyrics reveal instead an angry, broad-based rebellion that is now finding a political voice in the emerging youth movement.

The youth organizations described previously are examples of how some in the "Hip Hop generation" have appropriated this cultural stance, and the music, to work for social change. Nascent political attitudes embodied in this cultural form are crucial tools for any social movement that could be developed in the foreseeable future. To build a movement, adults both inside and outside of schools need to assist youth in turning this rebellion into informed, organized resistance.

Social Construction of New Identities through Participation in Transgressive Politics

Let me reiterate this important point from Chapter 8: As people march, sit-in, prepare petitions and speeches, meet with politicians and school boards, and otherwise engage in contentious politics, they typically develop identities as activists and, ultimately, if a movement develops, identities as part of that movement. As I have argued, we do not typically get people involved in activism or social movements through exposure to critical pedagogy, social justice curricula, or books like this one, although these are crucial to providing information and analysis. Rather, as labor movement, peace movement, and civil rights activists will tell you—people are radicalized by actually *participating* in contentious politics.

Robert Moses describes how involvement in civil rights work changed him: "... I was a 26-year-old teacher at ... an elite private school in the Bronx. ... It was the sit-in movement that led me to Mississippi for the first time in 1960. And that trip changed my life. I returned to the state a year later and over the next four years was transformed as I took part in the voter registration movement there" (2002, p. 4).

The power of participation to encourage activism implies that an initial component of building a social movement is to personally involve students, other youth, and adults in public protest and other strategic activities with which they can advocate for better opportunities.

The final chapter works at length with this understanding. It provides a variety of ways in which participation in social movement organizing can teach urban youth not only that they can improve their communities but that they are persons of worth, quality, and intelligence. Through political participation, youth become enmeshed in constructive social networks, and develop positive personal identities.

Creation of Innovative Action Repertoires

The repertoire of activities expressed by social movements develops over time, with each generation utilizing strategies of those who went before them and creating new ones out of their own experiences.

As the previous chapter demonstrates, community organizing was an important strategy in the repertoire of civil rights activists throughout the 20th century. The five movements already existing today also utilize community organizing as a central method of building power. Without a constituency, based in actual neighborhoods, towns, and cities, there is no movement. And without organizing, there is no constituency.

Even though masses of people across the U.S. demonstrated against invading Iraq in early 2003, and many activists fought the "Battle of Seattle" in 2000, these campaigns were not part of sustained community movements with organized constituencies; and they will not be, unless time and effort are spent to build bases in towns and cities around the country. Community organizing is a strategy that must remain central to any attempt to build a social movement.

Action strategies that might be useful in urban education struggles today include sit-down strikes of families and children in school buildings until demands for funding are met; "sick out" strikes, where students and families boycott schools until the threat of government withdrawal of funds because of absenteeism leads officials to meet demands; and picketing school, district, and political leaders at their homes. Or, students and community members could chain themselves to the metal fences surrounding urban schools. Hunger strikes may be necessary.

We could emulate the Freedom Rides of the civil rights movement and of minority unions in 2003—when a coalition of Black and immigrant workers hired buses to drive from California to Washington, DC. They stopped in cities along the way to bring attention to the problems workers face. They achieved much media attention and may affect pending legislation affecting the rights of immigrant workers.

We could appropriate this strategy, filling yellow school buses with students and families and driving through the city stopping at schools and neighborhoods that need urgent attention. We could organize street corner discussions and rallies at each stop, highlighting what needs to be done.

In the theoretical discussion of Chapter 8, I noted that civil rights history demonstrates that economic pressure has typically been a potent strategy in struggles against more powerful groups. Urban education is big business. Expenditures in each city for school district payrolls, purchases, facilities and maintenance, technology, and other goods and services are paid by taxpayers and keep hundreds of thousands of people employed nation-wide—and keep many business owners solvent. Perhaps there is a way to learn from the civil rights movement about the power of the economic boycott. Perhaps new strategies will emerge that threaten recipients of district monies with loss of income, and taxpayers with wasted resources, unless community demands are met. Useful, additional actions will arise during contestation, and urban youth will no doubt be instrumental in creating starkly expressive strategies.

Appropriation of Threat

Most urban youth do not engage in violence; and most violent acts that are carried out by Blacks and Latinos involve other residents of low-income communities. But the "thug" stereotype follows urban males throughout the media, and many Whites fear them. We could appropriate this perceived threat. Political organizing in the youth movement demonstrates that urban teenagers can move from anger, despair, and street life to well-informed resistance and organized political campaigns for equity. We would be remiss if we did not point out to Whites the diminution of the threat of violence by these youth that such politicization embodies.

Appropriation of Social Networks

This theoretical construct asks us to consider the power that would be generated if even half of the 7.5 million grassroots organizations and the several thousand Community Development Corporations were aligned together, acting toward the same goal. Linked by a common agenda, these groups would constitute a vast national network. Such a network would be a significant strand in a social movement.

There are other networks that could constitute other strands: The Leadership Conference on Civil Rights (LCCR), a venerable organization of 180 civil rights groups, represents the older generation of activists. Members have vast accumulated experience. They have produced a *Handbook for Activists* and a *Grassroots Tool Kit*, and maintain active student chapters on college campuses. The Leadership Conference has authored two prospective legislative bills that could lay the foundation of a platform for educational and economic justice (http://www.civil-rights.org).

As we know, the African American church has long provided networks supporting social justice mobilizing. Some argue, however, that the church may not be able to play a similar role today. Sociologist Omar McRoberts studied a low-income section of Boston, and found that, in contrast to the past, African Americans in the congregations of churches in that area do not typically live in the neighborhoods where they worship; they merely rent the buildings for services (2003, p. 4). Therefore, they are not as available or concerned about "social uplift" in the neighborhood where the church is located. McRoberts argues that Black churches therefore are not likely to take part in sustained political struggle to improve the inner city.

But as Andrew Billingsley demonstrates in *Mighty Like a River: The Black Church and Social Reform*, there also exist well over a thousand mostly large, well-established African American churches in U.S. cities, and a majority of them are deeply involved in community outreach (2002, p. 88). Billingsley argues that among Black churches, "community outreach activities are much more common than is generally believed, especially in urban areas. . . . [A] majority of contemporary Black churches have not abandoned community issues since the civil rights era" (p. 89).

Indeed, some of the most productive CDCs and community-based organizations today are part of, or offshoots of, religious organizations. Faith-based organizing (e.g., in the IAF, PICO, and GAMALIEL) is an important part of movement building today (see Freeman, 1994; Jacobson, 2003; Rooney, 1995; Shirley, 2002; Warren, 2003; and Wood, 2002).

I noted when discussing social networks in Chapter 8 that the civil rights movement was blessed with many family activist traditions. However, indications are that there is little agreement between members of old and young in the African American community today. There is often distance, suspicion, and even hostility that builds up between the generations around social goals and means. As in the 1960s, when White activists expressed contempt for people over 30 years old, today African American youth are often estranged from their civil rights "elders." The young define themselves against the old.

But it is crucial for movement building today that we overcome the boundaries of age, because men and women who fought the battles of the civil rights, labor, and community development movements in the 1950s and '60s have much to teach those who would be political today. And the organizations these elders built over the years could provide a network of "safe houses" and operational nodes in a national movement.

Social Contradictions as an Impetus for Radical Action

The penultimate theoretical construct I apply is the role of contradictions in stimulating political contention. Social justice teachers know that political and economic contradictions can be a fecund source of ideas for discussion, political education, and consciousness raising. However, contradictions can also catalyze action.

As I pointed out in Part I, for example, African Americans and Latinos are obtaining more education than ever before, but their situation in the economy has deteriorated in the last 15-20 years. This highlights the new truth that an historic faith in education as the path to middle-class status is no longer assured. This contradiction is anger-producing, and may be catalyzing—if we appropriate it as such.

Another contradiction of urban schooling that could be mobilizing is that even though society urges low-income minority youth to "stay in school," perseverance (unless one has the funds to complete college) is likely to provide very little reward to graduates. Many students are aware that without the availability of jobs and decent pay, lacking a college degree, and in the face of employer discrimination, the promises of education are severely compromised.

These and other contradictions plaguing folks day after day, if used strategically, can become mobilizing points for youth and their families. I will demonstrate in the final chapter numerous ways educators can assist youth and families to move from knowledge of the social traps they experience to concrete political contention to change the situation.

The Process of Legitimation

As I argued in Chapter 8, for success, the goals of a social movement should ultimately appear legitimate to a broad swath of the public. There may not be wide acceptance of the idea of, say, a wealth tax on the super rich. However, if people were made aware of how much wealth a very few have, how much more relative tax they paid in the past, and how much money equitable taxing might produce, a consensus for a wealth tax might develop.

But I do believe that there is a consensus among Americans that urban students deserve quality education. As I have noted, the NCLB lends federal legitimation to this goal. Moreover, the repeal of welfare and the "discovery" by policymakers that the jobs former recipients can obtain do not provide funds sufficient to support a family has created the basis for another emerging consensus—that full-time work should bring a person a living wage.

For maximum power, the various movements today—and the many grassroots and social justice groups that constitute them— need to unite, and acknowledge that the problems they tackle can be best resolved if they are tackled as intimately interrelated issues. For as I have been at pains to point out, the obstacles that urban residents face are complex and interrelated. The problems of urban education, jobs, lack of transportation, housing segregation, police brutality, and incarceration are tangled together in the fabric of everyday living in poor neighborhoods. These issues create a formidable knot of many tightly wound strands. Only when the knot itself is undone will the threads come free.

10

Putting Education at the Center

There is no [social] movement.
There needs to be a movement.
—Marion Bolden, District Superintendent,
Newark, NJ Public Schools. June 20, 2004

Why should we put education—and concerned educators—at
the center of efforts to build a unified movement for social justice?
Other analysts might place progressive labor unions, immigrant
rights, activist church groups, or the national living wage campaign at the center. But I believe there are compelling reasons that
urban education—and urban educators—ought to be a fulcrum
of movement building.

A most important reason is the theoretical location of urban
education. Urban schools are at the center of the maelstrom of
constant crises that beset low-income neighborhoods. Education
is an institution whose basic problems are caused by, and whose
basic problems reveal, the other crises in cities: poverty, joblessness and low-wages, and racial and class segregation. Therefore,
a focus on urban education can expose the combined effects of
public policies, and highlight not only poor schools but the entire
nexus of constraints on urban families. A well-informed mobilization centering on education would challenge macroeconomic
federal and regional policies and practices as part of an overall
plan to improve local educational opportunity.

Moreover, even though education is not guaranteed by the U.S. Constitution, it is often construed as a civil right, and can be located ideologically in the long and powerful tradition of civil rights struggle (Moses and Cobb, 2001, p. 1; see also http://www.civilrights.org). This legitimacy may lend movement building through education an acceptance that could affect public attitudes toward new policies regarding the need for jobs, decent wages, and affordable housing.

Further, many people involved in the movements described in the last chapter live in low-income urban areas and have children in underfunded and underachieving city schools. Like other adults, they are often willing to bear substantial hardship without fighting back; but, as parent organizing in cities across America reveals, they will "go to the mat for their kids" (Leigh Dingerson, Center for Community Change, personal communication, Aug. 25, 2004). This willingness to fight for the rights of their children means that putting education at the center may be a good mobilizing tool with which to attract parents' involvement in other issues as well.

Indeed, educators are in an excellent position to build a constituency for economic and educational change in urban communities. Teachers and principals have continual access to parents and urban youth. If they are respectful, caring, hardworking educators, trusted by students and parents, they have a unique opportunity to engage residents and youth in political conversations and activity.

A final reason to center movement building in education is that there is a rich tradition of liberal/left advocacy to build on. I, like many others, entered teaching "to change the world" (Oakes and Lipton, 2002). There are teachers in every city today who teach a critical, thought-provoking curriculum, and who utilize the classroom to discuss issues their students face. Hundreds of scholarly books and articles have been written offering insight and inspiration to teachers who concern themselves with social justice. In addition, there exist widely read progressive publications like *Rethinking Schools*, proactive organizations like National Coalition of Educational Activists and Educators for Social Responsibility, and professional conferences that enrich critical teaching. There is possibility here, and great promise in the work of these educators. We can take this work further in our appropriation of the institution for radical purposes.

For all these reasons, I believe that those of us in education who have social justice as a goal can play a crucial role in movement building for economic and educational rights of the poor. We can do this in our daily lives, as we "cast down our buckets" where we are. We can commit to the radical possibilities in our everyday work in schools, despite the onslaught of institutional mandates. To assist in this effort, the present chapter supplements existing critical pedagogical work with strategies used by community and education organizers.

STUDENT SELF-ESTEEM AND POLITICIZATION

As I noted in Chapter 8, social movement theorists argue that fear, despair, and negative valuations of self can be immobilizing, and may keep social actors who have cause to get involved in political contention from participating. Feelings of efficacy, righteous anger, and strength, on the other hand, are more likely to lead one to activism. A first step in movement building in urban schools, then, is to help students appreciate their own value, intelligence, and potential as political actors.

African American and Latino scholars write tellingly about the fears harbored by many students of color that they fit the stereotypes White society has of them—that they are incapable of high academic achievement, not interested in education, and to blame for their lack of advancement (see Boykin, 2003; Hale, 2001; King, 2002; Perry, 2003; Steele, 2003; Suarez-Orozco, 2002; Valdes, 1996; and Valenzuela, 2001). An important mechanism is that this "stereotype threat" can prevent students' full engagement in academic work, as they fear failure and fulfillment of the stereotype (see in particular Steele, 2003). This is tragic in and of itself. But I want to point out that blaming oneself, rather than locating causes of failure in the wider structure of opportunities, has another consequence: It can also mitigate against a perceived need to change the system.

Theresa Perry argues that in order to undermine ideology and practice of victim blaming, educators need to create a *counter narrative* to the story of failure and low intelligence of students of color. She notes that we could learn from successful all-Black schools in the antebellum South, where teachers emphasized the relation between education and freedom: "Freedom for literacy, and literacy for freedom" (2003, p. 92). Perry exhorts teachers to counter the damaging dominant social narrative by building an intentional classroom community spirit of education for "racial uplift, citizenship and leadership" (p. 93). In order to demonstrate to students that they are capable and worthy, "teachers must explicitly articulate, regularly ritualize, and pass on in formal public events the belief in minority students as scholars of high achievement and as of social value" (pp. 99, 100). A supportive and trusting environment provides "identity security" to students, who are then emotionally more ready to challenge the stereotypical myths (Steele, 2003).

As Lisa Delpit reminds us, however, we must also teach minority students the culture and knowledge held by powerful Whites and the middle and upper classes (Delpit, 1997). They need to understand this coded cultural capital and be able to parse it—just like affluent White students are taught to do (Anyon, 1980, 1981).

A healthy education of this sort would urge minority students toward a stance of *entitlement* regarding the responsibility of governments to provide equal opportunities; and this would encourage them to hold the system accountable. Thus, a politically energizing education for African Americans must explicitly recognize and acknowledge with students that they and their families are *not* free—and that social change is necessary. This is one reason a history of both oppression and resistance is so important. Students who are knowledgeable about dominant forms of power and how this power affects them can better move from self-blame to informed efforts at change. Teachers and administrators who would assist students in this development could begin by working with the community of which the students are a vital part.

WORKING WITH THE COMMUNITY

Teachers, administrators, and other professionals in urban public schools are not usually from the neighborhood. Their social class and often their race differentiate them from students, families, and other residents. In this sense, many of those who work to appropriate the educational institution for social justice are outsiders and bicultural brokers. They can contribute important resources and knowledge to that which students and families already possess. In education organizing across urban America, educators are increasingly playing a brokering, bridging role, as they join with parents and communities to combat policies that oppress.

When educators work with community residents as equals and as change agents to organize for better education, movement building is taking place; and as a not inconsequential outcome, schools typically improve and student achievement increases. Research suggests that there are several reasons for this raised student achievement, including community pressure for more resources and district accountability, increased parental engagement, and improved staff development and pedagogy (Gold, Simon, and Brown, 2002; Henderson and Berla, 1994; Henderson and Mapp, 2002).

I would like to highlight two other causes of the increased achievement. First, education organizing has been shown to lower the rate at which students move from one school to another (mobility), sometimes by as much as 50%. Studies show that in schools where educators work closely with the community as partners in change, parents and students often report that they do not want to leave the school because of their involvement in and satisfaction with the activities (Vail, January 4, 2004, p. 2; Hohn, 2003; Whalen, 2002).

Another reason for increased achievement in schools where parents and educators work together as change agents may be an increase in trust and respect between the parties. Tony Bryk and Barbara Schneider have demonstrated convincingly that trusting relationships in daily interactions in low-income urban schools are correlated with raised achievement over time (2002, pp. 98–99, 120).

Community and parent organizers regularly utilize several strategies that teachers and administrators might incorporate to work for change and build personal relationships and mutual trust. Teachers can involve parents and other residents in one-on-one conversations designed to identify their concerns, can hold meetings in parents' homes where groups of residents address these concerns, and can engage parents, other community members, and educators in "neighborhood walks"—during which participants tour the area around the school and reach a common understanding and vision of what changes are needed (Gold, Simon, and Brown, 2002, p. 22).

School principals who work with the Industrial Areas Foundation say that "an angry parent is an opportunity"—an opening to organize the community for increased accountability of officials and politicians (IAF Principal Claudia Santamaria, Cambridge, MA Conference, February 20, 2004). A major strategy utilized by the IAF that educators could apply is what organizers call "accountability sessions"—meetings to which district and elected officials or candidates for office are invited and asked to give their opinions on important issues. Candidates are asked to respond to yes/no questions, without speeches. Local media are invited, and report on the official and candidate responses, thus providing a public record to which the officials can later be held accountable (Gold and Simon, 2004, p. 2).

Some education organizers also work with parent groups and teachers to monitor district and state programs and policies by carrying out research that identifies discrepancies between stated goals of district, city, or state policies and programs, and the actual experience of students and teachers. These can also be useful as the basis for calling officials to account (for examples, see the Institute for Democracy, Education, and Access at http://www.idea.gseis.ucla.edu/, the National Center for Schools and Communities at http://www.ncscatfordham.org/pages/home. cfm, and the Institute for Education and Social Policy at http:// www.nyu.edu.iesp).

ACQUIRING COMMUNITY ORGANIZING SKILLS

The foregoing strategies provide an introduction to working with parents and communities as partners for change. This section provides suggestions for organizing parents in extended issue campaigns.

Chicago-based Cross City Campaign for Urban School Reform (Cahill, 1999) and the Institute for Education and Social Policy in New York (Zimmer and Mediratta, 2004) have prepared advice (based on many years of organizing experience) that is useful for educators interested in carrying out issue campaigns with community members.

A short summary follows:

1. Choose issues from the bottom up. Issues to pursue should come from parents, students, and other residents. Knock on doors in two-people teams (for example, one parent and one teacher or principal) to identify issues important to the community; and recruit people for home meetings to discuss the issues they feel are important and what to do about them. Visit area congregations to discuss local problems, and develop

relationships with members and clergy. Systematic personal contact and the building of personal relationships are key to successful engagement of residents. Keep parents in forefront.

2. Begin to build a community constituency for long-range reform through immediate, specific, and winnable issues. Frame broad demands like "better schools" more specifically to attract particular constituencies: bilingual programs for Latino parents, and after school job training and placement for parents and high school students. Building a base among parents and community members will provide a force and legitimacy to the demands you will make. Because you also want to develop working relationships with other educators, it may be best to start with a neighborhood issue rather than one that directly targets problems in the school.

3. Locate key school and district personnel who can assist you in gathering data to document the problems you want to address. Work with local community-based organizations to see what system information they already have. Collaborate with them in writing and disseminating a report, if possible.

4. Develop a program of needed changes and present this to authorities. Plan demonstrations and other activities that attempt to obtain concessions, promises, and behavioral responses from those in power in the district and city (I would add that one should attempt coalitions of organizing groups across the city, region, and state).

5. Develop a plan for what to do when people in power ignore you, refer you to others, delay you, or try to placate you. Officials may try to discredit you. Or they may attempt to buy off your leaders, or propose a substitute that does not meet your needs. Some of the strategies you could consider when this happens may be cooperative, like setting up meetings; but some may be confrontational—like pickets, demonstrations, political theater, press conferences, etc.

6. Keep the pressure on administrators and officials by demonstrations and actions of various sorts. A "presence in the streets" is necessary to hold their attention and get results (Zimmer and Mediratta, 2004, p. 3).

I want to emphasize that, whenever possible, link educational issues to community issues regarding jobs, housing, transportation, and investment. Education organizing by itself can improve schools in low-income areas to the point that housing values rise, businesses increasingly invest in the neighborhood, and low-income residents are pushed out by higher rents. This creep of gentrification is occurring on two blocks in Chicago's Logan Square area, in part because of the success of education organizing by LNSA. In response, LSNA has intensified its lobbying at the state level for housing reform (Hohn, 2003; Halsband, 2003). Gentrification resulting from education organizing and improved local schools is a reminder that without other public policy changes (in this case, housing policies to maintain low-income housing or policies providing better-paying jobs), successful school reform in low-income urban neighborhoods can have unfortunate, unintended consequences for residents.

COLLABORATION BETWEEN MAINSTREAM SCHOOL REFORMERS, COMMUNITY GROUPS, AND EDUCATION ORGANIZERS

One way to increase the breadth and depth of school reform is for mainstream school reformers to collaborate with those working to provide resident services and neighborhood development. The following two project descriptions are examples of how vital the synergy could be if curricular and pedagogical reforms were coupled with financial and social support of students outside of school.

In Washington, DC, Othello Poulard and the Center for Community Change created such a system of outside student support. With foundation funding, they provided extensive programs for 8th through 12th graders living in five local housing projects. Poulard and the Public Housing Graduates Demonstration program (PHG) built a system of daily after-school tutoring in each project building. They hired skilled, long-term tutors. Poullard provided emotional support and guidance with trained neighborhood residents serving as "Mighty Moms" or "Mighty Pops," hired as long-term mentors. These mentors kept an eye on the students and helped them with personal problems. "Big Brothers" and "Big Sisters" were provided and offered emotional and academic support. PHG exposed the students to colleges as well as middle-class culture, and trained them to use computers; the program provided computers for the students' homes. PHG offered athletics, and taught the youth how to avoid pregnancy and deal with violence. They provided health care, and financial support. As in middle-class and affluent families, youth were paid an allowance. They received $100 a month in 10th and 11th grade, and $200 a month in 12th grade. To qualify for the allowance they had to participate in almost daily after-school activities, along with weekend college readiness sessions and field trips. They also had to produce journals and detailed time sheets. They lost money every time they did not fulfill requirements (Center for Community Change, 2001, pp. 1–4).

The results of this extensive support system were extremely encouraging. Whereas before the program, only 40% of the public housing students who entered the 8th grade ever graduated from high school, 89.6% of PHG's students graduated by the end of a three-year evaluation (compared to 63% of students who attended the same schools but who were not in the program). PHG participants had a significantly higher grade point average and higher test scores than a control group; 70% of PHG students applied to college or trade school; all were accepted and everyone who applied for financial aid received it. Over three years, only one 12th grader failed to graduate because of pregnancy or incarceration (ibid., p. 5).

The second example is of school reformers linking with community developers to fight gentrification. The LEARN Charter school, serving a low-income population in a community in Chicago, partnered with a local community developer who helped revitalize the neighborhood by building over 1,600 affordable housing units and a major shopping center. Wanting to "keep people in the neighborhood," the developer also became involved in a $6.6 million project to build a major campus for the local public school. As a testament to the increasing strength of the neighborhood, the city decided to invest millions of dollars to rebuild local transportation lines—which would increase residents' access to jobs outside of the community (Halsband, 2003, p. 37).

As important as these connections between school and community can be, educational reform groups do not typically work with community organizations to create or link to programs providing external student and family support. School reformers and community organizers, in fact, rarely talk to each other; they typically operate in different social circles. Most school reform groups are from university, funding, or government arenas, and community organizers are usually from the neighborhood or political activist spheres. There is little communication or cooperation.

Educational reformers (especially equity-seeking groups like New Visions and Bay Area Coalition for Equitable Schools) and education organizers could teach each other important strategies, to the benefit of each. Organizers could teach school reformers about the power of public constituencies, about the power of an inflamed, informed community to demand and obtain programs from governments and school boards. For example, New Visions in New York City, a school reform group that obtained funding from Bill Gates and Soros Foundations to develop new small schools, was unfamiliar with existing community groups and parent organizing in the city. The New York City district had not informed parents in low-income neighborhoods that their high schools were about to be disbanded, and there was considerable community anger and resistance. Wisely, New Visions hired a doctoral student of mine, Madeline Perez (who has extensive experience organizing parents in Oakland, CA, and New York) to facilitate outreach and community meetings with residents in areas where new schools are to be developed. New Visions has also begun to develop relationships with strong faith-based organizations in New York City's neighborhoods. This school reform group may find that the understanding and increased trust that accrues from such overtures will be crucial to the success of the new schools.

We know all too well that over the last few decades, traditional school reform in U.S. cities has shown considerably less success than hoped for. One important reason for disappointing results is that most urban school reforms are not successful in part because the community is not behind them, and often actively mistrusts them. Community organizing can create the political will to implement reforms. Indeed, success would most likely be assured if politicians and education reform groups were to work with community members to come to a consensus as to what changes are needed.

One way to reach this consensus is for school reformers and politicians to create proposals for change on the basis of recommendations made by community research. Such research typically documents inequities in a powerful, personal manner, and highlights inadequate provision for low-income students and schools.

For example, in the mid-1990s, ACORN carried out and published three studies documenting that Black parents were not told about kindergarten gifted programs when they inquired of school personnel, while White parents were. These reports also demonstrated that the vast majority of students in New York City's three competitive high schools came from three White, middle-class districts, and that almost no low-income districts sent students to the special schools (Association of Community Organizations for Reform Now, 1996). These powerful reports could have been the basis for meaningful, community-backed school reform if taken up by mainstream educational groups and politicians.

It is also the case that education organizers have much to learn from school reformers. As political activists, education organizers typically are not trained in education; however, they need to know more about curriculum and pedagogical best practice, how public schools work internally in order to know what classroom reforms to advocate for, and how to work with administrators once they get their attention. Community pressure is not always enough (Mediratta and Fruchter, 2004, p. 4). Moreover, in order to work with school boards, mayors, and state legislatures, community organizers must be knowledgeable about educational research, practice, and jargon.

In order to facilitate exchanges between networks of school reformers and organizers, the Pacific Institute for Community Organizing (PICO), a national network of community-based organizations, held two multiday meetings of 100 educational researchers working on school reform issues and organizers from established community groups (Corbin, 2003, p. 3). The organizers learned from educational researchers about effective education practice, principles and tools for analyzing classrooms and schools, and ways that districts operate internally. Other such meetings need to be organized.

Any effort to create a social movement with potential to affect current policy and practice regarding urban schools and economic access must get concerned actors together, working in concert. Equity-seeking school reform networks and community activists advocating for school and neighborhood improvement are usually on the same side; they should acknowledge their commonalities and collaborate in the interest of increased opportunity and change.

Importantly, politically progressive classroom teachers are central here. They are in a position to work with both kinds of groups as they mentor youth activism.

CLASSROOMS AS MOVEMENT-BUILDING SPACES

Middle and high school teachers, in particular, can make a powerful contribution to movement-building by engaging students in civic activism. Both the civil rights movement and successful youth efforts to reduce the voting age from 21 to 18 (legalized in 1971) demonstrate that activism by young people can make a huge impact on American society. The activities in this section provide teachers with strategies to assist urban youth in moving from self-blame or angry rebellion to well-informed political engagement.

But, you might respond, urban students are not interested in political activity. To that I reply that behavioral resistance to typical methods of teaching does not necessarily transfer to alternative, more appealing methods. Moreover, I believe it is the case that most urban teens *want* an education—a high *quality* education. College readiness is the top priority of urban youth who are involved in organizing. A comprehensive assessment of 49 youth groups in 18 states found that the issues youth most frequently address have to do with education. Most (61%) want college preparation from their high school; the next issue is criminal and juvenile justice (49%), and then economic justice (18%) and immigrant rights (14%). Indeed, programs run by organizations in urban communities that promote teenage activism typically attract youth who are alienated from school. Teachers, then, may not find it difficult to interest students in political projects; and they may find that through such activities, students who are dropping out can be brought back in (Mattie Weiss, 2003; also Wheeler, 2003, available at (http://www.theinnovationcenter.org).

Numerous benefits accrue to youth who work for increased opportunities in their communities. Studies have documented that civic activism by low-income students of color typically fosters teenagers' positive personal development, and improves their academic engagement and, therefore, achievement (see, for example, Benson and Leffert, 1998; Forum for Youth Investment, 2004; Ginwright and James, 2002; Hilley, 2003; Lewis and Charp,

2003; Roth, Brooks-Gunn, and Murray, 1997; and Zeldin and Price, 1995).

There are several other benefits, as well. Organizing urban youth to work with others to improve their schools and neighborhoods gives teenagers *connections,* embedding them in constructive community networks. This connectedness is a worthy alternative to that offered by most street gangs (Hilley, 2003).

In addition, by organizing others to work responsibly for social change, minority youth counter the view that they constitute a social "problem." Teens also are encouraged to understand how the poverty of their families and their peers arises from systemic rather than personal failings. And it provides them with the concrete lesson that they can bring about changes in society, giving them a foundation for pursuing this kind of activity as adults.

A final benefit to working with students on political projects that aim to achieve youth and family rights puts educators and students on the same "team," and increases trust between them, which, as we have seen, has been found to increase academic achievement (Bryk and Schneider, 2002).

An example of teachers organizing students demonstrates several of these positive outcomes. In 1995, youth at Gratz High School in Philadelphia started the first chapter of what became a citywide Student Union (PSU). The original impetus for organizing was students' complaints about inadequate textbooks and dirty bathrooms. When the students asked administrators why there were no new textbooks, they were told it was their fault because "students tear them up." When students complained about the bathrooms, they were told "students mess them up." Students' first reaction was to agree with school administrators that they were themselves to blame. However, with their adviser's help they were encouraged to ask themselves the following questions: "Why didn't they consider it their school and their property? Why did they deface their school as if they didn't respect it or own it? Why didn't they feel comfortable at school?" After years and years in a failing system, the students were frustrated and self-blaming. Their adviser assisted them as they got to work to advocate for improvements in the school.

Since 1995, many changes have resulted from PSU's activism in Philadelphia high schools, including new student governments, creation of school ombudsmen to stop the harassment and abuse by school security officers, a district-level student platform on planned school reforms, a rally of 2,450 students at City Hall, which helped to defeat planned privatization of Philadelphia high schools, new networks of organized students in multiple city schools, and a statewide campaign to increase school funding to the level of nearby affluent suburbs (American Youth Policy Forum, 2002, p. 103).

As shown in research studying the benefits of youth organizing in Los Angeles, many of the Philadelphia students who became involved as activists and leaders had been on the verge of dropping out, but remained in school when it became clear that they had a voice. A number of teachers reported that these new youth leaders became academic "stars." Teachers and administrators reported respect for students who organize (Hayasaki, 2003, May 30, p. 4).

The following classroom activities can develop in students many of the skills utilized by community organizers in their movement-building work. The activities begin with research in the neighborhood, and lead to the development of issue campaigns to bring about new policy.

Mapping Community Assets

Finding and documenting community resources that could be useful for making the neighborhood a better place to live and work is an important first step. The classic source for asset mapping is Kretzman and McNight (1997). These activist-scholars point out that a thorough map of community begins with an inventory of the "gifts, skills and capacities of the community's residents ... few of which are being mobilized for community-building purposes. ... " (p. 5).

In addition to identifying the gifts and skills of individuals, households, and families, student researchers will compile an inventory of formal and informal institutions. These include churches, ethnic and religious associations, tenants groups, political organizations, advocacy and activist groups, among others. Politicians and political parties should be included, as should local branches of corporations, the chambers of commerce, and other interest groups. Mapping should also include businesses such as banks and restaurants, and public institutions such as libraries, parks, community colleges, and other types of schools; and nonprofit institutions such as hospitals and social service agencies. Physical characteristics, as well, are part of a community's assets—vacant and occupied land and buildings and other infrastructure such as streets and transportation systems.

Students travel in pairs or small groups to catalogue these assets. Then, the class as a whole raises important questions: How might the assets held by individuals, associations, institutions, and the physical environment be connected to each other? How might the community begin to imagine and institute new uses for these strengths? Mapping the environment means looking carefully at the political and cultural resources that can be mobilized to solve the particular problems faced by the community.

Teachers could focus the mapping on locating "opportunity structures" within the neighborhoods. These comprise an interrelated and interdependent web of systems (such as education and health care), markets (such as employment), and structures (such as transportation) (Powell, 2003, p. 1). Maps can be made of the locations of jobs and day care providers, the availability of transportation, and access to a variety of social services. Maps can reveal key demographic information such as poverty rates, race/ethnicity, age, language, employment status and rates, the cost of land development, who develops it, levels of criminal activity, school achievement levels, the price of housing, and the location of any job-training services. The spatial depiction of these systems provides a useful tool for students and teachers who want to identify impediments and assets related to solving problems that people in the community face (http://www1.umn.edu/irp/programs/oppmapping.html, pp. 1–3; see also http://www.communityyouthmapping.org/Youth/).

Power Analysis

Asset mapping is not an end in itself. It should be the basis for a "power analysis." Such an inquiry assesses the causes and solutions of current problems—whether these extend from the neighborhood and city to the metropolitan or federal levels.

A power analysis identifies a problem faced by students or other community residents and asks the following kinds of questions: Who is impacted by the problem? Who makes the decisions that affect the immediate situation? Who makes decisions that determine what those individuals or groups do and say? What kinds of informal influence or formal power do they have? What kinds of informal influence or formal power do community residents have over the situation? Whose interests are affected by decisions that have been made? Who are potential allies in an attempt to solve the problem?

To the asset map a group has made will be added specific individuals and organizations that could work together to solve the problem. When the map shows assets that are actual people with names, work, interests, and relationships to others, it becomes a *power* map (Bass and Boyte, http://www.cpn.org/tools/manuals/Youth/rules5.html, p. 6). As described below, the power map becomes a basis for political campaigns to improve the community.

After teachers and students map and analyze community issues and resources, they share their analysis with other community residents, to begin to build a base of support. They could share it with school and government officials, as well, in initial attempts to obtain improvements.

In general, students' research can be disseminated in any number of ways. For example, in Oakland, CA, a group of teachers, students, parents, and community members prepared a report that compared state spending on education (proposed cuts) and prisons (proposed increases). After confronting officials with their data, they put their report on the World Wide Web (http://www.may8.org; see also Bloom and Chajet, 2004, and http://www.whatkidscando.org/studentresearch).

Upon completion and sharing of research reports, students and teachers should not end their involvement in the issue. Indeed, they are just beginning. Movement building requires an ongoing relationship with the community. Students should continue their engagement with community issues by using their research to assist in developing issue campaigns with residents.

Developing an Issue Campaign

As I will describe in more detail below, activities teachers utilize to develop skills of political analysis and activism in students typically involve well-regarded pedagogical strategies. The process involves techniques of *problem-solving, data collection and analysis, and reflective action* (taking some action to learn about and communicate findings through writing, graphing, etc., and reflection on what has been accomplished in order to continue) (Youth Organizing, 2002, p. 10).

One key to developing an issue campaign with students is to break the overall task—say, a campaign for immigrant students' rights—into manageable pieces, and to obtain a student to take responsibility for each piece (Bobo, Kendall, and Max, 2001, p. 124). It is also a good idea to set up structures like committees with student leaders, to facilitate many youth having chances to develop skills. Have older teens teach younger ones. In some cases, college students help high school students plan issue campaigns (see http://www.publicachievement.org, in Schutz, 2004, p. 19).

In all organizing work with youth, make use of their own cultural modes. For example, my niece, who is a youth organizer in Oakland, CA, took a group of her students to a concert by the Hip Hop group Dead Prez, a politically progressive group (that does not utilize egregious sexual imagery). She reported that attending the concert was an "incredible political education" for the students because they related so well to the medium in which the political message was delivered (Yolanda Anyon, personal communication, February 25, 2004).

The following description of how to develop an issue campaign with students is taken from an interview with experienced youth organizer Kim McGillicuddy, one of 13 founding members of Youth Force in the Bronx. McGillicuddy now works with Youth Justice Coalition to Free LA. This group was formed to deal with what they call "California's undeclared war on youth," and is led by youth aged 8–24 who have been arrested, detained, incarcerated, or put on probation or parole.

McGillicuddy advises that a successful campaign with young people has a number of steps: It starts with identifying the students' constituency. Who do they feel they represent—immigrant students, families, all community residents? The youth then conduct a strength and needs assessment, identifying and mapping constituents' needs, skills, resources, and vision for change. Youth can develop, conduct, transcribe and assess surveys, interviews, and personal stories. Next, youth scan existing research in relation to concerns or issues identified in their community. They obtain demographic data, Geographic Information Systems (GIS) data, and evaluate research done by others. Often, their research requires investigating primary sources, something few schools teach or expect from urban students.

With the teacher's help, the class analyzes the data that surfaced from research activities—looking at everything they have found.

They use their asset and power maps. Through discussion, they decide whether they want to act on the concerns. If so, they begin to identify the specific issues the class will take on, and determine short- and long-term organizing goals. The goals may be worded as a youth platform or campaign demands.

Base-building is the next step. Youth determine what sort of organizational structure will best serve that goal. Base-building means creating and implementing recruitment and communications strategies in the neighborhood, creating informational curriculum, debating whether decisions will be made by majority rule or consensus, facilitating meetings, and recording and communicating decisions.

After researching the problems, identifying the issues, sketching out demands, and beginning to educate the larger community, youth now further develop the campaign's power analysis, including researching targets of the campaign. They ask who is the person or group that has the power to give us what we want and what do they believe. How have they voted in the past? From where do they gain their strength—financial resources, advice, support? Where are they vulnerable? Who are their allies, and ours—and who can we move? The answers to these questions, combined with the other analyses already done, should produce a short-term strategy, a long-term vision, and a final list of demands—all of which should be used to measure the group's success.

Teacher and students then develop their campaign action plan—including selecting tactics that will most effectively impact targets. Full debate is necessary to choose tactics, and the pros and cons of everything from taking one's demands to the target with an appointment, if possible, to civil disobedience, if necessary. Invite community-based organizations to become involved. If the issue has to do with education, invite both education organizers and school reform groups to join in.

Students may want to support their platform, or those of others with which they agree, by demonstrating publicly. The following anecdote is of a demonstration in Chicago in which teachers and students took part, although they did not plan it together. The target of the demonstration was the board of education, and the point was to publicize how the U.S. military budget supporting the war in Iraq was depleting money available for public education. The report conveys the excitement and potentiality of public political action with students.

The May 12 Rally at the Board of Education was excellent! Starting a little before 4PM, we teachers had about 35 spirited picketers in front of the Board, with our bullhorn, chants, and "bake sale" as we tried to raise enough funds to "compete" with the military budget. . . . We carried home-made "Victim of the War" posters of blown-up [disguised] photos of students . . . with words written below each such as "Dropped Out," "Homeless," and "Inmate."

THEN, the youth came charging down the street, 50 or so Youth First! members who had been rallying at [offices] up the street to demand equitable funding for education. They joined in with us (eclipsing us for a moment with their energy!), but we recovered and marched together for a while, waking up the Chicago Public Schools brass upstairs . . . in a loud and angry (but peaceful) picket.

[Significantly], this was teachers and students together, supporting each other. What was striking was that so many students commented how much they appreciated that the teachers were there, and that the teachers were so impressed by the Youth First! activists. (http://www.teachersforjustice.org/rallyupdate.php)

During demonstrations and other activities that develop a political campaign, youth build strong communications and media skills. The details, responsibilities, and opportunities are enormous—organizing community forums and school assemblies, educating residents door-to-door, writing stories or creating media such as newsletters, CDs, and videos, educating and cooperating with journalists, organizing meetings with city officials, testifying at public hearings, and integrating cultural expression into outreach (through open microphones, spoken word, slap tags, etc.); all these develop student communication skills.

Even the rallies and marches that the class may undertake involve lots of duties: deciding when, where, and why to rally; getting speakers and helping them to develop effective messages; setting up a sound system; getting permits from police, sanitation, and the parks department; handling security and negotiating with police; training people as marshals, coordinating legal support if there's a chance of arrests; and coming up with chants and posters.

The group is writing constantly: producing research reports, newsletters, Web sites, curricula, petitions, education guides, scripts for popular education skits, grant proposals, speeches, dialogue for videos. And because the youth are writing for a public audience, they are more concerned about getting it right; they are learning about the power of words well expressed. They learn math: They produce grant proposals and budgets, order supplies, fill vouchers, make requisitions, create estimates, enter data, crunch numbers, and prepare for reviews of their figures. And they practice critical thinking—learning to ask hard questions, make connections, and gather evidence. They learn tolerance for others while discovering and coming to appreciate their own identity and agency.

McGillicuddy notes that many urban youth "struggle with the oppression that they have suffered as well as hurt that they have caused others, and gain the understanding that their own liberation is dependent on the liberation of other people." She reports that "many of the youth who become involved in organizing are not just leaders, but local heroes." Few other "youth development" activities offer young people the chance, for example, to help rid their community of a toxic waste site or a corrupt police chief. "What better way for youth to overcome the isolation and anger they feel in communities where too many people clutch their bags and cross the street to avoid [them]!" (Interview of Kim McGillicuddy by What Kids Can Do staff, May 2003, available at http://www.whatkidscando.org/feataure stories/YOinterview.html; for other resources, see http://www. innercitystruggle.org and Goldwasser, 2004).

Most teacher-led activities will take place at the local level, in schools and communities. As Chapter 8 suggested for the civil rights movement, without *local* organizing there would not have been a mass movement. And so it is today. However, it is also true that without connection to citywide, regional, state, and national momentum and groups, many of the "wins" resulting from neighborhood organizing can be easily overruled by local officials. So, collaborations are crucial.

The next section asks education organizers to take the lead in pulling together not only progressive teachers and youth, but all others engaged in struggles for economic and educational opportunities in U.S. cities.

REGIONAL AND NATIONAL CONVENINGS

The education-organizing field is an increasing presence in U.S. cities. Sizeable numbers of groups are active, and many are part of regional and national networks like ACORN, IAF, and PICO. Yet the effect is not national. We need to find a way to use these networks to challenge policies and practices at the metropolitan and federal levels—since these are where underlying determinants of urban poverty and poor schools originate. Because of the intricate connections between urban education and these deep structural issues, moving to scale in educational organizing and reform will require collaboration with the already existing political movements for economic rights I have described—for jobs and housing, a living wage, and progressive union and immigrant concerns.

It is also the case, moreover, that collaboration with educational campaigns would strengthen these other movements. The Immigrant Freedom Ride in 2003, for example, was an exciting collaboration of progressive labor unions and other immigrant groups; and the tour across the country may have an impact on federal legislation regarding immigrants' wages and civil rights. But the campaign could have been considerably stronger if children of immigrants and their exclusion from an education that allows them access to jobs with decent wages had been linked.

How do various campaigns obtain unity of purpose and coordination of activity—these important prerequisites to a large-scale movement? One lesson of the civil rights movement is that "umbrella groups" are essential to coordinating those involved in local activism, and in bringing the struggle to regional and national scale. Currently, there are groups in each of the existing movements that function somewhat like proto-umbrella groups. As noted in chapter 9, the entities are called intermediaries and offer a wide range of supports to local organizations. They assist with research, policy and organizational development, training, legal assistance, alliance-building, and fundraising (Moore and Sandler, 2003, p. 4).

Among the intermediaries in the education organizing field that I believe have the capacity to join together to call others to the table are the New York University Institute for Education and Social Policy, the Washington, DC-based Center for Change, the Bay Area Coalition for Equitable Schools in California, Chicago's Cross City Campaign for Urban School Reform, and Southern Echo. Intermediaries that would be able to attract youth groups include LISTEN, the Movement Strategy Center, Youth Action, and The School of Unity and Liberation (HoSang, James, and Chow-Wang, 2004, p. 8).

As a new organization representing the youth and education movements, this umbrella group could reach out to unions, living wage proponents, and other community organizations, and begin a process of conversing that could lead to national conferences— the goal of which would be to discuss a national movement to unify the various campaigns under one banner with a common agenda.

Long ago, community organizing icon Saul Alinsky pioneered the use of conventions to establish unified agendas and strategies among groups (Shaw, 2001, p. 258), and such an approach seems crucial to the creation of synergy and impact today.

CONCLUSION

When I was a child, I listened to my parents' stories of organizing in factories and of being harassed by the police. One time, a sympathetic news reporter agreed to announce falsely that my father had been killed to waylay police efforts to find him. Growing up in the household of former 1930s radicals, I got my politics with mother's milk. Over the years, it seemed natural to get involved in social movements to right the wrongs I saw around me.

But most Americans do not have family lessons in organizing and political transgression. The majority of people who come to politically left beliefs have had to acquire them on their own, many through exposure to movements already in progress. Moreover, the ideological battering most people receive as school children, the mangled news they imbibe from newspapers and television, as well as racial and class distortions pouring from the media, make the chances of developing a faith in transgressive equity politics relatively small.

We can change the odds. My argumentation has aimed at a more radical consciousness in readers, particularly regarding poverty and urban education. I tried to develop an analysis that would explain how macroeconomic and regional policies and practices create conditions in urban areas that cannot be overcome by school reform alone. Several chapters delineated how public policies regarding jobs, wages, taxes, public transportation, housing, and investment prevent even equity-seeking educational policies from having a sustained positive effect and consequence. I argued, as a result, that public policies regarding economic and social equity ought to be among the strategies we propose in our attempts to increase urban school quality.

Following this explication of the power of macroeconomic policies and regional arrangements to trump urban school reform and conventional educational prescriptions, I presented an array of theoretically and historically derived processes whose enactment could involve increasing numbers of Americans in movement building.

Finally, I offered suggestions specifically for urban educators, whose position in city schools yields a strategic theoretical and practical advantage in organizing youth and communities. I took the liberty of suggesting that education organizers should instigate national unity by calling the various smaller social movements together.

The consequence of my overall analysis for the ways we conceptualize education policy is fundamental. Governments and corporate elites depend on education to deflect the pain inflicted by the economy. That cover does not work any longer for larger percentages of the population. The discovery by urban students as early as the fifth grade (Anyon, 1997) that education does not "matter" has a chilling effect on motivation; rightly contextualized, however, this realization can ultimately be politically activating.

To be adequate to the task of relevant prescription—as well as political mobilization—education policy cannot remain closeted in schools, classrooms, and educational bureaucracies. It must join the world of communities, families, and students; it must advocate for them and emerge from their urgent realities. Policies for which we press would therefore take on a larger focus: Education funding reform would include the companion need for financing of neighborhood jobs and decent wages. Small schools would be created as an important part of the coordinated efforts at neighborhood revitalization for low-income residents. Lawsuits to racially integrate districts will acknowledge housing segregation as fundamental and target legal challenges appropriately.

Policies that set the standards schools must meet would identify the money, materials, teachers, courses, and neighborhood needs that should be fulfilled in order to provide opportunities to learn at high levels. Educational accountability would be conceived as a public undertaking, centrally involving families, communities, and students, in consultation with district and government officials. And college would be understood as a continuation of government's financial responsibility for public education, thus providing a material basis for motivation and effort on the part of K-12 students and educators.

In this new paradigm of educational policy, the political potential of pedagogy and curriculum would be realized. Critical pedagogy would take to the streets, offices, and courtrooms where social justice struggles play out. Curriculum could build toward and from these experiences. Vocational offerings in high school would link to living wage campaigns and employers who support them. And educational research would not be judged by its ostensible scientific objectivity, but at least in part by its ability to spark political consciousness and change—its "catalytic validity" (Lather, 1991).

In this approach to school reform, "policy alignment" does not refer to the fit between education mandates issued by various levels of government and bureaucracy. The fit we seek is between neighborhood, family, and student needs and the potential of education policies to contribute to their fulfillment.

This reorientation of education policy is unabashedly radical, and brings me to a final point. Whether one is born to radicalism or acquires it along the way, the premises on which it rests affirm the deeply rooted connections and disjunctures between democracy and capitalism. A radical frame provides the understanding that, for example, economic exclusion and educational underachievement flow fundamentally from systemic causes, even in the face of what appears to be democratic process and individual failure. And a radical analysis points toward concrete, long-lasting solutions.

In 1967, at the height of the Vietnam War, Martin Luther King, Jr. argued that civil rights, poverty, and war are all part of the same problem. He preached that Americans need to fight these as part of the same struggle. But, he said, in order to do that we must "recapture the revolutionary spirit" of freedom and equality which defines true democracy.

If those of us who are angry about injustice can recapture this revolutionary spirit of democracy, and if we can act on it together, then we may be able to create a force powerful enough to produce economic justice and real, long-term school reform in America's cities.

Bibliography

Allard, Scott W. (2001, September). *Place, race and work: The dynamics of welfare reform in metropolitan Detroit*. Brookings Center on Urban and Metropolitan Policy. Washington, DC: Brookings Institution.

Alloway, Kristen, and Gebeloff, Robert. (2002, February 17). New Jersey's rising property tax dilemma. *The Star-Ledger.*

American Youth Policy Forum. (1997). *Some things do make a difference for youth: A compendium of evaluations of youth programs and practices*. Washington, DC.

American Youth Policy Forum. (2002, May 17). *Youth action for educational change: A Forum Brief*. Washington, DC.

Aminzade, Ron, Goldstone, Jack, and Perry, Elizabeth. (2001). Leadership dynamics and the dynamics of contention. In Ron Aminzade (Ed.), *Silence and voice in contentious politics* (pp. 126–154). Cambridge, MA: Cambridge University Press.

Anders, Gideon. (2002, June). *False hope: A critical assessment of HOPE VI public housing redevelopment program*. Oakland, CA: National Housing Law Project with the Poverty & Race Research Action Council in Washington, DC.

Anyon, Jean. (1980). Social class and the hidden curriculum of work. *Journal of Education, 162*(1), 7–92.

Anyon, Jean. (1981). Social class and school knowledge. *Curriculum Inquiry, 11*(1), 3–42.

Anyon, Jean. (1994a). Teacher development and reform in an inner city school. *Teachers College Record, 96*(1), 14–31.

Anyon, Jean . (1994b). The retreat of Marxism and socialist feminism: Postmodern and poststructural theories in education. *Curriculum Inquiry, 24*(2), 115–134.

Anyon, Jean. (1995a). Race, social class, and educational reform in an inner city school. *Teachers College Record, 97*(1), 69–94.

Anyon, Jean. (1995b). Inner city school reform: Toward useful theory. *Urban Education, 30*(1), 56–70.

Anyon, Jean. (1995c). Educational reform, theoretical categories, and the urban context. *Access: Critical perspectives on culture and policy studies in education* (New Zealand), *14*(1), 1–11.

Anyon, Jean. (1997). *Ghetto schooling: A political economy of urban educational reform*. New York: Teachers College Press.

Apple, Michael. (2001). *Educating the 'right' way: Markets, standards, God, and inequality*. New York: RoutledgeFalmer.

Applebaum, Eileen. (2000). *What explains employment developments in the U.S.?* Economic Policy Institute Briefing Paper. Washington, DC: Economic Policy Institute.

Araiza, Olivia E. (2002). *Bridging research and education organizing: Can we strengthen our combined power?* San Francisco: Justice Matters Institute.

Archer, Jeff. (2002, January 9). Group cites needy but high-performing schools. *Education Week*.

Ayres, William, Jean Ann Hunt, and Theresa Quin (Eds). (1998). *Teaching for social justice: A democracy and education reader*. New York: New Press.

Association of Community Organizations for Reform Now (1996). *Secret apartheid III: Follow up to failure*. New York.

Banchero, Stephanie, and Olszewski, Lori. (2000, August 28). 19,000 kids seek new schools. *The Chicago Tribune*.

Bankston, Carl and Caldas, Stephen. (1996). Majority African American schools and social injustice: The influence of *de facto* segregation on academic achievement. *Social Forces, 75*, 535–552.

Barnes, William, and Ledebur, Larry. (1998). *The new regional economies: The U.S. Common Market and the global economy*. London: Sage.

Baron, Harold. (1982). The demand for black labor: Historical notes on the political economy of racism. *Radical America, 5*(2), 1–46. Cited in McAdam 1982 (p. 88).

Bass, Melissa, and Boyte, Harry. 1995). *Making the rules: A public achievement guidebook for young people who intend to make a difference*. Waltham, MA: The Center for Democracy and Citizenship.

Bates, Beth. (2001). *Pullman porters and the rise of protest politics in black America, 1925–1945*. Chapel Hill: University of North Carolina Press.

Beam, John, Eskenazi, Mike, and Kamber, Tom. (2002). *Unlocking the schoolhouse door: The community struggle for a say in our children's education*. New York: National Center for Schools and Communities at Fordham University.

Bennett, Larry, and Reed Jr., Adolph. (2000). The complexities of a public housing community. In Stephen Steinberg (Ed.), *Race and ethnicity in the United States: Issues and debates* (pp. 127–134). Malden, MA: Blackwell Publications.

Benson, Peter and Leffert, Nancy. (1998). Beyond the 'village' rhetoric: Creating healthy communities for children and adolescents. *Journal of Applied Developmental Sciences, 2,* 138–159.

Berkshire, Jennifer. (2003, February 20). What happens to charities when foundations support trendy issues—and abandon yesterday's hot topics? *The Chronicle of Philanthropy.*

Bernadett, Proctor, and Dalaker, Joseph. (2002). *Poverty in the United States: 2001.* Current Population Reports, P60–219. U.S. Census Bureau. U.S. Government Printing Office. Washington, DC.

Bernstein, Jared. (2003). *The living wage movement: Pointing the way toward the high road.* Washington, DC: Economic Policy Institute.

Bernstein, Jared, Brockt, Chauna, and Apade-Aguilar, Mattie. (2000). *How much is enough? Basic family budget for working families.* Washington, DC: Economic Policy Institute.

Bernstein, Jared, Hartmann, Heidi, and Schmitt, John. (1999, September 16). *The minimum wage increase: A working woman's issue.* Issue Brief #133. Washington, DC: Economic Policy Institute and the Institute for Women's Policy Research.

Berube, Alan. *(*2003, January). *Rewarding work through the tax code: The power and potential of the Earned Income Tax Credit.* Center on Urban and Metropolitan Policy. Washington, DC: Brookings Institution.

Berube, Alan and Frey, William. (2002, August). *A decade of mixed blessings: Urban and suburban poverty in Census 2000.* Washington, DC: Brookings Institution.

Bigelow, Bill and Peterson, Bob (eds.). (2002). *Rethinking globalization: Teaching for justice in an unjust world.* Milwaukee, WI: Rethinking Schools.

Billingsley, Andrew. (2002). *Mighty like a river: The black church and social reform.* New York: Oxford University Press.

Blank, Martin, Mellaville, Atella, and Shah, Bela. (2003). *Making the difference: Research and practice in community schools.* Washington, DC: Coalition for Community Schools.

Blank, Martin, Brand, Betsy, Deich, Sharon, Kazis, Richard, Politz, Bonnie, and Trippe, Steve. (2003). *Local intermediary organizations: Connecting the dots for children, youth, and families.* Washington, DC: Institute for Educational Leadership.

Bloom, Janice. (2005). (Mis)reading social class in the journey towards college: Youth development in urban America. *Teachers College Record* (in press).

Bloom, Janice, and Chajet, Lori. (2003). Urban students tackle research on inequality: What you thought we didn't know. *Rethinking Schools.* Vol. 18, 1 (Fall): 31–32.

Bobo, Kim, Kendall, Jackie, and Max, Steve. (2001). *Organizing for social change: Midwest Academy manual for activists.* Santa Ana, CA: Seven Locks Press.

Bolger, Kerry, and Patterson, Charlotte. (1995). Psychosocial adjustment among children experiencing persistent and intermittent family economic hardship. *Child Development, 66,* 1107–1129.

Boo, Katherine. (2003, August 18). The marriage cure: Promoting wedlock in the projects. *The New Yorker.*

Bos, Johannes, Huston, Aletha, Duncan, Greg, Brock, Tom, and McLoyd, Vonnie. (1996). *New hope for people with low incomes: Two-year results of a program to reduce poverty and reform welfare.* New York: Manpower Development Research Corporation.

Bound, John, and Dresser, Laura. (1999). The erosion of the relative earnings of young African American women during the 1980s. In Irene Browne (Ed.), *Latinas and African American women at work.* New York: Russell Sage. Cited in Moss and Tilly 2001 (p. 6).

Bound, John, and Freeman, Richard. (1992). What went wrong? The erosion of relative earnings and employment for blacks. *Quarterly Journal of Economics, 107*(1), 201–232.

Boushey, Heather, Brocht, Chauna, Gunderson, Betheny, and Bernstein, Jared. (2001). *Hardships in America: The real story of working families.* Washington, DC: Economic Policy Institute.

Bowles, Jonathan. (2003, April 15). *Think tank: NYC's six closest suburbs gained 39,000 jobs over the past year while the city lost 58,000 jobs.* New York: Center for an Urban Future.

Boyd, Todd. (2002). *The new H.N.I.C.: The death of civil rights and the reign of hip hop.* New York: New York University Press.

Bracey, Gerald. (1997). The truth about America's schools: The Bracey reports, 1991–97. Bloomington, IN: Phi Delta Kappa Educational Foundation.

Bradford, Calvin and Associates, Inc. (2002, May). Risk or race? Racial disparities and the sub-prime refinance market. Washington, DC: The Center for Community Change.

Bradley, Robert. (1984). One hundred seventy-four children: A study of the relation between the home environment and early cognitive development in the first 5 years. In Allen Gottfried (Ed.), *The home environment and early cognitive development* (pp. 5–56). Orlando, FL: Academic Press.

Brooks-Gunn, Jeanne, Duncan, Greg, Leventhal, Tama, and Aber, Lawrence. (1997). Lessons learned and future directions for research on the neighborhoods in which children live. In Jeanne Brooks-Gunn, Greg Duncan, and Lawrence Aber (Eds.). *Neighborhood poverty, Volume 1: Contexts and consequences for children* (pp. 279–98). New York: Russell Sage.

Bryk, Anthony S., and Schneider, Barbara. (2002). *Trust in schools: A core resource for improvement.* New York: Russell Sage.

Burtless, Gary. (1995). Employment prospects of welfare recipients. In Demetra Smith Nightingale and Robert Havemann (Eds.), *The work alternative: Welfare reform and the realities of the job market.* Washington, DC: Urban Institute. Quoted by Lafer 2002 (p. 5).

Byron, Joan, Exeter, Hillary, and Mediratta, Kavitha. (2001, July/August). School facilities provide an entry point for community organizers. *Sheltorforce Online.* http://www.nhi.org/online issues/118ByronExterMediratta.html.

Cahill, Michele. (1999). *Community organizing for school reformers: Train the trainers manual.* Chicago, IL: Cross City Campaign for Urban School Reform.

Candovan, Candy, and Candovan, Guy. (1983). We shall overcome: An American freedom song. *Talkin' Union.*

Capelli, Peter. (1995). Is the 'skills gap' really about attitudes? *California Management Review, 37*(4), 18–24.

Cappelli, Peter. (1996). Technology and skill requirements: Implications for establishment of wage structures. In Philip Moss and Chris Tilly (Eds.), Earnings Inequality: Special Issue of the *New England Economic Review.* (May/June). Cited in Moss and Tilly 2001 (p. 47).

Carson, Clayborn. (2001). *In struggle: SNCC and the black awakening of the 1960s.* Fourth Printing. Cambridge: Harvard University Press.

Case, Anne, Lubotsky, Darren, and Paxson, Christina. Economic status and health in childhood. *Poverty Research News, 5,* 5. Available at http://www.wws.princeton.edu/~chw.

Caspi, Avshalom, Wright, Bradley, Moffit, Entner and Silva, Terrie. (1998). Early failure in the labor market: Childhood and adolescent predictors of unemployment in the transition to adulthood. *American Sociological Review, 63*(3), 424–451.

Castells, Manuel. (2000). *End of millennium: The information age: Economy, society and culture.* Vol. III. Oxford, UK: Blackwell Publishers.

Cauthen, Nancy and Lu, Hsien-Hen. (2001, August). *Living on the edge: Employment alone is not enough for America's low-income children and families.* Research Brief No. 1, Mailman School of Public Health, National Center for Children in Poverty. New York: Columbia University Press.

Center for Community Change (2001, May). *Saved by an education: A successful model for dramatically increasing high school graduation rates in low income neighborhoods.* Washington, DC.

Center for Community Change. (1998, June–July). *Organizing, 10,* 1.

Chafe, William, Gavins, Raymond, and Korstad, Robert. (2001). *Remembering Jim Crow: African Americans tell about life in the segregated South.* New York: The New Press.

Champernowne, David and Cowell, Frank (1999). *Economic inequality and income distribution.* Cambridge, UK: Cambridge University Press.

Chapman, Jeff. (2003, June 11). *States move on minimum wage: Federal inaction forces states to raise wage floor.* Washington, DC: Economic Policy Institute.

Chen, Don, and Jakowitsch, Nancy. (2000). *Transportation reform and smart growth: A nation at the tipping point.* Surface Transportation Policy Project in Collaboration with the Funders' Network For Smart Growth and Livable Communities.

Cherry, Robert and Rodgers, William. (2000). *Prosperity for all? The economic boom and African Americans.* New York: Russell Sage.

Chicago Institute on Urban Poverty. (1997). *Does privatization pay?* Chicago, IL.

Citizens for Tax Justice. (2002, March 15). *Corporate tax payments near record low this year.* Washington, DC.

Citizens for Tax Justice. (2002, April 17). *Surge in Corporate tax welfare drives corporate tax payments down to near record low.* Washington DC.

Citro, Constance, and Robert, Michael (Eds.). (1995). *Measuring poverty: A new approach.* Washington, DC: National Academy Press.

Clemetson, Lynette. (2003, September 2). Census shows ranks of poor rose in 2002 by 1.3 million. *New York Times.*

Coleman, James. (1993). *Equality and achievement in education* (Reprint ed.). Boulder, CO: Westview Press.

Collaborative Communications Group. (2003). *New relationships with schools: Organizations that build community by connecting with schools.* Washington, DC.

Collier-Thomas, Bette, and Franklin, V.P. (2001). *Sisters in the struggle: African American women in the civil rights-black power movement.* New York: New York University Press.

Community Affairs Department, Federal Reserve Bank of Kansas City. (2002, Summer). CDCs at the crossroads? *Community Affairs, 10,* 1.

Conon, David. (1995). *Black Moses: The story of Marcus Garvey and the universal Negro improvement association.* Madison: University of Wisconsin Press.

Consortium on Chicago School Research. (1996). *Charting reform in Chicago: The students speak.* Chicago.

Cooran, Mary, Heflin, Colleen, and Reyes, Belinda. (1999). Latino women in the U.S.: The economic progress of Mexican and Puerto Rican women. In Irene Browne (Ed.), *Latinas and African American women at work.* New York: Russell Sage.

Corbin, Gene. (2003). *Overcoming obstacles to school reform: A report on the 2002 Organizing for Educational Excellence Institute.* Philadelphia, PA: Temple University Center for Public Policy and the Eastern Pennsylvania Organizing Project Research for Democracy.

Costello, Jane, Compton, Scott, Keeler, Gordon, and Angold, Adrian. (2003, October 15). Relationships between poverty and psychopathology: A natural experiment. *Journal of the American Medical Association, 290*(15), 2023–2029.

Council of the Great City Schools. (2003). *Beating the odds III.* Washington, DC.

Danziger, Sheldon and Gottschalk, Peter. (1995). *America unequal.* Cambridge, MA: Harvard University Press.

Darder, Antonia, Torres, Rodolpho, and Baltodano, Marta. (2002). *The Critical Pedagogy Reader.* New York: RoutledgeFalmer.

Darling-Hammond, Linda. (2001). *The right to learn: A blueprint for creating schools that work.* San Francisco: Jossey-Bass.

Davis, Mike. (1993). Who killed L.A.? The war against the cities. *Crossroads, 32*, 2–19.

Dawkins, Casey. (2004). Recent evidence on the continuing causes of black-white residential segregation. *Journal of Urban Affairs. 26*(3), 379–400.

Delpit, Lisa. (1997). *Other people's children: Cultural conflict in the classroom.* New York: New Press.

Department of Labor (2002). *Occupation projections to 2010.* Washington, DC.

Dillon, Sam. (2003, April 30). Report finds number of black children in deep poverty rising. *New York Times.*

Dimitriadis, Greg. (2001). *Performing identity/performing culture: Hip hop as text, pedagogy, and lived practice.* New York: Peter Lang.

Downs, Anthony. (1994) *New visions for metropolitan America.* Washington, DC: Brookings Institution.

Downs, Anthony. (1999). Comment on Kenneth T. Rosen and Ted Dienstfrey, The economics of housing services in low-income neighborhoods. In Ronald Ferguson and William Dickens (Eds.), *Urban problems and community development* (pp. 463–469). Washington, DC: Brookings Institution.

Dreier, Peter. (1999). Comment. In Ronald Ferguson and William Dickens (Eds.), *Urban problems and community development* (pp. 178–187). Washington, DC: Brookings Institution.

Dreier, Peter. (2000, Summer). Why America's workers can't pay the rent. *Dissent,* 38–44.

Dreier, Peter, Swanstrom, Todd, and Mollenkopf, John. (2001). *Place matters: Metropolitics for the 21st century.* Lawrence: University Press of Kansas.

Dumas, Michael, and Anyon, Jean. (2005). Toward a critical approach to educational policy implementation: Implications for the (battle)field. In Meredith Honig (Ed.), *Defining the field of policy implementation.* Albany: State University of New York Press.

Duncan, Greg, and Brooks-Gunn, Jeanne (Eds.). (1997). *Consequences of growing up poor.* New York: Russell Sage.

Duncan, Greg, Brooks-Gunn, Jeanne, and Klebanov, Pamela. (1994). Economic deprivation and early childhood development. *Child Development, 65*, 296–318.

Economic Policy Institute. (1999, September 30). *Income picture.* Washington, DC.

Economic Policy Institute. (2000, February 17). *Entry level workers face lower wages.* Washington, DC.

Economic Policy Institute. (2002). *Minimum wage issue guide.* Washington, DC.

Economic Policy Institute. (2002, July 24). *Economic snapshots.* Washington, DC.

Economic Policy Institute. (2002, August 7). *Decline in job openings fuels unemployment.* Washington, DC.

Economic Policy Institute. (2004, July*). EPI issue guide: Minimum wage. Washington*, DC.

Economic Policy Institute. (2004, July 19). *Higher minimum wage most helps low-earning households.* Washington, DC.

Economic Policy Institute. (2004, July 21). *Jobs in the future: No boom in the need for college graduates.* Washington, DC.

Edelman, Marion Wright. (2002, July). *Child watch: The shame of child poverty in the richest land on earth.* Washington, DC: The Children's Defense Fund.

Education Trust. (2001, March). *The funding gap: Low-income and minority students receive fewer dollars.* Washington, DC.

Education Trust. (2004a). *Trends in student aid.* Washington, DC.

Education Trust. (2004b). *A matter of degrees: Improving graduation rates in four-year colleges and universities.* Washington, DC.

Education Trust. (2004c). *The funding gap 2004: Many states still shortchange low-income and minority students.* Washington, DC.

Edwards, Ditra, and Carlson, Neil. (2003, September 4). Rekindling the movement: 40 years after the dream. *Tom Pain—Common Sense: A Public Interest Journal.*

Ehrenreich, Barbara. (2001). *Nickel and dimed: On (not) getting by in America.* NewYork: Henry Holt, Owl Books.

Eisenhower Foundation. (1998). *Background report.* Washington DC.

Entwistle, Doris. (1985). The role of schools in sustaining early childhood program benefits. *Future of Children, 5*(3), 133–144.

Entwistle, Doris, and Alexander, Karl. (1997). *Children, schools, and inequality.* Boulder, CO: Westview Press.

Fairclough, Adam. (1995). *Race and democracy: The civil rights struggle in Louisiana, 1915–1972.* Athens: University of Georgia Press.

Fairclough, Adam. (2001). *Better day coming: Blacks and equality, 1890–2000.* New York: Penguin.

Ferguson, Ronald, and Dickens, William. (1999). *Urban Problems and Community Development.* Washington DC: Brookings Institution.

FINE Forum e-Newsletter. (2003 Fall). *Program spotlight: Preparing teachers for urban schools.* Issue 7 (pp. 1–3).

Fine, Michelle, Ed. (1994). *Chartering urban school reform: Reflections on public high schools in the midst of change.* New York: Teachers College Press.

Fisher, Peter. (2002). Tax incentives and the disappearing state corporate income tax. *Tax Analysts Reference.* (http://www.tax.org/ bestofstate.)

Fisher, Robert. (1997). *Let the people decide: Neighborhood organizing in America* (Updated ed.). Farmington Hills, MI: Twayne Publishers.

Fleetwood, Chad, and Shelley, Kristina. (2000, Fall).The outlook for college graduates, 1998–2008: A balancing act. *Occupational Outlook Quarterly, 44,* 3. Cited in Lafer 2002 (p. 61).

Fleischer, Wendy. (2001). *Extending ladders: Findings from the Annie E. Casey Foundation's jobs initiative.* Baltimore, MD: Annie E. Casey Foundation.

Forman, Murray. (2002). *The 'hood comes first: Race, space, and place in rap and hip-hop.* Middletown, CT: Wesleyan University Press.

The Forum for Youth Investment. (2004, May). *From youth activities to youth action.* Vol. 2, Issue 2.

The Foundation Center. (2003). Highlights of the Foundation Center's Foundation Yearbook. *Foundations today series.* New York: Foundation Center.

Fossey, Richard, and Bateman, Mark. (1998). *Condemning students to debt: College loans and public policy.* New York: Teachers College Press.

Freedman, Samuel. (1994). *Upon this rock: The miracles of a black church.* New York: HarperCollins.

Freeman, Richard. (1991). The earnings and employment of disadvantaged young men over the business cycle. In Christopher Jencks and Paul E. Peterson (Eds.), *The urban underclass.* Washington, DC: Brookings Institution (pp. 103–120).

Freeman, Richard. (1976). *Black elite: The new market for highly educated black Americans.* Report prepared for the Carnegie Commission on Higher education. New York: McGraw-Hill. Cited in Moss and Tilly 2001 (p. 35).

Freire, Paulo and Macedo, Donaldo. (1987). *Literacy: Reading the word and the world.* New York: Bergin and Garvey.

Frenkel, Stephen J., Korczynski, Maretk, Shire, Karen, and Tam, May. (1999). *On the front line: Organization of work in the information economy.* Ithaca, NY: Cornell University Press.

Galbraith, James K. (1998). *Created unequal: The crisis in American pay.* Twentieth Century Fund Book. New York: The Free Press, Simon and Schuster.

Gamson, William. (1990). *The strategy of social protest.* Belmont, CA: Wadsworth.

Gamson, William. (1992). *Talking politics.* Cambridge: Cambridge University Press.

Ganz, Marshall. (2000). Resources and resourcefulness: Strategic capacity in the unionization of California agriculture, 1959–1966. *American Journal of Sociology, 105*(4), 1003–1062.

Gecan, Michael. (2002). *Going public: An inside story of disrupting politics as usual.* Boston: Beacon.

Genovese, Eugene. (1976). *Roll, Jordan roll: The world the slaves made.* New York: Vintage Books.

Giles, Hollyce. (1998). ERIC Digest: Parent engagement as a school reform strategy. 135, EDO-UD-98-5. New York: ERIC Clearinghouse on Urban Education, 1–9.

Ginwright, Shawn. (2003, February). Youth organizing: Expanding possibilities for youth development. Occasional Papers Series on Youth Organzing, No. 3. New York: Funders' Collaborative on Youth Organizing.

Ginwright, Shawn, and Taj, James. (2002, Winter). From assets to agents of change: Social justice, organizing, and youth development. *New Directions for Youth Development, 96,* 27–46.

Giroux, Henry. (1997). *Pedagogy and the politics of hope.* New York: Westview.

Gittel, Marilyn. (1980). *Limits to participation: The decline of community organization and citizen participation.* New York: Sage.

Gittell, Marilyn. (1997, January). *Building civic capacity: Best CDC practices.* Howard Samuels State Management and Policy Center. Graduate School and University Center of the City University of New York.

Gittell, Marilyn and Gardner, Sarah. (1997). *The capacity of grassroots groups in the environmental movement.* Howard Samuels State Management and Policy Center. Graduate School and University Center of the City University of New York.

Gittell, Marilyn, Gross, Jill, and Newman, Kathe. (1994). *Race and gender in neighborhood development organizations.* Howard Samuels State Management and Policy Center. Graduate School and University Center of the City University of New York.

Gittell, Marilyn, Newman, Kathe and Ortega, Isolda. (1997). *Building civic capacity: Best CDC practices.* The Howard Samuels State Management and Policy Center, Graduate School and University Center of the City University of New York.

Gittell, Marilyn, Newman, Kathe, Ortega-Bustamante, Isolda, and Pierre-Louis, François. (1999). *The politics of community development: CDCs and social capital.* Howard Samuels State Management and Policy Center. New York: Graduate School and University Center of the City University of New York.

Gittell, Ross and Vidal, Avis. (1998). *Community organizing: Building social capital as a development strategy.* New York: Sage.

Gladieux, Lawrence. (2004). "Low-Income Students and the Affordability of Higher Education." In Richard Kahlenberg (Ed.) *America's untapped resource: Low-income students in higher education.* New York: The Century Foundation Press, 17–58.

Glaser, Edward, Kahn, Mattew, and Chu, Chenghuan. (2001, May). *Job sprawl: Employment location in U.S. metropolitan areas: Center on Urban and Metropolitan Policy.* Washington DC: Brookings Institution.

Goering, John and Feins, Judith (Eds.). (2003). *Choosing a better life? Evaluating the Moving to Opportunity social experiment.* Washington, DC: The Urban Institute Press.

Gold, Eva, and Simon, Elaine. (2004, January 14). Public accountability. *Education Week.*

Gold, Eva, Simon, Elaine, and Brown, Chris. (2002). *Strong neighborhoods and strong schools: The indicators project on education organizing.* Chicago: Cross City Campaign for Urban School Reform.

Goldwasser, Matthew. (2004). *A guide to facilitating action research for youth.* Philadelphia. PA: Research for Action.

Gottschalk, Peter. (1997, Spring). Inequality, income growth, and mobility: The basic facts. *Journal of Economic Perspectives, 11*(2), 21–40. Cited in Lafer 2002 (p. 60).

Gross, Jane. (2003, August 29). Free tutoring reaches only fraction of students. *New York Times.*

Greene, Jay P. (2001, November). *High school graduation rates in the United States.* Washington, DC and NY: Black Alliance for Educational Options and the Manhattan Institute.

Hahn, Steven. (2003). *A nation under our feet: Black political struggles in the rural South from slavery to the great migration.* Cambridge, MA: Harvard University Press.

Hale, Janice E. (2001). *Learning while black: Creating educational excellence for African American children.* Baltimore, MD: Johns Hopkins University Press.

Halsband, Robin. (2003 Nov/Dec). Charter schools benefit Community economic development. *Journal of Housing and Community Development* (pp. 34–38).

Haney, Walter. (2003, September 23). *Attrition of students from New York schools.* Invited Testimony at Public Hearing "Regents Learning Standards and High School Graduation Requirements" before the New York Senate Standing Committee on Education, Senate Hearing Room, 250 Broadway, 19th fl., New York, New York.

Harrington, Michael. (1963). *The other America: Poverty in the United States.* Baltimore, MD: Penguin.

Hayasaki, Erika. (2003, May 30). Schools see an awakening of student activism. *Los Angeles Times.*

Henderson, Anne, and Mapp, Karen. (2002). *A new wave of evidence: The impact of school, family, and community connections on student achievement.* Austin, TX: National Center for Family and Community Connections with Schools, Southwest Educational Development Laboratory.

Henderson, Anne, and Berla, Nancy. (1994). *A new generation of evidence: The family is critical to student achievement.* Washington, DC: Center for Law and Education.

Hilley, John. (2004, May). Teens taking action in Tennessee. *Forum Focus* 2 (2), 7–8. (http://www.forumforyouthinvestment.org).

Hohn, Joshua. (2003*). Chicago neighborhood discovers delicate balance between success of community schools and resident displacement.* Available at http://www.communityschools.org.

Holusha, John. (2003, March 16). New vitality around old railroad stations. *New York Times.*

Holzer, Harry. (1996). *What employers want: Job prospects for less educated workers.* New York: Russell Sage.

Holzer, Harry, and Stoll, Michael. (2001). *Employers and welfare recipients: The effects of welfare reform in the workplace.* San Francisco: Public Policy Institute of California.

Holzer, Harry, and Stoll, Michael. (2003). *The employment rate of adult African American men.* Washington DC: The Urban Institute.

hooks, bell. (1994). *Teaching to transgress: Education as the practice of freedom.* New York: Routledge.

Hosang, Daniel. (2003). Youth and community organizing today. *Occasional Papers Series on Youth Organizing No. 2.* The Funders Collaborative on Youth Organizing.

Hosang, Daniel, James, Taj, and Chow-Wang, Mamie. (2004, February 9).*Youth organizing for public education reform: A preliminary scan and assessment.* Available from the Mosaic and Movement Strategy Center, Edward W. Hazen Foundation, and Surdna Foundation.

Houser, Robert, Brown, Brett, and Prosser, William. (1998). *Indicators of children's well-being.* New York: Russell Sage.

Hout, Michael. (1988). More universalism, less structural mobility: The American occupational structure in the 1980s. *American Journal of Sociology, 93*(3), 1358–1400.

Howell, David. (1994, Summer). The skills myth. *American Prospect, 18,* 84–87.

Howell, David, Houston, Ellen, and Milberg, William. (1999). *Demand shifts and earnings inequality: Wage and hours growth by occupation in the U.S., 1970–97.* CEPA Working Paper No. 6. New York: Center for Economic Policy Analysis at The New School University.

Howell, David, and Wolff, Edward. (1991). Trends in the growth and distribution of skills in the U.S. workplace, 1960–1985. *Industrial and Labor Relations Review, 44*(3), 486–502.

Hungerford, Thomas. (1993). U.S. income mobility in the seventies and eighties. *Review of Income and Wealth, 39* (4) 401–417.

Huston, Aletha, Duncan, Greg, Bos, Robert, McLoyd, Johannes, and Crosby, Danielle. (2001). Work-based anti-poverty programs for parents can enhance the school performance and social behavior of children. *Child Development, 72,* 318.

Huston, Aletha, Miller, Cynthia, Richburg-Hayes, Lashawn, Duncan, Greg, and Eldred, Carolyn (2001). *Summary Report, New Hope for families and children: Five-year results of a program to reduce poverty and reform welfare.* New York: Manpower Development Research Corporation.

Ingels, Steven J. (2002). *Coming of Age in the 1990s: The 8th Grade Class of 1988 12 Years Later.* U.S. Department of Education, National Center for Education Statistics.

The Initiative for a Competitive Inner City. (1998). *The business case for pursuing retail opportunities in the inner city.* Boston: Boston Consulting Group.

Jackson, Kenneth. (2000). Gentleman's agreement: Discrimination in metropolitan America. In Bruce Katz (Ed.), *Reflections on Regionalism.* Washington, DC: Brookings Institution (pp. 185–217).

Jackson, Kenneth. (1995). *Crabgrass frontier: The suburbanization of the United States.* New York: Oxford University Press.

Jacobson, Dennis. (2003). *Doing justice: Congregations and community organizing.* Minneapolis, MN: Fortress Press.

Jargowsky, Paul. (1998). *Poverty and place: Ghettos, barrios, and the American city.* New York: Russell Sage.

Jehl, Jeanne, Blank, Martin, and McCloud, Barbara. (2001, July). *Education and community building: Connecting two worlds.* Washington, DC: Institute for Educational Leadership.

Jencks, Christopher. (1991). Is the American underclass growing? In Christopher Jencks and Paul E. Peterson (Eds.), *The urban underclass.* Washington DC: Brookings Institution (pp. 28–102).

Jencks, Christopher and Phillips, Meredith. (1998). *The black/white test score gap.* Washington DC: Brookings Institution.

Jenkins, J.C. and Halcli, A. (1999), Grassrooting the system? The development and impact of social movement philanthropy, 1953–1990. In E.C. Lagemann, *Philanthropic foundations: New scholarship, New Possibilities.* Bloomington: Indiana University Press, (pp. 229–256); cited in Robert O. Bothwell 2000. Foundation Funding of Grassroots Organizations. Available at http:// comm-org.utoledo. edu/papers2001/bothwell.htm).

Johnson, Michael, Ladd, Helen, and Ludwig, Jens. (2002). The benefits and costs of residential mobility programs. *Housing Studies, 17*(1), 125–138.

Johnson, Nolas, Carey, Kevin Mazerov, Michael, McNichol, Elizabeth, Tenny, Daniel, and Zahradnik, Robert. (2002, February 26). *State income tax burdens on low-income families in 2001.* Washington, DC: Center on Budget and Policy Priorities.

Johnston, David Cay. (1999, September 5). Gap between rich and poor found substantially wider. *New York Times.*

Joint Center for Housing Studies of Harvard University. (2001). *State of the nation's housing.* Cambridge, MA.

Kahlenberg, Richard. (2003). *All together now: Creating middle-class schools through public school choice.* Washington DC: Brookings Institution.

Kanter, Rosabeth Moss. (1995). *World class: Thriving locally in the world economy.* New York: Simon and Schuster.

Kanter, Rosabeth Moss. (2000). Business coalitions as a force for regionalism. In Bruce Katz (Ed.), *Reflections on regionalism* (pp. 154–181). Washington DC: Brookings Institution.

Katz, Bruce. (2003, January 9). American cities: Federal neglect imperils their rise. *Baltimore Sun.*

Katz, Bruce. (2000, Summer). Enough of the small stuff: Toward a new urban agenda. *Brookings Review, 18*(3), 4–9. Washington DC: Brookings Institution.

Katz, Bruce, Puentes, Robert, and Bernstein, Scott. (2003, March). *TES-21 reauthorization: Getting transportation right for metropolitan America.* Washington, DC: Brookings Institution.

Kelley, Robin (1990). *Hammer and hoe: Alabama communists during the great depression.* Chapel Hill: University of North Carolina Press.

Kelley, Robin (1994). *Race rebels: Culture, politics, and the black working class.* New York: Free Press.

Kelley, Robin (2002, Fall). Building bridges: The challenge of organized labor in communities of color. *New Labor Forum*, 42–58.

King, Joyce (1995, Rev. Ed.). *Black mothers to sons: Juxtaposing African American literature with social practice.* New York: Peter Lang.

Kingsley, Thomas, and Petit, Kathryn. (2003, May). *Concentrated poverty: A change in course.* Neighborhood Change in Urban America Series. Washington DC: The Urban Institute.

Kirp, David, Dwyer, John, and Rosenthal, Larry. (1995). *Our town: Race, housing, and the soul of suburbia.* New Brunswick, NJ: Rutgers University Press.

Kitwana, Bakari. (2002). *The hip hop generation: Young blacks and the crisis in African American culture.* New York: Basic Civitas Books.

Klandermans, Bert, Kriesi, Hanspeter, and Tarrow, Sidney (Eds.). (1988). *From structure to action: Social movement participation across cultures.* Greenwich, CT: JAI.

Klein, Kim. (2000, November). Why are big-money philanthropies afraid of community organizers? *City Limits,* (1), (p. 2).

Klerman, Lorraine. (1991; 2003 Repr. ed.). The health of poor children: Problems and programs. In Aletha Huston (Ed.), *Children and Poverty: Child development and public policy.* New York: Cambridge University Press.

Kohn, Alphie. Only For My Kid. *Phi Delta Kappan*, 79, 568–577.

Kozol, Jonathan. (1992). *Savage inequalities: Children in America's schools.* St. Helens, OR: Perennial Press.

Kretzmann, John, and McNight, John. (1997). *Building communities from the inside out: A path toward finding and mobilizing a community's assets.* Chicago: Acta Publications.

Ladd, Helen (1994). Fiscal Impacts of local population growth: A conceptual and empirical analysis. *Regional Science and Urban Economics, 24,* 661–686.

Ladd, Helen, and Ludwig, Jens. (2003). The effects of Moving to Opportunity on educational opportunities in Baltimore. In John Goering and Judith Feins (Eds.), *Choosing a better life?* (pp. 117–152). Washington, DC: The Urban Institute.

Ladd, Helen, and Yinger, John. (1989). *America's ailing cities: Fiscal health and the design of urban policy.* Baltimore, MD: Johns Hopkins University Press.

Lafer, Gordon. (2002). *The job training charade.* Ithaca, NY: Cornell University Press.

Lardner, James. (1998, March 16). Too old to write code? *U.S. News and World Report.* Cited in Lafer 2002 (p. 250).

Lareau, Annette. (2003). *Unequal childhoods: Class, race, and family life.* Berkeley, CA: University of California Press.

Lather, Patti. (1991). *Getting Smart: Research and pedagogy with/in the postmodern.* New York: Routledge.

Ledebur, Larry, and Barnes, William (1993). *All in it together.* Washington, DC: National League of Cities.

Lee, Valerie, Burkam, David (2002). *Inequality at the starting gate: Social background and achievement at kindergarten entry.* Washington, DC: Educational Policy Institute.

Lemann, Nicholas. (1994, January 9). The myth of community development. *New York Times Magazine,* 27–31, 50, 54, 60.

Leonhardt, David. (2003, April 26, 2003). As companies reduce costs, pay is falling top to bottom. *New York Times.*

LeRoy, Greg. (2001). *Talking to union leaders about smart growth.* Sprawl Watch Clearinghouse Monograph Series. Available at http://www.sprawlwatch.orgnewsletterdec01.html

LeRoy, Greg, and Slocam, Tyson. (1999). *Economic development in Minnesota: High subsidies, low wages, absent standards.* Washington, DC: Good Jobs First.

Letwin, Daniel. (1997). *The challenge of interracial unionism: Alabama coal miners, 1878–1921.* Chapel Hill: University of North Carolina Press.

Levin-Waldman, Oren. (1999). *Do institutions affect the wage structure? Right-to-work laws, unionization, and the minimum wage.* Public Policy Brief No. 57. Annondale-on-Hudson, NY: Jerome Levy Economics Institute of Bard College.

Levy, Frank. (1999). *The new dollars and dreams: American incomes and economic change.* New York: Russell Sage.

Levy, Frank and Murnane, Richard. (1994). Skills, demography, and the economy: Is there a mismatch? In Lewis Solomon and Alec Levinson (Eds.). *Labor markets, employment policy, and job creation.* Boulder: Westview. Cited in Lafer 2002 (p. 52).

Lewin, Tamar and Medina, Jennifer. (2003, July 31). To cut failure rate, schools shed students. *New York Times.*

Lewis, Charles and Allison, Bill, and the Center for Public Integrity. (2001). *Cheating of America: How tax avoidance and evasion by the super rich are costing the country billions—and what you can do about it.* New York: William Morrow.

Lewis-Charp, Heather. (2003). *Extending the reach of youth development through civic activism: Outcomes of the youth leadership for development initiative.* San Francisco, CA: Social Policy Research Associates.

Lewis, Earl. (1957, Summer). The Negro voter in Mississippi. *Journal of Negro Education, 26,* 329–350. Cited in Payne, 1995 (p. 18).

Lipman, Pauline. (2003). *High stakes education: Inequality, globalization, and urban school reform.* New York: RoutledgeFalmer.

Lipman, Pauline. (1998). *Race, class, and power in school restructuring.* Albany: State University of New York Press.

LISTEN. (2004, March). *From the frontlines: Youth organizers speak.* Washington, DC.

Logan, John. (2001, December 18). *Ethnic diversity grows, neighborhood integration lags behind.* Report by the Lewis Mumford Center for Comparative Urban and Regional Research. Albany: State University of New York.

Logan, John. (2002, July 24). *The suburban advantage: New census data show unyielding city-suburb economic gap.* Report by the Lewis Mumford Center for Comparative Urban and Regional Research. Albany: State University of New York.

Logan, John. (2002, October 15). *Separate and unequal: The neighborhood gap for blacks and Hispanics in metropolitan America.* Report by the Lewis Mumford Center for Comparative Urban and Regional Research. Albany: State University of New York.

Logan Square Neighborhood Association. (2004). *Literacy ambassadors: A parent-to-parent approach to building literacy.* Chicago, IL.

Logan Square Neighborhood Association. (no date). *A Community-centered, holistic approach to immigrant families in public schools.* Chicago, IL.

Lopez, Elena. (2003). Transforming schools through community organizing: A research review. FINE Family Network, Harvard University Graduate School of Education.

Loprest, Pamela. (1999). *Families who left welfare: Who are they and how are they doing?* Washington, DC: Urban Institute.

Lu, Hsien-Hen. (2003). *Low-income children in the United States.* National Center for Children in Poverty. New York: Columbia University, Mailman School of Public Health.

Luce, Robert, and Luce, Stephanie. (1998). *The living wage: Building a fair economy.* New York: The New Press.

Ludwig, Jens, Duncan, Greg, and Ladd, Helen. (2003). The effects of Moving to Opportunity on children and parents in Baltimore. In John Goering and Judith D. Feins (Eds.), Choosing a better life? (pp. 153–177). Washington, DC: The Urban Institute.

Marable, Manning and Mullings, Leith. (2000). *Let nobody turn us around: Voices of resistance, reform, and renewal—an African American anthology.* New York: Rowman and Littlefield.

Marris, Peter, and Rein, Martin. (1973). *Dilemmas of social reform: Poverty and community action in the United States.* Chicago: Aldive.

Marx, Gary, and Useem, Bert. (1971). Majority involvement in minority movements. *Journal of Social Issues, 27,* 81–104.

Massey, Douglas, and Denton, Nancy. (1993). *American apartheid: Segregation and the making of the American underclass.* Cambridge, MA: Harvard University Press.

Masten, Ann and Coatsworth, Douglas. (1995). The structure and coherence of competence from childhood through adolescence. *Child Development, 66,* 1635–1659.

Mauer, Marc. (2003a, May/June). Some punishments begin after prison. *The Crisis,* 16–17.

Mauer, Marc. (2003b). *Invisible punishment: The collateral consequences of mass imprisonment.* New York: New Press.

Mayer, Susan. (1997). What money can't buy: Family income and children's life chances. Cambridge, MA: Harvard University Press.

McAdam, Doug. *Freedom summer.* (1988). New York: Oxford University Press.

McAdam, Doug. (1982, 2nd ed., 1999). *Political process and the development of black insurgency, 1930–1970.* Chicago: University of Chicago Press.

McArdle, Nancy, and Stuart, Guy. (2002). *Race, place, and segregation: Redrawing the color line in our nation's metros.* Research Report to the Civil Rights Project, Harvard University.

McGirr, Lisa. *Suburban warriers: The origins of the new American Right.* Princeton, NJ: Princeton University Press.

McGrath, Daniel, and Kuriloff, Peter. (1999, November). They're going to tear down the doors of this place: Upper-middle-class parent school involvement and the educational opportunities of other people's children. *Educational Policy, 13*(5), 603–629.

McKenzie, Evan. (1994). *Privatopia: Homeowner associations and the rise of residential private government.* New Haven, CT: Yale University Press.

McLaren, Peter. (1997). *Revolutionary multiculturalism: Pedagogies of dissent for the new millennium.* New York: Westview.

McLaren, Peter. (2002). *Life in schools: An introduction to critical pedagogy in the foundations of education* (4th ed.). Boston: Allyn and Bacon.

McLoyd, Vonnie. (1998a). Children in poverty: Development, public policy, and practice. In I. Siegel and K. Renninger (Eds.), *Handbook of child psychology,* 4th Ed. New York: Wiley.

McLoyd, Vonnie (1998b). Socioeconomic disadvantage and child development. *American Psychologist, 53,* 185–204.

McLoyd, Vonnie and Jayartne, Toby. (1994). Unemployment and work interruption among African-American single mothers: Effects on parenting and adolescent socio-emotional functioning. *Child Development, 65,* 562–589.

McNair Barnett, Bernice. (1993, June). Invisible Southern black women leaders in the civil rights movement: The triple constraints of gender, race, and class. *Gender and Society, 7,* 162–182.

McRoberts, Omar. (2003). *Streets of glory: Church and community in a black urban neighborhood.* Chicago, IL: University of Chicago Press.

Medina, Jennifer, and Lewin, Tamar. (2003, August 1). High school under scrutiny for giving up on its students. *New York Times.*

Mediratta, Kavitha, and Karp, Jessica. (2003). *Parent power and urban school reform: The story of Mothers on the Move.* New York: Institute for Education and Social Policy.

Mediratta, Kavitha, Fruchter, Norm, and Lewis, Anne. (2002). *Organizing for school reform: How communities are finding their voices and reclaiming their public schools.* New York: Institute for Education and Social Policy.

Mediratta, Kavitha, and Fruchter, Norm. (2003, January 17). *From school governance to community accountability: Building relationships that make schools work.* New York: New York University Institute for Education and Social Policy, and the Drum Major Institute for Public Policy.

Medoff, Peter, and Sklar, Holly. (1994). *Streets of hope: The fall and rise of an urban neighborhood.* Boston: South End Press.

Melucci, Alberto. (1999). *Challenging codes: Collective action in the information age.* Cambridge, UK: Cambridge University Press.

Meyer, Rachel. (2002, August 17). *Collective action and the making of interracial solidarity.* Paper presented at the American Sociological Association Annual Meeting, Chicago, IL.

Michaloupolos, Charles, Tattri, Doug, Miller, Cynthia, and Robins, Philip. (2002). *Making work pay: Final report on the self-sufficiency project for long-term welfare recipients.* New York: Manpower Development Research Corporation.

Mickelson, Roslyn (2001a). Subverting *Swann:* First- and second-generation segregation in the Charlotte-Mecklenburg schools. *American Educational Research Journal, 38,* 215–252.

Mickelson, Roslyn (2001b). How middle school segregation contributes to the race gap in academic achievement. Paper presented at the meeting of the American Sociological Association. Anaheim, CA.

Mickelson, Roslyn (2003, April). The academic consequences of desegregation and segregation: Evidence from the Charlotte-Mecklenburg schools. *North Carolina Law Review, 81*(4), 120–165.

Mishel, Lawrence, Bernstein, Jared, and Boushey, Heather. (2003). *The state of working America: 2002/2003.* Ithaca, NY: Cornell University Press.

Mishel, Lawrence, Bernstein, Jared, Schmitt, John. (2001). *The state of working America: 2000/2001.* Ithaca, NY: Cornell University Press.

Mishel, Lawrence, and Teixeira, Ruy. (1991). *The myth of the coming labor shortage: Jobs, skills, and incomes of America's workforce 2000.* Washington, DC: Economic Policy Institute.

Monthly Labor Review. (2002, October). Editor's comments. 10, 121. Quoted in Lafer, 2002 (p. 47).

Moore, Rosanna, and Sandler, Susan. (2003). *Supporting the education organizing movement: An exchange between intermediaries.* San Francisco: Justice Matters Institute.

Morris, Aldon. (1984). *The origins of the civil rights movement: Black communities organizing for change.* New York: Free Press.

Morris, Aldon, and Staggenborg, Suzanne. (2002). Leadership in social movements. (available at http://www.cas.northwestern.edu/sociology/faculty/files/leadershipessay.pdf).

Morris, Pamela, Huston, Aletha, Duncan, Greg, Crosby, Daniell, and Bos, Johannes. *How welfare and work policies affect children: A synthesis of research.* Washington, DC: Manpower Development Research Corporation.

Morris, Pamela, and Michalopoulos, Charles. (2000). *The self-sufficiency project at 36 months: Effects on children of a program that increased parental employment and income.* Ottawa: Social Research and Demonstration Corporation.

Moss, Philip, and Tilly, Chris. (2001) *Stories employers tell: Race, skill, and hiring in America.* New York: Russell Sage.

Moses, Bob. (2001, May/June). Quality education is a civil rights issue. *Harvard Education Letter* (pp. 1–2).

Moses, Robert, and Charles Cob, Jr. (2002). *Radical equations: Civil rights from Mississippi to the Algebra Project.* Boston: Beacon Press.

Moss, Philip, and Tilly, Chris. (1996). 'Soft' skills and race: An investigation of Black men's employment problems. *Work and Occupations, 23*(3), 252–276. In Moss and Tilly 2001, (p.47).

Murnane, Richard, and Levy, Frank. (1996). *Teaching the new basic skills: Principles for educating children to thrive in a changing economy.* New York: Free Press.

Nash, Gary. (1979). *Urban crucible: Social change, political consciousness, and the origins of the American revolution.* Cambridge, MA: Harvard University Press.

National Center for Educational Statistics. *The condition of education: An annual snapshot, 2003.* Washington, DC: U.S. Department of Education.

National Center for Children in Poverty. (2004, May). *Low-income children in the United States (2004).* New York: Mailman School of Public Health, Columbia University.

National Center for Public Policy and Higher Education. (2002). *Losing ground: A national status report on the affordability of American higher education.* San Jose: CA: National Center.

National Jobs For All Coalition. (2002, October). *Uncommon sense.* New York City: (http://www.njfac.org.

Natriello, Gary, McDill, Edward, and Pallas, Aaron. (1990). *Schooling disadvantaged children: Racing against catastrophe.* New York: Teachers College Press.

Newman, Katherine. (2000). *No shame in my game: The working poor in the inner city.* New York: Vintage.

Newman, Katherine. (1993). *Declining fortunes: The withering of the American dream.* New York: Basic Books.

Newman, Maria. (August 2, 2002). Trenton court upholds law on moderately priced housing. *New York Times.*

Niedt, Christopher. (1999). *The effects of the living wage in Baltimore.* Working Paper No. 119. Washington, DC: Economic Policy Institute.

Nolan, Kathleen, and Anyon, Jean. Learning to do time: Willis' cultural reproduction model in an era of deindustrialization, globalization, and the mass incarceration of people of color. In Nadine Dolby and Greg Dimitriadis (with P. Willis) (Eds.). (2004). *Learning to labor in new times.* New York: RoutledgeFalmer.

Oakes, Jeannie. (1990). *Multiplying inequalities: The effects of race, social class, and tracking on opportunities to learn mathematics and science.* Santa Monica, CA: RAND.

Oakes, Jeannie, and Lipton, Martin (2002). *Teaching to change the world.* New York: McGraw-Hill.

O'Connor, Anahad. (2003, October 21). Rise in income improves children's behavior. *New York Times.*

Offner, Paul, and Holzer, Harry. (2002, April). *Left behind in the labor market: Recent employment trends among young black men.* Center on Urban and Metropolitan Policy. Washington, DC: Brookings Institution.

Olson, Lynne. (2001). *Freedom's daughters: The unsung heroines of the civil rights movement from 1830 to 1970.* New York: Scribner.

Orfield, Gary. (1996, April). Metropolitan school desegregation: Impacts on metropolitan society. *Minnesota Law Review, 80*(4), 825–873.

Orfield, Gary. (2001). *Schools more separate: Consequences of a decade of re-segregation.* Cambridge, MA: The Civil Rights Project at Harvard University.

Orfield, Gary. (2001, April 3). Housing segregation: Causes, effects, possible cures. Cambridge, MA: The Civil Rights Project, Harvard University. National Press Club.

Orfield, Myron. (1997). *Metropolitics: A regional agenda for community and stability.* Washington, DC: Brookings Institution.

Orfield, Myron. (2002). *American metropolitics: The new suburban reality.* Washington, D.C: Brookings Institution.

Orr, Marion. (1999). *Black social capital: The politics of school reform in Baltimore, 1986–1998.* Lawrence: University Press of Kansas.

Osterman, Paul. (1995). Skill, training, and work organization in American establishments. *Industrial Relations, 34,* 2–13.

Osterman, Paul. (2001). *Working in America: A blueprint for the new labor market.* Cambridge, MA: MIT Press.

Osterman, Paul, and Lautsch, Brenda. (1996). *Project quest: A report to the Ford Foundation.* Cambridge, MA: MIT Sloan School of Management. Cited in Moss and Tilly 2001 (p. 259).

Pack, Janet Rothenberg. (1995). *Poverty and urban expenditures.* Philadelphia: University of Pennsylvania, Wharton Real Estate Center. Cited in Orfield 2002 (p. 27).

Parson, Gail. (2003). *Outside the law: How lenders dodge community reinvestment.* Milwaukee, WI: National Training and Information Center.

Pawasarat, John, and Quinn, Lois. (2001). *Exposing urban legends: The real purchasing power of central city neighborhoods.* Washington, DC: Brookings Institution.

Payne, Charles. (1995). *I've got the light of freedom: The organizing tradition and the Mississippi freedom struggle.* Berkeley: University of California Press.

Perry, Theresa. (2003). *Young, gifted, and black: Promoting high achievement among African-American students.* New York: Beacon.

Persky, Joseph, and Kurban, Haydar. (2001, November). *Do federal funds better support cities or Suburbs?* Washington, DC: Brookings Institution Center on Urban and Metropolitan Policy.

Pettit, Kathryn, Kingsley, Tomas, and J. Coulton, Claudia. (2003, May 30). Neighborhoods and health: Building evidence for local policy. Washington, DC: The Urban Institute.

Philadelphia Children Achieving Challenge. (1996). *A first-year evaluation report.* Philadelphia, PA.

Phillips, Kevin. (1990). *The politics of rich and poor: Wealth and the American electorate in the Reagan aftermath.* New York: Random House.

Phillips, Kevin. (2002). *Wealth and democracy: A political history of the American rich.* New York: Broadway Books, Random House.

Phillips, Meredith, Brooks-Gunn, Jeanne, Greg, Duncan, Klebanov, Pamela, and Crane, Jonathan. (1998). Family background, parenting practices, and the black/white test score gap. In Christopher Jencks and Meredith Phillips (Eds.), *The black/white test score gap.* Washington, DC: Brookings. (pp. 103–145).

Phillips, Meredith, Crouse, James, and Ralph, John. (1998). Does the black/white test score gap widen after children enter school? In Christopher Jencks and Meredith Phillips. *The black/white test score gap,* (pp. 229–272). Washington, DC: Brookings Institution.

Pigeon, Marc-Andre, and Wray, Randall. (1999). Down and out in the U.S.: An inside look at the out of the labor force population. Public Policy Brief No. 54. Annandale-on-Hudson, NY: The Jerome Levy Economics Institute of Bard College.

Pittman, Karen. (2002, July). Balancing the equation: Communities supporting youth, youth supporting communities. In J.P. Terry (Ed.), *CYD Anthology 2002.* (pp. 19–24). Sudbury, MA: Institute for Just Communities.

Pittman, Karen. (2003, May). Youth consultants for change. *Youth Today, 12*(5), 43.

Piven, Frances Fox, and Cloward, Richard. (1979). *Poor people's movements: Why they succeed, how they fail.* New York: Vintage Books, 1979.

Policy Link. (2000). *Community based initiatives promoting regional equity: Profiles of innovative programs from across the country.* Oakland, CA.

Policy Link. (2001). *Dealing with neighborhood change.* Oakland, CA.

Policy Link. (2002). *Regional equity success stories: Los Angeles.* Oakland, CA.

Pollin, Robert. (1998, November 23). Living wage, live action. The *Nation.* Quoted in Lafer 2002, (p. 84).

Popkin, Susan, Katz, Bruce, Cunningham, Mary, Brown, Karen, Gustafson, Jeremy, and Turner, Margery. (2004). *A decade of HOPE VI: Research findings and policy challenges.* Washington, DC: The Urban Institute.

Porter, Michael E. (1995a, May–June). The competitive advantage of the inner city. *Harvard Business Review, 73,* 55–71.

Porter, Michael E. (1995b, Fall). An economic strategy for America's inner cities: Addressing the controversy. *Review of Black Political Economy, 24*(2/3), 1–17.

Powell, John A. (2000). Addressing regional dilemmas for minority communities. In Bruce Katz (Ed.), *Reflections on regionalism* (pp. 218–248). Washington, DC: Brookings Institution.

Powell, John A. and M. Graham, Kathleen. (2002). Urban fragmentation as a barrier to equal opportunity. In *Citizens Commission on Civil Rights* (Ed.) (pp. 79–97) Washington, DC: Citizens Commission on Civil Rights.

Proctor, Bernadett, and Dalaker, Joseph. (2002). *Poverty in the United States: 2001.* U.S. Census Bureau, Current Population Reports (pp. 60–219), U.S. Government Printing Office, Washington, DC.

Pryor, Frederic, and Schaffer, David. (1999). *Who's not working and why: Employment, cognitive skills, wages and the changing U.S. labor market.* New York: Cambridge University Press.

Puentes, Robert. (2003). *An Intelligent transportation policy.* Washington, DC: Brookings Institution.

Raines, Howell. (1983). *My soul is rested: Movement days in the deep South remembered.* New York: Viking Press.

Ravitch, Diane. (2000 Reprint). *The great school wars: A history of the New York City public schools.* Baltimore, MD: Johns Hopkins University Press (pp. 179–182).

Reich, Robert B. (2002, November 23). Whose tax cuts? *The American Prospect* (13).

Rheingold, Howard. (2002). *Smart mobs: The next social revolution.* New York: Perseus Publishers.

Robnett, Belinda. (1997). *How long? How long? African American women in the struggle for civil rights.* New York: Oxford University Press.

Rooney, Jim. (1995). *Organizing the South Bronx.* Albany: State University of New York Press.

Rose, Kalim, and Silas, Julie. (2001, February). *Achieving equity through smart growth: Perspectives from philanthropy.* Oakland, CA: Policy Link and Funders' Network for Smart Growth and Livable Communities.

Rosenbaum, James. (2001). *Beyond college for all: Career paths for the forgotten half.* New York: Russell Sage.

Roth, Jodie, and Brooks-Gun, Jeanne. (1998). Promoting healthy adolescence: Synthesis of youth development program evaluations. *Journal of research on adolescence* 8 (423–459).

Rothstein, Richard. (1999, October 27). Shortage of skills? A high-tech myth. *New York Times.*

Rouse, Jacqueline. (2001). We seek to know in order to speak the truth: Nurturing the seeds of discontent—Septima P. Clarke and participatory leadership. In Bettye Collier-Thomas and V.P. Franklin (Eds.), *Sisters in the struggle: African American women in the civil rights-black power movement* (pp. 96–120). New York: New York University Press.

Rusk, David. (1993). *Cities without suburbs.* Washington, DC: Woodrow Wilson Center Press.

Rusk, David. (1998, July). *Abell report: To improve poor children's test scores, move poor families*. Baltimore, MD: Abell Foundation.

Rusk, David. (1999). *Inside game/outside game: Winning strategies for saving urban America*. Washington, DC: Brookings Institution.

Rusk, David. (2000). Growth management: The core regional issue. In Bruce Katz (Ed.) *Reflections on Regionalism* (pp. 78–106). Washington, DC: Brookings Institution.

Rubin, Herbert (2000). *Renewing hope within neighborhoods of despair: The community-based development model*. Albany: State University of New York Press.

Rubinowitz, Leonard, and Rosenbaum, James. (2002). *Crossing the class and color line: From public housing to white suburbia*. Chicago: University of Chicago Press.

Sammartino, Frank J. (2001). *Designing tax cuts to benefit low-income families*. Washington, DC: The Urban Institute.

Sampson, Robert, Morenoff, Jeffrey, and Gannon-Rowley, Thomas. (2002). Assessing 'neighborhood effects': Social processes and new directions in research. *Annual Review of Sociology, 28*, 443–78.

Sanders, Korenman, and Miller, Jane. (1997). Effects of long-term poverty on physical health of children in the national longitudinal survey of youth. In Greg Duncan and Jeanne Brooks-Gunn (Eds.), *Consequences of growing up poor.* (pp. 70–99). New York: Russell Sage.

Sanders, Mavis, and Adia Harve. (2004, May). Beyond the school walls. *Teachers College Record, 104*(7), 1345–1368.

Sandia Laboratories. (1993). Perspective on education in America. *Journal of Educational Research, 86*(5), 259–310.

Sassen, Saskia. (2001). *Global city: New York, London, Tokyo*. Princeton: Princeton University Press.

Savitch, Harold, Collins, David, Sanders, Donald, and Markham, Janice (1993). Ties that bind: Central cities, suburbs, and the new metropolitan region. *Economic Development Quarterly, (7)*, 4, 341–358.

Sawicky, Max and Cherry, Robert. (2001, December 21). *Making work pay with tax reform*. Issue Brief No.173. Washington, DC: Economic Policy Institute.

Schemo, Diana Jean. (2003, July 11). Questions on data cloud luster of Houston schools. *New York Times*.

Schensul, Jean and Margaret LeCompte. (1999). *Ethnographer's toolkit*. Walnut Creek, CA: Altamira Press.

Schutz, Aaron. (2004. Jan/Feb). Rethinking domination and resistance: Challenging postmodernism. *Educational Researcher (pp. 15–23)*.

Seeger, Pete. Appleseed Recordings, http://www.appleseedrec.com/ petecd/bruce.html.

Sharatrand, Angela, Weiss, Heather, Kreider, Holly, and Lopez, Elena. (1997). *New skills for new schools: Preparing teachers in family involvement*. FINE Forum (http://www.gse.harvard.edu/hfrp/puts/onlinepubs/skills/chptr3.html).

Shaw, Randy. (2001). *The activists' handbook: A primer* (Updated ed.). Berkeley: University of California Press.

Shirley, Dennis. (1997). *Community organizing for urban school reform.* Austin: University of Texas Press.

Shirley, Dennis. (2002). *Valley Interfaith and school reform : Organizing for power in South Texas.* Austin: University of Texas Press.

Shor, Ira. (1992). *Empowering education: Critical teaching for social change.* Chicago: University of Chicago Press.

Short, Kathleen, Iceland, John, and Garner, Thesia. (1999). *Experimental poverty measures.* Washington, DC: U.S. Census Bureau.

Shulman, Beth. (2000, July). It's not just money: Thirty-five million workers in low-wage jobs. Adapted from Beth Shulman, "Working without a social contract. *Perspectives on Work* (4),1. (Quoted in *Uncommon Sense* 26. (p. 2) [http://www.njfac.org]).

Shuman, Michael. (1998, January 12). Why do progressive foundations give too little to too many? *The Nation.*

Sklar, Holly, Mykyta, Laryssa, and Wefald, Susan. (2001). *Raise the floor: Wages and policies that work for all of us.* New York: Ms. Foundation for Women.

Skocpol, Theda. (1991). Targeting within universalism: Politically viable policies to combat poverty in the United States. In Christopher Jencks and Paul E. Peterson (Eds.), *The Urban Underclass* (pp. 420–434).Washington, DC: Brookings Institution.

Sleeter, Christine, and McLaren Peter (eds.). (1995). *Multicultural education: Critical pedagogy and the politics of difference.* Albany: State University of New York Press.

Smeeding, Timothy, Rainwater, Lee, and Burtless, Gary. (2001, May). *United States poverty in a cross-national context.* Paper prepared for the International Research on Poverty Conference, Understanding poverty in America: Progress and problems.

Smith, James, and Welch, Finis (1989). Black economic progress after Myrdal. *Journal of Economic Literature, 27*(2) 519–64. Cited in Moss and Tilly 2001 (p. 5).

Snow, David, Rochford, Burke, Worden, Steven, and Benford, Robert. (1986). Frame alignment processes, micromobilization, and movement participation. *American Sociological Review, 51,* 464–481.

Social Policy Research Associates. (2003, December). *Lessons in leadership: How young people change their communities and themselves: An evaluation of the Youth Leadership for Development Initiative.* Executive Summary. Takoma Park, MD: Innovation Center for Community and Youth Development.

Southern, Eileen. (1971). *The music of black Americans: A history* (2nd ed.). New York: Norton.

Spring, Joel. (2000). *The American school, 1642–2000* (5th ed.). New York: McGraw-Hill.

Squires, Gregory. (2003). Racial profiling, insurance style: Insurance redlining and the uneven development of metropolitan areas. *Journal of Urban Affairs, 25*(4), 391–410.

The Staff of Black Star Publishing. *The political thought of James Forman.* (1970). Detroit: Black Star Publishing.

Stipic, Deborah, and Ryan, Rosaleen. (1997). Economically disadvantaged preschoolers: Ready to learn but further to go. *Developmental Psychology, 33*(4), 711–723.

Stuart, Guy. (2000). *Segregation in the Boston metropolitan area at the end of the 20th century.* The Civil Rights Project, Harvard University.

Stuart, Guy. (2002). *Integration or re-segregation: Metropolitan Chicago at the turn of the new century.* Research Report to The Civil Rights Project, Harvard University.

Suarez-Orozco, Carola and Suarez-Orozco, Marcelo M. (2002). *Children of immigration.* Boston, MA: Harvard University Press.

Sugland, Barbara, Zaslow, Martha, and Brooks-Gunn, Jeanne. (1995). The early childhood HOME inventory and HOME short form in differing socio-cultural groups: Are there differences in underlying structure, internal consistency of subcases, and patterns of prediction? *Journal of Family Issues, 16*(5), 632–663.

Suro, Roberto, Singer, Audrey. (2002, July). *Latino growth in metropolitan America: Changing patterns, new locations.* Washington, DC: Brookings Institution.

Swanstrom, Todd, and Sauerkopf, Richard. (2000). The urban electorate in presidential elections. Conference paper for the Urban Affairs Association, Indianapolis, Indiana, April 1993. In Manuel Pastor, Jr. (Ed.), *Regions that work: How cities and suburbs can grow together.* Minneapolis: University of Minnesota Press.

Swarts, Heidi. (2002, January/February). Shut out from the economic boom: Comparing community organizations' success in the neighborhoods left behind. *Snapshots: Research Highlights from the Nonprofit Sector Research Fund,* (21), The Aspen Institute.

Thorbecke, Willem. (2000). *A dual mandate for the federal reserve: The pursuit of price stability and full employment.* Public Policy Brief No. 60. Annondale-on-Hudson, NY: Jerome Levy Economics Institute of Bard College.

Torre, Maria Elena, and Fine, Michelle. (2003 Summer). Youth reframe questions of educational justice through participatory action research. FINE Family Network, *The Evaluation Exchange.* Vol. IX, No. 2.

Traugott, Mark, (Ed.). (1995). *Repertoires and cycles of collective action.* Durham, NC: Duke University Press.

Turner, Margery Austin. (2002, November). *Discrimination in metropolitan housing markets: National results from phase I of HDS2000.* Washington, DC: U.S. Department of Housing and Urban Development.

United States Conference of Mayors. (2002, June 6). *The role of metro areas in the US economy.* Washington, DC.

U.S. Congress. (1998). Federal Transit Act of 1998, Section 3002, Amendments to Title 49, United States Code, Congressional Findings.

U.S. Department of Education. (2000). *Digest of Education Statistics, 2000.*

U.S. Department of Education. (2003). *Overview of public elementary and secondary schools and districts: School year 2001–2002.* Washington, DC: National Center for Education Statistics, Common Core of Data, Local education agency universe survey, 2001–2002.

U.S. Department of Education. National Center for Education Statistics. (2004). The Condition of Education 2004 (NCES 2004–077). Washington, DC: U.S. Government Printing Office.

U.S. General Accounting Office. (2001, March). *Welfare reform: Moving hard-to-employ recipients into the workforce.* Report GAO-01–386. Washington, DC: U.S. General Accounting Office.

U.S. General Accounting Office. (2004, February). *Comparison of the Reported Tax Liabilities of Foreign- and U.S.-controlled Corporations, 1996–2000; United States General Accounting Office.* Report to Congressional Requesters GAO-04–358.

U.S. Department of Transportation. 1998. Office of Small and Disadvantaged Business Utilization Press Release.

Valdes, Guadaloupe. (1996). *Con respeto: Bridging the distances between culturally diverse families and schools: An ethnographic portrait.* New York: Teachers College Press.

Valenzuela, Angela. (2001). *Subtractive schooling: U.S.-Mexican youth and the politics of caring.* Albany: State University of New York Press.

Vidal, Avis. (1992). *Rebuilding communities.* New York: Community Development Research Center, New School for Social Research.

Vincent, Theodore. (1972). *Black power and the Garvey movement.* San Francisco: Ramparts Press.

Voith, Richard. (1998). Do suburbs need cities? *Journal of Regional Science, 38*(3), 465–464.

Voith, Richard. (1992). City and suburban growth: Substitutes or complements. *Business Review, 2*(1), 1–3. Philadelphia: Federal Reserve Bank of Philadelphia.

Waldman, Amy. (1999, October 20). Long line in the Bronx, but for jobs, not the Yankees. *New York Times.*

Walker, Christopher. (1993). Nonprofit housing development: Status, trends, and prospects. *Housing Policy Debate, 4*(3), 369–414.

Wallin, Denise, Schill, Michael, and Daniels, Glynic. (2002). *State of New York City's housing and neighborhoods.* New York: Furman Center for Real Estate and Urban Policy, New York University School of Law.

Warren, Mark. (2001). *Dry bones rattling: Community building to revitalize American democracy.* Princeton, NJ: Princeton University Press.

Weiner, Tim. (2001, August 14). In Tijuana, a new kind of drug peril. *New York Times.*

Weir, Margaret. (1999). Power, money, and politics in community development. In Ronald Ferguson and William Dickens (Eds.), *Urban Problems and community development* (pp. 139–178). Washington, DC: Brookings Institution.

Weisbrot, Mark, and Sforza-Roderick, Michelle. 1998. *Baltimore's Living Wage Law.* Washington, DC: Preamble Center.

Weiss, Mattie. (2003). *Youth rising.* Oakland, CA: Applied Research Center.

Weissbourd, Robert. (1999). *The market potential of inner-city neighborhoods: Filling the information gap.* Boston: Shorebank Corporation.

Wells, Amy Stuart and Serna, Irene. (1996). The Politics of culture: understanding local political resistance to detracking in racially mixed schools. *Harvard Educational Review, 66,* 93–118.

Wells Fargo Bank. (1996). *The underground economy: A California growth industry?* Cited in Weissbourd, 1999 (p. 3).

Whalen, Samuel P. (2002, April). Report of the evaluation of the Polk Bros. Foundation's full service schools initiative: Executive Summary. Chapin Hall Center for Children at the University of Chicago. Available at http://www.communityschools.org.

What Kids Can Do. (2004). *Youth organizing: An emerging model for working with youth.* Providence, RI: What Kids Can Do.

Wheeler, Wendy. (2003). *Lessons in leadership: How young people change their communities and themselves.* Tacoma Park, MD: The Innovation Center.

White, Kevin. (1982). The relationship between socioeconomic status and academic achievement. *Psychological Bulletin, 91,* 46–81.

Williams, Juan. (2003, July/August). A great day in Washington: The March on Washington for Jobs and Freedom was America at its best. *The Crisis,* 24–30.

Wilson, William Julius. (1997). *When work disappears: The world of the new urban poor.* New York: Vintage.

Wolff, Edward. (1994). Trends in household wealth in the United States, 1962–83 and 1983–99. *Review of Income and Wealth, 40*(2), 143–174.

Wolff, Edward. (1995). *Top heavy: The increasing inequality of wealth in America and what can be done about it.* Washington, DC: Brookings Institution.

Wolff, Edward. (2002 Rev. Ed.). *Top heavy: The increasing inequality of wealth in America and what can be done about it.* New York: New Press.

Wolff, Edward. (2003). *Recent trends in living standards in the United States.* Annandale-on-Hudson, NY: Bard College, Jerome Levy Economics Institute.

Wood, Richard. (2002). *Faith in action: Religion, race, and democratic organizing in America*. Chicago: University of Chicago Press.

Woodward, C. Van. (1966). *The strange career of Jim Crow*. London: Oxford University Press.

Wright, Caspi, and Silva, Moffit. (1998). Early failure in the labor market: Childhood and adolescent prediction of unemployment and the transition to adulthood. *American Sociological Review* (63), 424–451.

Yaro, Robert D. (2000). Growing and governing smart: A case study of the New York region. In Bruce Katz (Ed.), *Reflections on Regionalism* (3), 43–77.

Youth Organizing (2002). Youth Organizing, 3:2.

Youth Organizing (2002). Expanding possibilities for youth development (3), Washington, DC: Brookings Institution, 10.

Zeldin, Shephard and Price, Lauren. (1995). Creating supportive communities for adolescent development: Challenges to scholars. *Journal of Adolescent Research* 10, (6–15).

Zellner, Wendy, and Bernstein, Aaron. (2000, March 13). Up against the Wal-Mart. *Business Week* (p. 78).

Zepezauer, Mark and Naiman, Arthur. (1996). *Take the rich off welfare*. Tuscon, AZ: Odonian Press.

Zimmer, Amy, and Mediratta, Kavitha. (2004). *Lessons from the field of school reform organizing*. New York: Institute for Education and Social Policy.

Index

229